My 365 Yummy Beef Dinner Recipes

(My 365 Yummy Beef Dinner Recipes - Volume 1)

Nancy Meza

Copyright: Published in the United States by Nancy Meza/ © NANCY MEZA

Published on September, 09 2020

All rights reserved. No part of this publication may be reproduced, stored in retrieval system, copied in any form or by any means, electronic, mechanical, photocopying, recording or otherwise transmitted without written permission from the publisher. Please do not participate in or encourage piracy of this material in any way. You must not circulate this book in any format. NANCY MEZA does not control or direct users' actions and is not responsible for the information or content shared, harm and/or actions of the book readers.

In accordance with the U.S. Copyright Act of 1976, the scanning, uploading and electronic sharing of any part of this book without the permission of the publisher constitute unlawful piracy and theft of the author's intellectual property. If you would like to use material from the book (other than just simply for reviewing the book), prior permission must be obtained by contacting the author at author@olympicrecipes.com

Thank you for your support of the author's rights.

Content

365 AWESOME BEEF DINNER RECIPES 8

1. African Beef Curry 8
2. All American Bacon Cheeseburgers 8
3. All Day Meatball Stew 9
4. All Day Meatballs 9
5. Almost Stuffed Peppers 10
6. Asian Barbecued Short Ribs 10
7. Asian Beef And Noodles 11
8. Asian Orange Beef 11
9. Asparagus Beef Lo Mein 12
10. Asparagus Steak Oscar 12
11. BBQ Brisket Flatbread Pizzas 13
12. Bacon Cheese Meatball Sliders 14
13. Bacon Cheeseburger Roll Ups 14
14. Bacon Cheeseburger Tater Tot Bake 15
15. Bacon Swiss Burgers 15
16. Bacon Blue Cheese Stuffed Burgers 16
17. Bacon Topped Meat Loaf 16
18. Baked Ziti With Fresh Tomatoes 17
19. Balsamic Steak With Red Grape Relish 17
20. Balsamic Seasoned Steak 18
21. Barbecue Beef Brisket 18
22. Barbecue Style Beef Brisket 19
23. Barbecued Beef Brisket 19
24. Barbecued Beef And Beans 20
25. Bavarian Beef Roast 21
26. Beef Rice Stuffed Cabbage Rolls 21
27. Beef Tater Bake 22
28. Beef 'n' Asparagus Pasta 22
29. Beef 'n' Chili Beans 23
30. Beef 'n' Sausage Lasagna 23
31. Beef Bourguignon 24
32. Beef Burgundy Stew 25
33. Beef Burritos 26
34. Beef Cabbage Roll Ups 26
35. Beef Osso Bucco 27
36. Beef Pizza Loaf 27
37. Beef Potpie 28
38. Beef Roast Au Poivre With Caramelized Onions 28
39. Beef Roast With Gravy 29
40. Beef Stew For Two 30
41. Beef Tips On Rice 30
42. Beef On A Stick 31
43. Beef Or Venison Stew 31
44. Beefy Hash Brown Bake 32
45. Berry Nice Brisket 32
46. Best Ever Roast Beef 33
47. Biscuit Topped Beef Casserole 33
48. Biscuit Topped Italian Casserole 34
49. Blue Cheese Burgers 35
50. Blue Cheese Flat Iron Steak 35
51. Blue Cheese Stroganoff 36
52. Blue Cheese Stuffed Steaks For Two 36
53. Brief Burritos 37
54. Brisket With Cranberry Horseradish Gravy 37
55. Broccoli Primavera With Cheese Sauce 38
56. Broiled Pizza Burgers 38
57. Broiled Sirloin 39
58. Bubbly Golden Mexican Beef Cobbler 39
59. Burgers For A Bunch 40
60. Burrito Lasagna 40
61. Cajun Meat Loaf 41
62. California Tamale Pie 42
63. Camping Haystacks 42
64. Cheeseburger Skillet Dinner 42
65. Cheesy Lasagna 43
66. Cheesy Spinach Stuffed Meat Loaf 43
67. Chicken Fried Steak Gravy 44
68. Chili Mac Cheese 45
69. Chili Sauce Meat Loaf 45
70. Chilies Rellenos Casserole 46
71. Chipotle Rubbed Beef Tenderloin 46
72. Chunky Pasta Sauce 47
73. Church Supper Hot Dish 47
74. Cider Beef Stew 48
75. Classic Cashew Beef For Two 48
76. Classic Lasagna 49
77. Coffee Roast Beef 49
78. Coffee Braised Roast Beef 50
79. Coffee Braised Short Ribs 51
80. Colorful Beef Stir Fry 51
81. Colossal Cornburger 52
82. Company Pot Roast 52
83. Confetti Casserole 53
84. Confetti Meat Loaf 53
85. Coriander Crusted Beef With Spicy Cranberry Relish 54
86. Corn 'n' Beef Pasta Bake 55

#	Recipe	Page
87.	Corned Beef Dinner	55
88.	Corned Beef Potato Dinner	55
89.	Cream Cheese And Swiss Lasagna	56
90.	Creamy Beef Lasagna	57
91.	Creamy Reuben Casserole	57
92.	Crescent Topped Casserole	58
93.	Crunchy Beef Bake	58
94.	Curly Noodle Dinner	59
95.	Deviled Baked Steak	59
96.	Deviled Swiss Steak	59
97.	Double Duty Layered Enchilada Casserole	60
98.	Dressed Up Meatballs	61
99.	Easy Grilled Flank Steak	61
100.	Easy Lasagna	62
101.	Easy Spaghetti	62
102.	Enchilada Casser Ole!	62
103.	Fabulous Fajitas	63
104.	Fajita Skillet	63
105.	Family Style Meat Loaf Dinner	64
106.	Fancy Skillet Steaks	65
107.	Fast Philly Cheesesteak Pizza	65
108.	Fiesta Beef Bowls	66
109.	Fiesta Grilled Flank Steak	66
110.	Flank Steak With Cilantro Salsa Verde	67
111.	Flank Steak With Couscous	67
112.	Flank Steak With Horseradish Sauce	68
113.	Flavorful Italian Pot Roast	68
114.	Flavorful Meat Loaf	69
115.	Florentine Meatballs	69
116.	Fourth Of July Bean Casserole	70
117.	French Beef Stew	70
118.	French Onion Shepherd's Pie	71
119.	Gala Beef Tenderloin Filets	71
120.	Garlic Beef Enchiladas	72
121.	Garlic Beef Stroganoff	73
122.	Garlic Lover's Beef Stew	73
123.	Garlic Mushroom French Beef Stew	74
124.	Garlic Pepper Tenderloin Steaks	74
125.	German Style Beef Roast	75
126.	Gorgonzola Beef Wellingtons	75
127.	Grandma Schwartz's Rouladen	76
128.	Grandma's Beef Stew	77
129.	Greek Pasta And Beef	77
130.	Grilled Beef Tenderloins	78
131.	Grilled Ribeyes With Herb Butter	79
132.	Grilled Steaks With Marinated Tomatoes	79
133.	Ground Beef Spiral Bake	80
134.	Guinness Corned Beef And Cabbage	80
135.	Hamburger Rice Skillet	81
136.	Hash Brown Beef Pie	81
137.	Hawaiian Beef Dish	82
138.	Haystack Supper	82
139.	Healthy Italian Pot Roast	83
140.	Hearty Burritos	84
141.	Hearty Cheese Tortellini	84
142.	Hearty Green Chili Stew	85
143.	Hearty Lasagna	85
144.	Hearty Shepherd's Pie	86
145.	Hearty Skillet Stew	86
146.	Hearty Slow Cooker Lasagna	87
147.	Hearty Stuffed Green Peppers	88
148.	Hearty Vegetable Beef Ragout	88
149.	Herb Stuffed Red Peppers	89
150.	Herbed Roast Beef	89
151.	Herbed Sirloin Tip	90
152.	Hobo Knapsacks	90
153.	Home Style Meat Loaf	91
154.	Home Style Roast Beef	91
155.	Homemade Apple Cider Beef Stew	92
156.	Homemade Pizza	93
157.	Homemade Ragu Bolognese	93
158.	Honey Garlic Meatballs	94
159.	Horseradish Encrusted Beef Tenderloin	94
160.	Hot Tamale Casserole	95
161.	Hungarian Stuffed Cabbage	96
162.	Idaho Tacos	96
163.	Indian Fry Bread Tacos	97
164.	Iowa Ham Balls Main Dish	97
165.	Italian Beef	98
166.	Italian Beef Tortellini Stew	98
167.	Italian Beef With Mushrooms	99
168.	Italian Mushroom Meat Loaf	99
169.	Italian Noodles	100
170.	Italian Pot Roast	100
171.	Italian Turkey Burgers	101
172.	Italian Style Beef Liver	101
173.	Jack N Jill Burgers	102
174.	Lakes Burgoo	102
175.	Lasagna With White Sauce	103
176.	Layer Cake Meat Loaf	103
177.	Layered Potato Beef Casserole	104
178.	Life Preserver Meat Loaves	105
179.	Lighter Lasagna Corn Carne	105

#	Title	Page
180.	Lots A Veggies Stew	106
181.	Louisiana Round Steak	106
182.	Macaroni Scramble	107
183.	Makeover Li'l Cheddar Meat Loaves	107
184.	Mardi Gras Beef	108
185.	Marinated Iowa Beef	108
186.	Marinated Ostrich Steak	109
187.	Matthew's Best Ever Meat Loaf	109
188.	Meat 'n' Potato Kabobs	110
189.	Meat Loaf From The Slow Cooker	111
190.	Meat Loaf Patty	111
191.	Meat Loaf Potato Surprise	112
192.	Meat Loaf For 120	113
193.	Meat Loaf For A Mob	113
194.	Meat Lover's Pizza Casserole	113
195.	Meatball Pie	114
196.	Meatball Submarine Casserole	115
197.	Meaty Macaroni	115
198.	Mexican Beef Cobbler	116
199.	Mexican Lasagna	116
200.	Mexicana Skillet Stew	117
201.	Microwave Meatball Stew	117
202.	Microwave Swiss Steak	118
203.	Midwest Meatball Casserole	118
204.	Mini Cheese Meat Loaves	119
205.	Minute Steaks Parmesan	119
206.	Moist Hungarian Goulash	120
207.	Mom's Beef Stew	121
208.	Mushroom Pizza Burgers	121
209.	Mushroom Pot Roast	122
210.	Mushroom Ribeyes	122
211.	Mushroom Steak	123
212.	Mustard Crusted Prime Rib With Madeira Glaze	123
213.	Nacho Cheese Beef Bake	124
214.	Nebraska Beef Rolls	125
215.	New Year's Eve Tenderloin Steaks	125
216.	Okie Beans	126
217.	Old Fashioned Beef Brisket	126
218.	Old World Corned Beef And Vegetables	127
219.	One Pot Saucy Beef Rotini	127
220.	Orange Flank Steak	128
221.	Oven Stew And Biscuits	128
222.	Papa Burger	129
223.	Pepper Jack Smothered Cheeseburgers	129
224.	Pepper Jack Meat Loaf	130
225.	Peppered Meatballs	130
226.	Peppered Ribeye Roast	131
227.	Peppered Steaks With Salsa	131
228.	Peppy Potato Casserole	132
229.	Philly Cheesesteak Rolls	133
230.	Philly Steak Potatoes	133
231.	Picante Cranberry Meatballs	134
232.	Pineapple Beef Stir Fry	134
233.	Pineapple Red Pepper Beef Stir Fry	135
234.	Pineapple Sirloin Kabobs	135
235.	Pinwheel Pizza Loaf	136
236.	Pizza Burgers	136
237.	Pizza Hot Dish	137
238.	Pizza Lasagna	137
239.	Pizza With Hash Brown Crust	138
240.	Plantation Supper	138
241.	Portobello Beef Burgundy	139
242.	Portobello Pizza Burgers	139
243.	Potato Beef Lasagna	140
244.	Pressure Cooker Beef Brisket In Beer	140
245.	Presto Beef Stew	141
246.	Prime Rib Of Beef	141
247.	Prime Rib With Horseradish Cream	142
248.	Quick Chili Mac	142
249.	Quick Corned Beef Hash	143
250.	Quick Spaghetti Skillet	143
251.	Quick Tater Tot Bake	144
252.	Quicker Mushroom Beef Stew	144
253.	Reuben Hot Dish	145
254.	Reuben Noodle Casserole	145
255.	Rice Mix Meatballs	146
256.	Roasted Garlic Herb Prime Rib	146
257.	Roasted Tenderloin And Red Potatoes	147
258.	Round Steak 'N' Dumplings	147
259.	Santa Fe Stew	148
260.	Saucy Skillet Lasagna	149
261.	Saucy Swiss Steak	149
262.	Sauerbraten	150
263.	Sauerbraten Patties	151
264.	Savory Braised Beef	151
265.	Savory Grilled T Bones	152
266.	Savory Meatballs	152
267.	Savory Spaghetti Sauce	153
268.	Savory Vegetable Beef Stew	153
269.	Scotch Braised Beef	154
270.	Sesame Beef 'n' Veggie Kabobs	154
271.	Sesame Beef Stir Fry	155
272.	Sesame Beef And Mushroom Noodles	156

273. Short Ribs With Dumplings 156
274. Sicilian Meat Roll 157
275. Simple Salisbury Steak 157
276. Sloppy Joe Biscuit Cups 158
277. Slow Cooker Beef Tostadas 158
278. Slow Cooker Beef With Red Sauce 159
279. Slow Cooker Burgundy Beef 160
280. Slow Cooker Chipotle Beef Carnitas 160
281. Slow Cooker Corned Beef Supper 161
282. Slow Cooker Pot Roast 161
283. Slow Cooker Sauerbraten 162
284. Slow Cooker Steak 'n' Gravy 162
285. Slow Cooked Barbecued Beef Brisket 163
286. Slow Cooked Green Chili Beef Burritos . 163
287. Slow Cooked Meatball Stew 164
288. Slow Cooked Spaghetti Sauce 164
289. Slow Cooked Stuffed Flank Steak 165
290. Slow Simmered Burgundy Beef Stew 165
291. Smoky Chuck Roast 166
292. Smothered Round Steak 166
293. South Of The Border Stuffed Peppers ... 167
294. Southern Pot Roast 168
295. Southwest Beef Brisket 168
296. Southwest Zucchini Boats 169
297. Southwestern Beef Burritos 169
298. Southwestern Burgers 170
299. Spaghetti Goulash 171
300. Spaghetti Hot Dish 171
301. Spaghetti Squash Meatball Casserole 172
302. Spaghetti With Italian Meatballs 172
303. Spiced Pot Roast 173
304. Spicy Beef Brisket 174
305. Spicy Beef Burritos 174
306. Spicy Orange Beef 175
307. Spicy Shepherd's Pie 175
308. Spinach Beef Bake 176
309. Spinach Beef Stew 176
310. Spinach Steak Pinwheels 177
311. Spinach Beef Spaghetti Pie 177
312. Spiral Pepperoni Pizza Bake 178
313. Star Of The North Pasties 179
314. Steak Pinwheels 179
315. Steak Potpie 180
316. Steak Tortillas 180
317. Steak And Black Bean Burritos 181
318. Steaks With Cherry Chipotle Glaze 181
319. Stew For A Crowd 182
320. Stout Shiitake Pot Roast 182
321. Stuffed Flank Steak With Mushroom Sherry Cream 183
322. Summer Beef Skewers 184
323. Summer Steak Kabobs 184
324. Super Spaghetti Sauce 185
325. Supreme Roast Beef 185
326. Sweet And Savory Pulled Beef Dinner ... 186
327. Swift Spaghetti 186
328. Swiss Steak Burgers For 2 187
329. Swiss Steak Dinner 187
330. Taco Bake 188
331. Taco Crescents 188
332. Taco Meat Loaves 189
333. Taco Muffins 189
334. Tacoritos For Two 190
335. Tamale Pie For Two 191
336. Tangy Meatballs 191
337. Tangy Sirloin Strips 192
338. Tangy Stuffed Peppers 192
339. Tasty Tacos 193
340. Tater Topped Casserole 193
341. Tender Barbecued Brisket 194
342. Teriyaki Beef Stir Fry For 3 194
343. Teriyaki Flank Steak 195
344. Texas Beef Stew 195
345. Texas Style Brisket 196
346. Thick Beef Stew 196
347. Three Cheese Meatball Mostaccioli 197
348. Three Pepper Beef Wraps 198
349. Tomato Beef And Rice Casserole 198
350. Tortilla Pie 199
351. Tortilla Salsa Meat Loaf 199
352. Traditional Boiled Dinner 200
353. Ultimate Pot Roast 200
354. Unstuffed Peppers 201
355. Upside Down Beef Pie 201
356. Veal Cutlets Supreme 202
357. Vegetable Steak Stir Fry 202
358. Veggie Steak Fajitas 203
359. Whiskey Sirloin Steak 203
360. Winter Oven Beef Stew 204
361. Worms For Brains 204
362. Yankee Pot Roast 205
363. Zeus Burgers 205
364. Zippy Peanut Steak Kabobs 206
365. Zucchini Beef Lasagna 207

INDEX 208
CONCLUSION 211

365 Awesome Beef Dinner Recipes

***

1. African Beef Curry

Serving: 4 servings. | Prep: 15mins | Ready in:

Ingredients

- 1 pound beef stew meat, cut into 1/2-inch cubes
- 1 can (14-1/2 ounces) diced tomatoes, undrained
- 1 small onion, chopped
- 1 small sweet red pepper, chopped
- 1 small green pepper, chopped
- 1 to 2 tablespoons curry powder
- 1/2 teaspoon salt
- Hot cooked rice
- Raisins, chopped salted peanuts and sweetened shredded coconut, optional

Direction

- Mix the first seven ingredients in a big pot. Heat to a boil. Cover, decrease heat, and simmer until meat is tender, 1 1/2-2 hours. Eat with rice. If desired, use coconut, raisins, and peanuts to garnish.

Nutrition Information

- Calories: 205 calories
- Protein: 23g protein. Diabetic Exchanges: 3 lean meat
- Total Fat: 8g fat (3g saturated fat)
- Sodium: 474mg sodium
- Fiber: 3g fiber)
- Total Carbohydrate: 10g carbohydrate (5g sugars
- Cholesterol: 70mg cholesterol

2. All American Bacon Cheeseburgers

Serving: 4 servings. | Prep: 15mins | Ready in:

Ingredients

- 2 tablespoons finely chopped onion
- 2 tablespoons ketchup
- 1 garlic clove, minced
- 1 teaspoon sugar
- 1 teaspoon Worcestershire sauce
- 1 teaspoon steak sauce
- 1/4 teaspoon cider vinegar
- 1 pound ground beef
- 4 slices sharp cheddar cheese
- 4 hamburger buns, split and toasted
- 8 cooked bacon strips
- Optional toppings: lettuce leaves and tomato, onion and pickle slices

Direction

- Mix the initial 7 ingredients in a big bowl. Break the beef up on top of the mixture and combine thoroughly. Form into 4 patties.
- Let burgers grill with cover, over moderate heat or broil for 4-7 minutes per side 3-inch away from the heat or till juices run clear and a thermometer register 160°. Put cheese on top. Grill for an additional of 1 minute or till cheese melts. Put on buns together with desire toppings and bacon then serve.

Nutrition Information

- Calories: 472 calories
- Cholesterol: 98mg cholesterol

- Protein: 33g protein.
- Total Fat: 25g fat (10g saturated fat)
- Sodium: 947mg sodium
- Fiber: 1g fiber)
- Total Carbohydrate: 27g carbohydrate (7g sugars

3. All Day Meatball Stew

Serving: 8 servings (3 quarts). | Prep: 20mins | Ready in:

Ingredients

- 2 packages (12 ounces each) frozen fully cooked Italian meatballs
- 5 medium potatoes, peeled and cubed
- 1 pound fresh baby carrots
- 1 medium onion, halved and sliced
- 1 jar (4-1/2 ounces) sliced mushrooms, drained
- 2 cans (8 ounces each) tomato sauce
- 1 can (10-1/2 ounces) condensed beef broth, undiluted
- 3/4 cup water
- 3/4 cup dry red wine or beef broth
- 1/2 teaspoon garlic powder
- 1/4 teaspoon pepper
- 2 tablespoons all-purpose flour
- 1/2 cup cold water

Direction

- Put mushrooms, onion, carrots, potatoes and meatballs into a 5- or 6-qt. slow cooker. Mix the pepper, garlic powder, wine, water, broth and tomato sauce in a large bowl; drizzle over top. Cook on low heat with a cover for 8-10 hours, or till vegetables are tender.
- Blend together water and flour until the mixture is smooth; gradually stir it into stew. Cook on high heat with a cover for 30 minutes, or till thickened.

Nutrition Information

- Calories: 384 calories
- Protein: 19g protein.
- Total Fat: 20g fat (9g saturated fat)
- Sodium: 1317mg sodium
- Fiber: 5g fiber)
- Total Carbohydrate: 35g carbohydrate (7g sugars
- Cholesterol: 41mg cholesterol

4. All Day Meatballs

Serving: 6 servings. | Prep: 25mins | Ready in:

Ingredients

- 1 cup milk
- 3/4 cup quick-cooking oats
- 3 tablespoons finely chopped onion
- 1-1/2 teaspoons salt
- 1-1/2 pounds ground beef
- 1 cup ketchup
- 1/2 cup water
- 3 tablespoons cider vinegar
- 2 tablespoons sugar

Direction

- In a large bowl, combine the first four ingredients. Crumble beef over mixture and mix well. Form into balls, 1-inch each. In a 5-quart slow cooker, place those balls.
- In a small bowl, combine the water, ketchup, sugar and vinegar. Pour mixture over meatballs. Cook while covered on low mode for approximately 6 to 8 hours until meat is no longer pink.

Nutrition Information

- Calories: 346 calories
- Protein: 26g protein.
- Total Fat: 16g fat (6g saturated fat)
- Sodium: 1139mg sodium
- Fiber: 2g fiber)

- Total Carbohydrate: 24g carbohydrate (11g sugars)
- Cholesterol: 81mg cholesterol

5. Almost Stuffed Peppers

Serving: 4-6 servings. | Prep: 5mins | Ready in:

Ingredients

- 1 pound ground beef
- 2 cups water
- 1 can (14-1/2 ounces) diced tomatoes, undrained
- 1 large green pepper, cut into 1/4-inch slices
- 1 medium onion, thinly sliced
- 1-1/2 teaspoons salt
- 1/2 teaspoon Italian seasoning
- 1/2 teaspoon pepper
- 1-1/2 cups uncooked instant rice

Direction

- Cook the beef in a large skillet over medium heat until not pink anymore; drain. Take out; then put aside and keep it warm.
- Blend the seasonings, onion, green pepper, tomatoes, and water in the same skillet; boil. Then turn down the heat; without the cover, simmer until the vegetables become tender. Add rice and stir; put a cover on skillet and take away from the heat. Allow to stand for 5 minutes. Add beef and stir; bring back to the heat and cook until heated through.

Nutrition Information

- Calories: 240 calories
- Protein: 16g protein.
- Total Fat: 7g fat (3g saturated fat)
- Sodium: 140mg sodium
- Fiber: 3g fiber)
- Total Carbohydrate: 27g carbohydrate (4g sugars
- Cholesterol: 37mg cholesterol

6. Asian Barbecued Short Ribs

Serving: 8 servings. | Prep: 25mins | Ready in:

Ingredients

- 4 pounds bone-in beef short ribs
- 1 tablespoon canola oil
- 1 medium onion, sliced
- 3/4 cup ketchup
- 3/4 cup water, divided
- 1/4 cup reduced-sodium soy sauce
- 2 tablespoons lemon juice
- 1 tablespoon brown sugar
- 1 teaspoon ground mustard
- 1/2 teaspoon ground ginger
- 1/4 teaspoon salt
- 1/8 teaspoon pepper
- 1 bay leaf
- 2 tablespoons all-purpose flour

Direction

- In a Dutch oven, brown all sides of ribs in oil in batches. Take away the ribs and eliminate the pan drippings. In that pan, sauté onion for about 2 minutes, or until soft. Move the ribs back to the pan.
- Stir the bay leaf, pepper, salt, ginger, mustard, brown sugar, lemon juice, soy sauce, a half cup of water and ketchup; pour over ribs.
- Bake with cover at 325° for about 1-3/4 to 2 hours, or till meat becomes soft.
- Take the ribs away and keep warm. Eliminate bay leaf. Scoop off fat from the pan drippings. Whisk the leftover water and flour in a small bowl until smooth; slowly mix into drippings. Let it boil; cook and combine for 2 minutes or until condense. Serve along with ribs.

Nutrition Information

- Calories: 240 calories
- Cholesterol: 55mg cholesterol
- Protein: 20g protein.
- Total Fat: 13g fat (5g saturated fat)
- Sodium: 854mg sodium
- Fiber: 1g fiber)
- Total Carbohydrate: 11g carbohydrate (9g sugars

7. Asian Beef And Noodles

Serving: 4 servings. | Prep: 5mins | Ready in:

Ingredients

- 1 pound lean ground beef (90% lean)
- 2 packages (3 ounces each) Oriental ramen noodles, crumbled
- 2-1/2 cups water
- 2 cups frozen broccoli stir-fry vegetable blend
- 1/4 teaspoon ground ginger
- 2 tablespoons thinly sliced green onion

Direction

- Cook beef till not pink in a big skillet on medium heat; drain. Add 1 ramen noodle's flavoring packet contents; mix till melted. Remove beef; put aside.
- Boil contents of leftover flavoring packet, noodles, ginger, veggies and water in the same skillet. Lower heat; cover. Simmer till noodles are tender for 3-4 minutes, occasionally mixing. Put beef in pan; heat through. Mix in onion.

Nutrition Information

- Calories: 377 calories
- Protein: 27g protein. Diabetic Exchanges: 3 lean meat
- Total Fat: 15g fat (7g saturated fat)
- Sodium: 624mg sodium
- Fiber: 3g fiber)
- Total Carbohydrate: 31g carbohydrate (3g sugars
- Cholesterol: 56mg cholesterol

8. Asian Orange Beef

Serving: 6 servings. | Prep: 20mins | Ready in:

Ingredients

- 3 large navel oranges
- 1 bunch green onions
- 3 tablespoons sugar
- 2 tablespoons cornstarch
- 3 tablespoons reduced-sodium soy sauce
- 3 garlic cloves, minced
- 1 tablespoon minced fresh gingerroot
- 1-1/2 pounds beef sirloin steak, cut into 1/2-inch cubes
- 1 tablespoon canola oil
- 3 cups hot cooked rice

Direction

- From 2 oranges, grate peel finely; put aside. Cut thin orange peel strips from leftover orange as garnish; put aside. From all oranges, squeeze juice. Cut onions to separate green and white parts. Slice white parts thinly; cut the green parts for garnish to 1-in. lengths.
- Sauce: Mix cornstarch and sugar in a small bowl; mix in orange juice till smooth. Mix in white onion parts, grated orange peel, ginger, garlic and soy sauce; put aside.
- Stir-fry beef till not pink in oil in a big nonstick skillet/wok coated in cooking spray. Mix sauce; put in pan. Boil; mix and cook till thick for 2 minutes. Serve with rice; garnish using leftover onions and orange peel strips.

Nutrition Information

- Calories: 351 calories
- Sodium: 352mg sodium

- Fiber: 3g fiber)
- Total Carbohydrate: 44g carbohydrate (15g sugars
- Cholesterol: 64mg cholesterol
- Protein: 25g protein. Diabetic Exchanges: 3 lean meat
- Total Fat: 8g fat (2g saturated fat)

9. Asparagus Beef Lo Mein

Serving: 4 servings. | Prep: 10mins | Ready in:

Ingredients

- 1 beef top sirloin steak (1 pound), cut into thin strips
- 2 packages (3 ounces each) beef ramen noodles
- 2/3 cup hoisin sauce
- 2-1/4 cups water, divided
- 2 tablespoons olive oil, divided
- 1 pound fresh asparagus, trimmed and cut into 2-1/2-inch pieces
- 1 small garlic clove, minced

Direction

- Toss 1/2 tsp. seasoning from ramen seasoning packet and beef; throw leftover opened packet. Mix 1/4 cup water and hoisin sauce in a small bowl.
- Boil leftover water in a saucepan. Add contents of unopened seasoning packet and noodles; cook for 3 minutes, uncovered. Take off heat; stand till noodles are tender, covered.
- Meanwhile, heat 1 tbsp. oil on medium high heat in a big skillet; stir-fry beef for 3-4 minutes till brown. Remove from pan.
- Heat leftover oil on medium high heat in same pan; stir-fry garlic and asparagus for 1-3 minutes till crisp tender. Mix in hoisin sauce mixture; boil. Cook till slightly thick; mix in beef then heat through. Serve on noodles.

Nutrition Information

- Calories: 511 calories
- Protein: 31g protein.
- Total Fat: 21g fat (7g saturated fat)
- Sodium: 1367mg sodium
- Fiber: 3g fiber)
- Total Carbohydrate: 48g carbohydrate (13g sugars
- Cholesterol: 47mg cholesterol

10. Asparagus Steak Oscar

Serving: 4 servings. | Prep: 15mins | Ready in:

Ingredients

- 1 envelope bearnaise sauce
- 1 pound fresh asparagus, trimmed
- 1/4 pound fresh crabmeat
- 2 tablespoons butter
- 1/2 teaspoon minced garlic
- 1 tablespoon lemon juice
- 4 beef tenderloin steaks (1 inch thick and 3 ounces each)
- 1/8 teaspoon paprika

Direction

- Make the béarnaise sauce following the package instructions. In a steamer basket, put in asparagus; arrange the basket over a big saucepan with an inch of water; boil. Cover and let it steam for 8-10 minutes until the asparagus is tender-crisp.
- In a big pan with butter, cook crab for 3-4 minutes until warmed through; add garlic. Sauté for another minute. Pour in lemon juice; stir. Keep the mixture warm.
- On medium heat, grill steaks while covered or broil four inches from heat for 6-8mins per side until it reaches the preferred doneness (an inserted thermometer in the steak should register 170° Fahrenheit for well-done, 160 degrees F for medium done, and 145° Fahrenheit for medium rare). Add asparagus,

crab mix, and béarnaise sauce on top. Season with paprika.

Nutrition Information

- Calories: 376 calories
- Protein: 27g protein.
- Total Fat: 25g fat (14g saturated fat)
- Sodium: 524mg sodium
- Fiber: 1g fiber)
- Total Carbohydrate: 11g carbohydrate (4g sugars
- Cholesterol: 116mg cholesterol

11. BBQ Brisket Flatbread Pizzas

Serving: 2 flatbread pizzas (6 slices each). | Prep: 03hours00mins | Ready in:

Ingredients

- 2 cups barbecue sauce, divided
- 1/2 cup cider vinegar
- 1/2 cup chopped green onions, divided
- 1/2 cup minced fresh cilantro, divided
- 2 pounds fresh beef brisket
- 1 teaspoon salt
- 1 teaspoon pepper
- 1 large red onion, cut into thick slices
- 1 teaspoon olive oil
- 2 cups shredded smoked Gouda cheese
- DOUGH:
- 2-3/4 to 3-1/4 cups all-purpose flour
- 1 tablespoon sugar
- 3 teaspoons salt
- 1 package (1/4 ounce) quick-rise yeast
- 1-1/4 cups warm water (120° to 130°)
- 2 tablespoons olive oil

Direction

- Mix quarter cup cilantro, quarter cup green onions, vinegar and a cup of the barbecue sauce in a big sealable plastic bag. Scatter pepper and salt on brisket; put to the bag. Enclose the bag and coat by flipping. Chill for 8 hours or up to overnight.
- Let drain and throw away the marinade. With drip pan, have grill ready for indirect heat. Put brisket on top of pan; grill with cover for an hour, on indirect low heat. To coals, put 10 briquettes. Place cover and let grill for an additional of 1-1/4 hours or till meat is tender once pricked with fork, putting additional briquettes if necessary. Once cool enough to hold, put meat apart using 2 forks; reserve.
- In the meantime, mix yeast, salt, sugar and 2-3/4 cups flour in a big bowl. Put oil and water; whisk barely till smooth. Mix in sufficient leftover flour to make a soft dough, dough will become gooey.
- Transfer to a floured surface area; knead for about 6 to 8 minutes, till pliable and smooth. Put in an oiled bowl, flipping one time to oil the surface. Put on cover and allow to rise in a warm area till doubled in size, approximately an hour. Deflate dough; split in half. Roll every half into a 15-inch round.
- Over moderate heat, grill every round with the cover on, for 1 to 2 minutes per side or till slightly browned. Reserve. Brush oil on onion; grill till soft for 4 to 5 minutes, flipping one time. Take off from heat; slice and reserve.
- Scatter the rest of barbecue sauce on the grilled side of every crust. Put the shredded brisket, onion, cheese and the rest of cilantro and green onions on top.
- Put the pizza on the grill; place cover and on indirect moderate heat, cook for 8 to 10 minutes or till cheese melts and crust is slightly browned. Through cooking, turn pizza midway to guarantee an evenly browned crust. Redo with the rest of the pizza.

Nutrition Information

- Calories: 322 calories
- Sodium: 1184mg sodium
- Fiber: 2g fiber)

- Total Carbohydrate: 28g carbohydrate (6g sugars
- Cholesterol: 54mg cholesterol
- Protein: 24g protein.
- Total Fat: 12g fat (5g saturated fat)

12. Bacon Cheese Meatball Sliders

Serving: 6 servings. | Prep: 50mins | Ready in:

Ingredients

- 12 frozen bread dough dinner rolls
- 1 egg
- 1 teaspoon water
- 1 tablespoon sesame seeds
- KABOBS:
- 3/4 cup seasoned bread crumbs
- 6 bacon strips, cooked and crumbled
- 2 eggs, lightly beaten
- 1-1/2 teaspoons Worcestershire sauce
- 1/2 teaspoon garlic salt
- 1-1/2 pounds ground sirloin
- 1 medium sweet red pepper or green pepper, cut into 1-inch pieces
- 1 small red onion, cut into 1-inch pieces
- 6 slices process American cheese, cut into quarters

Direction

- Thaw dough following the directions on package. Divide each roll into 2 equal pieces; form into balls. On lightly greased baking sheets, arrange dough balls 2 inches apart. Use clean kitchen towels to cover; let them rise for about 30 minutes in warm place until almost doubled.
- Remove cover; press gently to slightly flatten. Mix together water and egg; use it to brush on tops. Use sesame seeds to sprinkle. Put into the oven at 400 degrees to bake until golden brown in color, about 8 to 10 minutes. Transfer to wire racks.
- Mix together the first 5 kabob ingredients in a large bowl. Add crumbled beef to the mixture and stir well to combine. Form into 24 patties. On 24 soaked wooden or metal skewers, thread alternately onion, red pepper and patties, insert patties sideways.
- Use cooking oil to moisten a paper towel; lightly coat the grill rack with long-handled tongs. Put kabobs on grill grate over medium-high heat with a cover until no longer pink, about 4 to 5 minutes per side. Take them away from the grill grate; add cheese on top of patties right away. Cut buns in half; assemble sliders to serve.

Nutrition Information

- Calories: 612 calories
- Total Carbohydrate: 57g carbohydrate (10g sugars
- Cholesterol: 187mg cholesterol
- Protein: 42g protein.
- Total Fat: 25g fat (9g saturated fat)
- Sodium: 1834mg sodium
- Fiber: 4g fiber)

13. Bacon Cheeseburger Roll Ups

Serving: 8 servings. | Prep: 25mins | Ready in:

Ingredients

- 1 pound ground beef
- 6 bacon strips, diced
- 1/2 cup chopped onion
- 1 package (8 ounces) process cheese (Velveeta), cubed
- 1 tube (16.3 ounces) large refrigerated buttermilk biscuits
- 1/2 cup ketchup
- 1/4 cup yellow mustard

Direction

- Cook the onion, bacon, and beef in a large skillet on medium heat until the meat is not pink anymore; then drain. Put in cheese; stir and cook until it melts. Take away from the heat.
- Pound the biscuits into 5-inch circles; put 1/3 cup of the beef mixture atop each. Fold the ends and sides over the filling and roll them up. On a baking sheet coated with cooking spray, arrange with seam side down.
- Bake at 400 degrees until golden brown, or for 18-20 minutes. Mix mustard and ketchup in a small bowl; then serve alongside roll-ups.

Nutrition Information

- Calories: 429 calories
- Total Fat: 24g fat (10g saturated fat)
- Sodium: 1372mg sodium
- Fiber: 1g fiber)
- Total Carbohydrate: 32g carbohydrate (11g sugars
- Cholesterol: 63mg cholesterol
- Protein: 21g protein.

14. Bacon Cheeseburger Tater Tot Bake

Serving: 12 servings. | Prep: 25mins | Ready in:

Ingredients

- 2 pounds ground beef
- 1 large onion, chopped and divided
- 1 can (15 ounces) tomato sauce
- 1 package (8 ounces) process cheese (Velveeta)
- 1 tablespoon ground mustard
- 1 tablespoon Worcestershire sauce
- 2 cups shredded cheddar cheese
- 12 bacon strips, cooked and crumbled
- 1 package (32 ounces) frozen Tater Tots
- 1 cup grape tomatoes, chopped
- 1/3 cup sliced dill pickles

Direction

- Preheat oven at 400 degrees. Sauté 1 cup of onion and beef in a large skillet put over medium heat for 6-8 minutes or until the onions are soft and the beef is brown and starting to crumble. Drain excess oil. Add in processed cheese, tomato sauce, Worcestershire sauce and mustard and mix for 4-6 minutes until cheese has melted.
- Transfer in a greased 3-1/2-quartz or 13x9-inch baking dish. Top off with bacon and cheddar cheese. Put Tater Tots on top. Put the baking dish uncovered in the preheated oven and bake for 35-40 minutes until it is bubbling. Finish off with a toppings of pickles, remaining onion and tomatoes.

Nutrition Information

- Calories: 479 calories
- Sodium: 1144mg sodium
- Fiber: 3g fiber)
- Total Carbohydrate: 24g carbohydrate (4g sugars
- Cholesterol: 92mg cholesterol
- Protein: 27g protein.
- Total Fat: 31g fat (12g saturated fat)

15. Bacon Swiss Burgers

Serving: 2 servings. | Prep: 5mins | Ready in:

Ingredients

- 1 teaspoon chopped jarred jalapeno pepper
- 1 bacon strip, cooked and crumbled
- 1/4 teaspoon salt
- 1/8 teaspoon coarsely ground pepper
- 1/2 pound ground beef
- 2 slices Swiss cheese
- Mayonnaise
- 2 sourdough rolls, split
- Tomato slices, optional

Direction

- Mix together pepper, salt, bacon and jalapeno pepper in a large bowl. Add crumbled beef to the mixture and stir well to combine. Form into 2 patties.
- Broil the burgers 4 inches from heat or put burgers on grill grate over medium heat with a cover until no longer pink and a thermometer reaches 160 degrees, about 6 minutes per side. Add cheese on top. Add mayonnaise to rolls and spread evenly. Put tomato slices to your liking and burgers on rolls to serve.

Nutrition Information

- Calories: 409 calories
- Total Carbohydrate: 24g carbohydrate (1g sugars
- Cholesterol: 83mg cholesterol
- Protein: 31g protein.
- Total Fat: 20g fat (10g saturated fat)
- Sodium: 734mg sodium
- Fiber: 1g fiber)

16. Bacon Blue Cheese Stuffed Burgers

Serving: 4 servings. | Prep: 30mins | Ready in:

Ingredients

- 1-1/2 pounds lean ground beef (90% lean)
- 3 ounces cream cheese, softened
- 1/3 cup crumbled blue cheese
- 1/3 cup bacon bits
- 1/2 teaspoon salt
- 1/2 teaspoon garlic powder
- 1/4 teaspoon pepper
- 1 pound sliced fresh mushrooms
- 1 tablespoon olive oil
- 1 tablespoon water
- 1 tablespoon Dijon mustard
- 4 whole wheat hamburger buns, split
- 1/4 cup mayonnaise
- 4 romaine leaves
- 1 medium tomato, sliced

Direction

- Form beef into 8 thin patties. Mix bacon bits, blue cheese, and cream cheese together; on the center of 4 patties, spoon the mixture. Use remaining patties to top and firmly press edges for sealing. Mix pepper, garlic powder, and salt together; dredge over patties.
- Cover and grill burgers over medium heat or broil 4 inches from the heat for 5-7 minutes per side till juices are clear and a thermometer reads 160 degrees.
- In the meantime, sauté mushrooms with oil in a large skillet till softened. Stir mustard and water in.
- Place burgers on buns with mushroom mixture, tomato, romaine, and mayonnaise for serving.

Nutrition Information

- Calories: 701 calories
- Cholesterol: 149mg cholesterol
- Protein: 48g protein.
- Total Fat: 43g fat (15g saturated fat)
- Sodium: 1280mg sodium
- Fiber: 5g fiber)
- Total Carbohydrate: 31g carbohydrate (7g sugars

17. Bacon Topped Meat Loaf

Serving: 8 servings. | Prep: 10mins | Ready in:

Ingredients

- 1/2 cup chili sauce
- 2 large eggs, lightly beaten
- 1 tablespoon Worcestershire sauce
- 1 medium onion, chopped

- 1 cup shredded cheddar cheese
- 2/3 cup dry bread crumbs
- 1/2 teaspoon salt
- 1/4 teaspoon pepper
- 2 pounds lean ground beef (90% lean)
- 2 bacon strips, halved

Direction

- In the big bowl, mix initial eight ingredients. Break up the beef on top of the mixture and combine them well. Form into the loaf in the ungreased 13x9-inch baking dish. Add the bacon on top.
- Bake, while uncovered, at 350 degrees till the thermometer reaches 160 degrees and the meat is not pink anymore or for 70 to 80 minutes. Drain off; allow it to rest for 10 minutes prior to cutting.

Nutrition Information

- Calories: 329 calories
- Cholesterol: 127mg cholesterol
- Protein: 28g protein.
- Total Fat: 17g fat (8g saturated fat)
- Sodium: 692mg sodium
- Fiber: 1g fiber)
- Total Carbohydrate: 13g carbohydrate (5g sugars

18. Baked Ziti With Fresh Tomatoes

Serving: 6 servings. | Prep: 01hours10mins | Ready in:

Ingredients

- 1 pound ground beef
- 1 cup chopped onion
- 3 pounds plum tomatoes, peeled, seeded and chopped (about 15 tomatoes)
- 1-1/2 teaspoons salt
- 1 teaspoon dried basil
- 1/4 teaspoon pepper
- 8 ounces uncooked ziti
- 2 cups shredded part-skim mozzarella cheese, divided
- 2 tablespoons grated Parmesan cheese

Direction

- In a Dutch oven, cook the onion and beef over medium heat till the meat is not pink anymore; let it drain. Mix in the pepper, basil, salt and tomatoes. Decrease heat to low; cook with cover while from time to time stirring for 45 minutes.
- Cook ziti as stated on package directions; let it drain. Put in a large bowl. Whisk in 1 cup of mozzarella cheese and sauce. Move to a greased 3-quart baking dish; scatter top with the leftover mozzarella cheese and Parmesan cheese.
- Bake with cover at 350° for about 15 minutes. Then bake with no cover for 15 more minutes, or up to heated through.

Nutrition Information

- Calories: 375 calories
- Total Fat: 14g fat (7g saturated fat)
- Sodium: 851mg sodium
- Fiber: 2g fiber)
- Total Carbohydrate: 33g carbohydrate (5g sugars
- Cholesterol: 60mg cholesterol
- Protein: 29g protein.

19. Balsamic Steak With Red Grape Relish

Serving: 4 servings. | Prep: 15mins | Ready in:

Ingredients

- 1 beef top sirloin steak (3/4 inch thick and 1 pound)

- 3/4 cup reduced-fat balsamic vinaigrette, divided
- 2-1/2 cups seedless red grapes, halved
- 4 green onions, chopped (about 1/2 cup)
- 1/2 cup crumbled blue cheese
- 1/4 teaspoon salt
- 1/4 teaspoon coarsely ground pepper

Direction

- In a big ziplock plastic bag, put in 1/2 cup of vinaigrette and the steak. Seal the ziplock bag and turn to coat the steak with the vinaigrette then let it rest for 10 minutes. While the steak is marinating on the side, mix the green onions, cheese and grapes together in a small bowl.
- Drain the marinated steak and throw away the vinaigrette marinade. Season the marinated steak with pepper and salt. Put the steak on a grill over medium heat then cover and grill or put the steak on a broiler and let it broil 4 inches away from the heat for 4-7 minutes on both sides until the preferred meat doneness is achieved (a thermometer inserted in the meat should indicate 160°F for medium, 170°F for well-done and 145°F for medium-rare).
- Slice the steak thinly. Serve it with the remaining vinaigrette and grape relish on the side.

Nutrition Information

- Calories: 332 calories
- Protein: 28g protein.
- Total Fat: 14g fat (6g saturated fat)
- Sodium: 659mg sodium
- Fiber: 1g fiber)
- Total Carbohydrate: 22g carbohydrate (18g sugars
- Cholesterol: 59mg cholesterol

20. Balsamic Seasoned Steak

Serving: 4 servings. | Prep: 10mins | Ready in:

Ingredients

- 1 beef top sirloin steak (3/4 inch thick and 1 pound)
- 1/4 teaspoon coarsely ground pepper
- 2 tablespoons balsamic vinegar
- 2 teaspoons steak sauce
- 2 ounces sliced reduced-fat Swiss cheese, cut into thin strips

Direction

- Preheat broiler. Put steak onto broiler pan; sprinkle pepper. Broil for 7 minutes 4-in. from heat. Meanwhile, mix steak sauce and vinegar.
- Flip steak; drizzle 1 tbsp. vinegar mixture. Broil for 4-6 minutes till meat gets desired doneness; 160° medium, 135° medium rare on a thermometer.
- Put steaks onto cutting board; stand for 5 minutes. Slice steak to 1/4-in. slices; put in broiler pan, slices near each other. Drizzle leftover vinegar mixture on slices; put cheese over. Broil for 30-60 seconds till cheese melts.

Nutrition Information

- Calories: 188 calories
- Sodium: 116mg sodium
- Fiber: 0 fiber)
- Total Carbohydrate: 2g carbohydrate (1g sugars
- Cholesterol: 70mg cholesterol
- Protein: 26g protein. Diabetic Exchanges: 3 lean meat
- Total Fat: 8g fat (3g saturated fat)

21. Barbecue Beef Brisket

Serving: 6 servings. | Prep: 20mins | Ready in:

Ingredients

- 1 fresh beef brisket (3 pounds)
- 1 cup barbecue sauce
- 1/2 cup finely chopped onion
- 2 tablespoons Worcestershire sauce
- 1 tablespoon prepared horseradish
- 1 teaspoon salt
- 1/2 teaspoon pepper
- 3 tablespoons cornstarch
- 1/4 cup cold water

Direction

- Cut brisket in half; put in 5-qt. slow cooker. Mix pepper, salt, horseradish, Worcestershire sauce, onion and barbecue sauce; put on beef. Cover; cook till meat is tender for 6-7 hours on low.
- Remove beef; keep warm. Boil cooking juices in big saucepan. Mix water and cornstarch till smooth; mix into pan slowly. Boil; mix and cook till thick for 2 minutes. Slice meat across grain; serve with gravy.

Nutrition Information

- Calories: 486 calories
- Fiber: 1g fiber)
- Total Carbohydrate: 12g carbohydrate (7g sugars
- Cholesterol: 136mg cholesterol
- Protein: 40g protein.
- Total Fat: 29g fat (11g saturated fat)
- Sodium: 933mg sodium

22. Barbecue Style Beef Brisket

Serving: 16-20 servings. | Prep: 20mins | Ready in:

Ingredients

- 1 tablespoon all-purpose flour
- 1 fresh beef brisket (5 pounds)
- 2 to 4 teaspoons Liquid Smoke, optional
- 1/2 teaspoon celery seed
- 1/4 teaspoon pepper
- 1 cup chili sauce
- 1/4 cup barbecue sauce

Direction

- Put the flour in a big oven roasting bag; flip it well to coat the bag. Scrub the brisket with the Liquid Smoke if preferred, pepper and celery seed; drop inside the bag. Put in a roasting pan. Stir the barbecue sauce and chili sauce and pour the mixture over brisket. Secure the bag.
- Score six slits measuring 1/2-in. on top of the bag using a knife. Let it bake for 3-1/2 to 4 hours at 325° or until the meat have softened. Let it sit for 5 minutes. Take the brisket out from bag carefully. Cut the meat across the grain thinly.

Nutrition Information

- Calories: 159 calories
- Fiber: 0 fiber)
- Total Carbohydrate: 4g carbohydrate (3g sugars
- Cholesterol: 48mg cholesterol
- Protein: 23g protein. Diabetic Exchanges: 3 lean meat.
- Total Fat: 5g fat (2g saturated fat)
- Sodium: 250mg sodium

23. Barbecued Beef Brisket

Serving: 6 servings. | Prep: 20mins | Ready in:

Ingredients

- 1/2 cup packed brown sugar
- 1/2 cup ketchup
- 1/4 cup water
- 1/4 cup cider vinegar
- 1/4 cup canola oil

- 3 tablespoons dark corn syrup
- 2 tablespoons prepared mustard
- 1 tablespoon prepared horseradish
- 1 garlic clove, minced
- BRISKET:
- 2 tablespoons canola oil
- 1 fresh beef brisket (2 to 2-1/2 pounds), trimmed

Direction

- Mix the first nine ingredients in a small saucepan; cook and combine over medium heat for 3 - 4 minutes, or till brown sugar dissolves. Move to a disposable foil pan.
- In a big frying pan, heat oil over medium heat. Brown both sides of the brisket. Line in a foil pan, flip to coat in sauce. Use foil to tightly cover the pan.
- Set the pan on a grill rack over indirect medium heat. Let it grill with cover for 2 to 2-1/4 hours, or till meat soften.
- Take away from heat. Take brisket from the pan; tent with foil then allow to rest for 10 minutes. Meanwhile, skim off the fat from sauce in pan. Slice the brisket against the grain diagonally into thin pieces; serve along with sauce.

Nutrition Information

- Calories: 437 calories
- Total Fat: 20g fat (4g saturated fat)
- Sodium: 392mg sodium
- Fiber: 0 fiber)
- Total Carbohydrate: 32g carbohydrate (26g sugars
- Cholesterol: 64mg cholesterol
- Protein: 31g protein.

24. Barbecued Beef And Beans

Serving: 8-10 servings. | Prep: 15mins | Ready in:

Ingredients

- 1 pound ground beef
- 1 medium onion, finely diced
- 1 garlic clove, minced
- 1/2 cup barbecue sauce
- 1/2 cup ketchup
- 1/4 cup molasses
- 1/2 cup packed brown sugar
- 1 jar (32 ounces) northern beans, rinsed and drained
- 1 can (28 ounces) baked beans
- 1 can (16 ounces) red kidney beans
- 1 can (15-3/4 ounces) lima beans, rinsed and drained
- 1 can (15 ounces) garbanzo beans or chickpeas, rinsed and drained
- 1 can (14-1/2 ounces) cut green beans, drained

Direction

- In a skillet, cook garlic, onion and beef over medium heat until beef is not pink anymore. Drain; then in a large greased casserole or roaster, place the beef. Stir in the ketchup, barbecue sauce, brown sugar and molasses. Add all beans and well mix.
- Uncovered while baking at 325° for nearly 30 minutes. Bake while covered for another 30 minutes.

Nutrition Information

- Calories: 433 calories
- Cholesterol: 28mg cholesterol
- Protein: 23g protein.
- Total Fat: 7g fat (2g saturated fat)
- Sodium: 1220mg sodium
- Fiber: 15g fiber)
- Total Carbohydrate: 72g carbohydrate (27g sugars

25. Bavarian Beef Roast

Serving: 8 servings. | Prep: 20mins | Ready in:

Ingredients

- 1 beef rump roast or bottom round roast (3 pounds)
- 1 garlic clove, cut into thin slivers
- 1 teaspoon canola oil
- 1 cup chopped carrots
- 1 cup thinly sliced celery
- 1 cup chopped onion
- 1 cup sherry or beef broth
- 1/2 cup minced fresh parsley
- 1 tablespoon sugar
- 2 teaspoons caraway seeds
- 1 teaspoon salt
- 1/2 teaspoon ground cardamom

Direction

- Cut thin slits in meat using a sharp knife; in each slit, place a piece of garlic. In a Dutch oven or large saucepan, brown meat in oil on all sides; drain. Add the onion, celery and carrots. Combine the parsley, sherry or broth, caraway seeds, sugar, cardamom and salt; pour over meat.
- Allow to boil. Lessen heat; simmer with cover for about 165 minutes or until meat is tender. Take meat out and slice. Skim fat from cooking liquid and serve vegetables together with meat.

Nutrition Information

- Calories: 228 calories
- Total Carbohydrate: 6g carbohydrate (0 sugars
- Cholesterol: 82mg cholesterol
- Protein: 28g protein. Diabetic Exchanges: 3 lean meat
- Total Fat: 9g fat (3g saturated fat)
- Sodium: 360mg sodium
- Fiber: 1g fiber)

26. Beef Rice Stuffed Cabbage Rolls

Serving: 6 servings. | Prep: 20mins | Ready in:

Ingredients

- 12 cabbage leaves
- 1 cup cooked brown rice
- 1/4 cup finely chopped onion
- 1 large egg, lightly beaten
- 1/4 cup fat-free milk
- 1/2 teaspoon salt
- 1/4 teaspoon pepper
- 1 pound lean ground beef (90% lean)
- SAUCE:
- 1 can (8 ounces) tomato sauce
- 1 tablespoon brown sugar
- 1 tablespoon lemon juice
- 1 teaspoon Worcestershire sauce

Direction

- In boiling water, cook cabbage in batches until crisp-tender, about 3-5 minutes. Strain; cool a little bit. Cut the thick vein from the bottom of each cabbage leaf, creating a V-shaped cut.
- Mix pepper, salt, milk, egg, onion, and rice together in a big bowl. Add the beef; stir gently but well. On each cabbage leaf, put approximately 1/4 cup beef mixture. Overlap the cut edges of leaf by gathering them together; fold over the filling. Fold in the sides and roll up.
- In a 4- or 5-quart slow cooker, put 6 rolls with the seam-side down. Combine the sauce ingredients in a bowl; pour half of sauce mixture over the cabbage rolls. Put the rest of the rolls and sauce on top. Cover and cook on low until the cabbage is soft and a thermometer displays 160° when you insert it into the beef, about 6-8 hours.

Nutrition Information

- Calories: 204 calories
- Protein: 18g protein. Diabetic Exchanges: 2 lean meat
- Total Fat: 7g fat (3g saturated fat)
- Sodium: 446mg sodium
- Fiber: 2g fiber)
- Total Carbohydrate: 16g carbohydrate (5g sugars
- Cholesterol: 83mg cholesterol

27. Beef Tater Bake

Serving: 8 servings. | Prep: 10mins | Ready in:

Ingredients

- 4 cups frozen Tater Tots
- 1 pound ground beef
- 1/4 teaspoon garlic powder
- 1/8 teaspoon pepper
- 1 can (10-3/4 ounces) condensed cream of broccoli soup, undiluted
- 1/3 cup 2% milk
- 1 package (16 ounces) frozen chopped broccoli, thawed
- 1 can (2.8 ounces) French-fried onions, divided
- 1 cup shredded Colby-Monterey Jack cheese, divided
- 1 medium tomato, chopped

Direction

- Preheat oven to 400°. In an ungreased baking dish of 13x9-inch, spread Tater Tots evenly. Uncovered while baking for around 10 minutes.
- In the meantime, in a large skillet over medium heat, cook and crumble beef for nearly 5 to 7 minutes until there is not pink anymore; and then drain. Stir in broccoli, soup, seasonings, milk, 3/4 cup onions, tomato and 1/2 cup cheese; heat through. Then pour over potatoes.
- Covered while baking for another 20 minutes. Have cheese and the remaining onions to sprinkle. Uncovered during bake for approximately 5 to 10 minutes until cheese is melted.

Nutrition Information

- Calories: 400 calories
- Sodium: 805mg sodium
- Fiber: 4g fiber)
- Total Carbohydrate: 29g carbohydrate (3g sugars
- Cholesterol: 50mg cholesterol
- Protein: 17g protein.
- Total Fat: 24g fat (9g saturated fat)

28. Beef 'n' Asparagus Pasta

Serving: 4 servings. | Prep: 10mins | Ready in:

Ingredients

- 3 cups uncooked bow tie pasta
- 1 tablespoon cornstarch
- 3/4 cup reduced-sodium beef broth, divided
- 1 beef top sirloin steak (1 pound), cut into 2-inch strips
- 1 tablespoon olive oil
- 1 pound fresh asparagus, trimmed and cut into 1-inch pieces
- 4 green onions, chopped
- 4 garlic cloves, minced
- 1 cup sliced fresh mushrooms
- 1 large tomato, diced
- 1 teaspoon dried basil
- 1/2 teaspoon dried oregano
- 1/2 cup dry red wine or additional reduced-sodium beef broth
- 2 tablespoons sliced ripe olives, drained
- 1/2 teaspoon salt
- 1/4 teaspoon pepper

Direction

- Following package directions to cook pasta. Mix together 1/4 cup of broth with cornstarch until smooth, then set aside.
- In the meantime, stir-fry beef with oil in a big nonstick wok or skillet until beef is not pink anymore or for a minute. Put in garlic, onions and asparagus, then stir-fry for 2 minutes. Put in oregano, basil, tomato and mushrooms, then stir-fry until vegetables are tender-crisp, or for 2 more minutes.
- Put in the leftover broth, pepper, salt, olives and wine. Stir cornstarch mixture and stir into the skillet gradually. Bring the mixture to a boil, then cook and stir until thickened, or for 2 minutes. Drain pasta and serve together with beef mixture.

Nutrition Information

- Calories: 451 calories
- Protein: 32g protein.
- Total Fat: 11g fat (3g saturated fat)
- Sodium: 477mg sodium
- Fiber: 4g fiber)
- Total Carbohydrate: 51g carbohydrate (5g sugars
- Cholesterol: 64mg cholesterol

29. Beef 'n' Chili Beans

Serving: 6-8 servings. | Prep: 15mins | Ready in:

Ingredients

- 3 pounds beef stew meat, cut into 1-inch cubes
- 2 tablespoons brown sugar
- 1-1/2 teaspoons ground mustard
- 1 teaspoon salt
- 1 teaspoon paprika
- 1/2 teaspoon chili powder
- 1/4 teaspoon pepper
- 1 large onion, chopped
- 2 cans (10 ounces each) diced tomatoes and green chilies, undrained
- 1 can (16 ounces) Ranch Style beans (pinto beans in seasoned tomato sauce)
- 1 can (15-1/4 ounces) whole kernel corn, drained

Direction

- Place the beef in a slow cooker (3 qt). Combine the paprika, brown sugar, chili powder, mustard, salt, and pepper; sprinkle over the beef and toss to coat. Top with corn, beans, onion, and tomatoes.
- Cover and cook on low for 6-8 hours until meat is tender.

Nutrition Information

- Calories: 373 calories
- Total Fat: 14g fat (5g saturated fat)
- Sodium: 1047mg sodium
- Fiber: 5g fiber)
- Total Carbohydrate: 22g carbohydrate (8g sugars
- Cholesterol: 106mg cholesterol
- Protein: 37g protein.

30. Beef 'n' Sausage Lasagna

Serving: 12 servings. | Prep: 45mins | Ready in:

Ingredients

- 1 pound ground beef
- 1 pound Johnsonville® Ground Mild Italian sausage
- 1 medium green pepper, chopped
- 1 medium onion, chopped
- 1 jar (26 ounces) spaghetti sauce
- 1 package (8 ounces) cream cheese, cubed
- 1 cup 4% cottage cheese
- 2 large eggs, lightly beaten
- 1 tablespoon minced fresh parsley
- 6 lasagna noodles, cooked and drained
- 2 cups shredded white cheddar cheese

- 3 teaspoons Italian seasoning, divided
- 2 cups shredded part-skim mozzarella cheese

Direction

- On medium heat, cook onion, beef, green pepper, and sausage in a big pan until the meat is not pink; drain. Reserve a cup of spaghetti sauce; pour the remaining sauce with the meat mixture. Let it simmer for 10 mins, uncovered, until the mixture is thick.
- On medium heat, melt cream cheese in a small pot; take off heat. Mix in parsley, eggs, and cottage cheese.
- In a 13-in by 9-inch greased baking dish, pour in meat sauce and add 3 noodles on top. Spread cheddar cheese and 1 1/2tsp Italian seasoning; pour in cream cheese mixture. Add the leftover noodles and saved spaghetti sauce in a layer. Top with mozzarella and leftover Italian seasoning.
- Bake in 350 degrees F oven, covered, for 35 mins. Remove cover and bake for another 10-15 mins or more until the dish is bubbly. Set aside for 15 mins. Serve.

Nutrition Information

- Calories:
- Sodium:
- Fiber:
- Total Carbohydrate:
- Cholesterol:
- Protein:
- Total Fat:

31. Beef Bourguignon

Serving: 6–8 servings | Prep: | Ready in:

Ingredients

- One 6-ounce chunk of bacon
- 1 tablespoon of olive oil or cooking oil
- 3 pounds lean stewing beef, cut into 2-inch cubes
- 1 carrot, sliced
- 1 onion, sliced
- 1 teaspoon salt
- 1/4 teaspoon pepper
- 2 tablespoons flour
- 3 cups of a full-bodied young red wine
- 2 to 3 cups brown beef stock or canned boullion
- 1 tablespoon tomato paste
- 2 cloves mashed garlic
- 1/2 teaspoon thyme
- A crumbled bay leaf
- 18 to 24 small white onions, brown-braised in stock
- 1 pound quartered fresh mushrooms sautéed in butter
- 9–10 inch fireproof casserole 3 inches deep

Direction

- Remove rind; cut bacon to lardons, 1 1/2-in. long and 1/4-in. thick sticks. Simmer bacon and rind in 1 1/2-qt. water for 10 minutes. Drain then dry.
- Preheat an oven to 450°.
- Sauté bacon in oil on medium heat to lightly brown for 2-3 minutes. Use slotted spoon to remove to side dish; put aside casserole. Reheat before sautéing beef till fat is nearly smoking.
- In paper towels, dry beef; if it's damp, it won't brown. A few pieces at a time, sauté in hot oil and bacon fat till all sides are browned nicely. Add to bacon.
- Brown sliced veggies in same fat, pouring sautéing fat out.
- Put bacon and beef back in casserole; toss with pepper and salt. Sprinkle on flour, tossing again to lightly coat beef in flour. Put casserole in center of preheated oven, uncovered, for 4 minutes. Toss meat then put back in oven for 4 minutes to cove meat with light crust and brown flour. Remove casserole and put oven to 325°.

- Mix enough bouillon/stock and wine in to barely cover meat. Add bacon rind, herbs, garlic and tomato paste; simmer on top of stove. Cover casserole and put in lower third of the preheated oven. Regulate heat so liquid very slowly simmers for 2 1/2-3 ours. If fork easily pierces meat, it is done.
- Prep mushrooms and onions as beef cooks; put aside till needed.
- Put casserole's contents into sieve set above saucepan when meat is tender.
- Wash casserole out; put bacon and beef back in it. Distribute mushrooms and cooked onions over meat.
- Skim off fat from sauce; simmer for 1-2 minutes, skimming extra fat off while rising. You should get 2 1/2 cups sauce that's thick enough to lightly coat spoon. Boil down rapidly if too thin, mix a few tbsp. stock in if too thick. For seasoning, carefully taste.
- At this point, you can prep recipe in advance.
- Immediate serving: Cover casserole; simmer, basting veggies and meat with sauce a few times for 2-3 minutes. Serve in its casserole or put stew on platter surrounded by rice/noodles/potatoes then decorate with parsley.
- Later serving: Cover and refrigerate when cold; simmer with cover 15-20 minutes before serving. Very slowly simmer for 10 minutes, basting meat and veggies with sauce occasionally.

Nutrition Information

- Calories: 881
- Saturated Fat: 36 g(178%)
- Sodium: 752 mg(31%)
- Fiber: 4 g(15%)
- Total Carbohydrate: 24 g(8%)
- Cholesterol: 243 mg(81%)
- Protein: 44 g(88%)
- Total Fat: 65 g(99%)

32. Beef Burgundy Stew

Serving: 2 servings. | Prep: 10mins | Ready in:

Ingredients

- 1/4 cup all-purpose flour
- 1/4 teaspoon salt
- 1/4 teaspoon pepper
- 3/4 pound beef top sirloin steak, cut into thin strips
- 2 tablespoons canola oil, divided
- 1 medium onion, thinly sliced
- 1 garlic clove, minced
- 2/3 cup beef broth
- 2/3 cup burgundy wine or additional beef broth
- 1/2 teaspoon dried basil
- Hot cooked egg noodles

Direction

- Combine pepper, salt, and flour in a big plastic resealable bag; Add a few pieces of beef at a time, then shake to coat them.
- Brown the beef on all sides with 1 tablespoon of oil using a small skillet. Remove the beef and set them aside. Use the same skillet to sauté garlic and onion with the remaining oil until soft.
- Return the beef into the pan and stir in basil, wine, and broth, then boil. Turn the heat down and simmer while covered until the meat is soft, or for about 25 - 30 minutes. Serve this along with egg noodles.

Nutrition Information

- Calories: 486 calories
- Protein: 36g protein.
- Total Fat: 23g fat (5g saturated fat)
- Sodium: 648mg sodium
- Fiber: 2g fiber)
- Total Carbohydrate: 21g carbohydrate (6g sugars
- Cholesterol: 94mg cholesterol

33. Beef Burritos

Serving: Makes 6 servings. | Prep: 20mins | Ready in:

Ingredients

- 2 medium avocado s (about 1 lb.), peeled, pitted
- 1/4 cup BREAKSTONE'S or KNUDSEN Sour Cream
- 1 clove garlic, minced
- 1/2 tsp. ground cumin
- 1/4 cup chopped cilantro
- 6 flour tortilla s (6 inch), warmed
- 2 cups shredded cooked roast beef, warmed
- 1 cup KRAFT Mexican Style Finely Shredded Cheddar Jack Cheese
- 1/2 cup salsa

Direction

- Mash together cumin, garlic, sour cream and avocados until well combined, then stir in cilantro.
- Spread on each tortilla with 2 tbsp. of avocado mixture, then put 1/3 cup of meat and 1 tbsp. of cheese on top of each. Roll up and tuck in both sides of each tortilla as you roll it up.
- Put any leftover avocado mixture and cheese on top, then serve together with salsa.

Nutrition Information

- Calories: 400
- Sugar: 2 g
- Saturated Fat: 8 g
- Sodium: 460 mg
- Fiber: 6 g
- Total Fat: 23 g
- Total Carbohydrate: 27 g
- Cholesterol: 65 mg
- Protein: 22 g

34. Beef Cabbage Roll Ups

Serving: 6 servings. | Prep: 30mins | Ready in:

Ingredients

- 1 head cabbage
- 1 large potato, peeled and shredded
- 1 large carrot, shredded
- 1/2 cup finely chopped celery
- 1/2 cup finely chopped green pepper
- 1/2 cup finely chopped onion
- 2 eggs, lightly beaten
- 2 garlic cloves, minced
- 3/4 teaspoon salt
- 1/2 teaspoon pepper
- 1 pound lean ground beef (90% lean)
- 2 cans (8 ounces each) tomato sauce
- 1/2 teaspoon dried basil
- 1/2 teaspoon dried parsley flakes

Direction

- Boil the water, add the cabbage. Cook until the leaves are separated from the head. Remove the thick vein of the 12 large leaves' bottom to create a V shape cut and set aside. Store the rest of cabbage in fridge for future use. Mix the pepper, salt, garlic, eggs, onion, green pepper, celery, carrot and potato together in a big bowl. Break the beef into crumbs over the mixture and blend well.
- Form into 12 logs. Lay one log on each cabbage leaf, overlap the leaf's cut ends. Fold in the sides, starting with the cut end and roll carefully to cover the filling. Use toothpick to secure.
- Use cooking spray to grease a 13x9-inch baking dish. Lay the cabbage on the prepared dish. Spoon the tomato sauce over roll-ups. Dredge parsley and basil on top. Set oven at 350°, bake while covered until the cabbage gets tender and the thermometer reaches 160°, about 30 to 35 minutes.

Nutrition Information

- Calories: 251 calories
- Total Carbohydrate: 25g carbohydrate (8g sugars
- Cholesterol: 108mg cholesterol
- Protein: 21g protein.
- Total Fat: 8g fat (3g saturated fat)
- Sodium: 584mg sodium
- Fiber: 6g fiber)

35. Beef Osso Bucco

Serving: 6 servings. | Prep: 30mins | Ready in:

Ingredients

- 1/2 cup all-purpose flour
- 3/4 teaspoon salt, divided
- 1/2 teaspoon pepper
- 6 beef shanks (14 ounces each)
- 2 tablespoons butter
- 1 tablespoon olive oil
- 1/2 cup white wine or beef broth
- 1 can (14-1/2 ounces) diced tomatoes, undrained
- 1-1/2 cups beef broth
- 2 medium carrots, chopped
- 1 medium onion, chopped
- 1 celery rib, sliced
- 1 tablespoon dried thyme
- 1 tablespoon dried oregano
- 2 bay leaves
- 3 tablespoons cornstarch
- 1/4 cup cold water
- GREMOLATA:
- 1/3 cup minced fresh parsley
- 1 tablespoon grated lemon zest
- 1 tablespoon grated orange zest
- 2 garlic cloves, minced
- Polenta, optional

Direction

- Mix together pepper, 1/2 teaspoon salt and flour in a large resealable plastic bag. Place a few pieces of beef in the bag at a time, shake to coat.
- Brown beef in oil and butter in a large skillet. Transfer drippings and meat to a 6-qt. slow cooker. Add wine to the skillet, stirring to loosen browned bits from pan; and pour over meat. Add bay leaves, oregano, thyme, celery, onion, carrots, broth, tomatoes and the remaining salt.
- Cook with a cover on low until meat is tender, about 7-9 hours. Remove bay leaves.
- Skim fat from cooking juices; pour juices in the large saucepan. Bring to a boil. Mix water and cornstarch together until smooth; stir gradually into the pan. Bring to a boil; cook while stirring until thickened, about 2 minutes.
- Mix the gremolata ingredients in a small bowl. Serve beef with sauce and gremolata, and over polenta if preferred.

Nutrition Information

- Calories: 398 calories
- Total Carbohydrate: 17g carbohydrate (5g sugars
- Cholesterol: 112mg cholesterol
- Protein: 47g protein.
- Total Fat: 15g fat (6g saturated fat)
- Sodium: 640mg sodium
- Fiber: 4g fiber)

36. Beef Pizza Loaf

Serving: 8 servings. | Prep: 10mins | Ready in:

Ingredients

- 2 large eggs
- 1 cup whole milk
- 1 cup crushed butter-flavored crackers (about 25 crackers)
- 1 medium onion, chopped
- 1/2 cup grated Parmesan cheese
- 1-1/2 teaspoons salt

- 1 teaspoon minced fresh oregano or 1/4 teaspoon dried oregano
- 2 pounds ground beef
- 1 cup pizza sauce
- 1 cup shredded part-skim mozzarella cheese
- Sliced fresh mushrooms and green pepper, optional

Direction

- Blend the first 7 ingredients in a bowl. Crumble the beef and place over the mixture, combine thoroughly. Then pat it into an 8-inch square baking pan coated with cooking spray.
- Bake at 350 degrees without a cover until the meat is not pink anymore and a thermometer registers 160 degrees, 50 minutes; drain.
- Top with pizza sauce. Dust with the mozzarella cheese. Bake until the cheese melts, 10 more minutes.
- At the same time, if you want, in a skillet, sauté green pepper and mushrooms. Gently place the meat loaf into a serving platter with 2 large spatulas. Put green pepper and mushrooms on top.

Nutrition Information

- Calories: 398 calories
- Cholesterol: 147mg cholesterol
- Protein: 31g protein.
- Total Fat: 23g fat (10g saturated fat)
- Sodium: 851mg sodium
- Fiber: 1g fiber)
- Total Carbohydrate: 14g carbohydrate (5g sugars

37. Beef Potpie

Serving: 2 servings. | Prep: 20mins | Ready in:

Ingredients

- 1 tablespoon butter
- 1 teaspoon dried minced onion
- 1 tablespoon all-purpose flour
- 1/8 teaspoon pepper
- 2/3 cup beef broth
- 1 cup frozen mixed vegetables, thawed
- 1/2 cup cubed cooked roast beef
- CRUST:
- 1 egg
- 2 tablespoons milk
- 1/2 cup biscuit/baking mix

Direction

- Melt butter in a small saucepan. Put in onion cook for a minute. Toss in pepper and flour until mixed. Gradually mix in broth. Take to a boil; cook and mix until thickened, about 2 minutes. Blend in beef and vegetables; heat through. Move to 2 greased custard cups of 10 ounce.
- Mix milk and egg in a small bowl. Toss in biscuit mix until smooth. Spoon over the meat mixture uniformly. Put on an ungreased baking sheet. Bake for 25 to 30 minutes at 400°, until top is golden brown and the pie is bubbly.

Nutrition Information

- Calories: 364 calories
- Cholesterol: 154mg cholesterol
- Protein: 22g protein.
- Total Fat: 15g fat (7g saturated fat)
- Sodium: 804mg sodium
- Fiber: 5g fiber)
- Total Carbohydrate: 35g carbohydrate (5g sugars

38. Beef Roast Au Poivre With Caramelized Onions

Serving: 6 servings. | Prep: 30mins | Ready in:

Ingredients

- 2 tablespoons each whole black and pink peppercorns or 1/4 cup whole black peppercorns
- 3 dried chipotle chilies, stems removed
- 1 tablespoon coriander seeds
- 1 tablespoon dried minced onion
- 1 tablespoon dried thyme
- 1-1/2 teaspoons salt
- 1 teaspoon dried orange peel
- 3 tablespoons steak sauce
- 1 beef tri-tip roast (2 to 3 pounds)
- ONIONS:
- 4 large onions, thinly sliced
- 3 tablespoons olive oil
- 1/2 cup chardonnay or other white wine
- 2 teaspoons dried thyme
- 1/2 teaspoon pepper
- 1/8 teaspoon salt
- 2 tablespoons minced fresh parsley

Direction

- Put the coriander, chilies and peppercorns in a blender. Put on cover and process until grounded roughly. Stir in the orange peel, salt, thyme and onion.
- Rub the seasoning mixture and steak sauce over roast; refrigerate with a cover for 8 hours or overnight.
- Put roast on a rack placed in a shallow roasting pan. Bake without a cover for 1 to 1-1/2 hours at 425°, or until the meat's doneness reaches desired level (for medium-rare meat, a thermometer should show 145°; 160° for medium; 170° for well-done).
- In the meantime, cook while frequently stirring onions with oil in a large skillet on low heat for 30-35 minutes, or until turn golden brown. Mix in wine and bring to a boil. Lower the heat; cook while stirring for 1-2 minutes, or until liquid is boiled away. Stir in the salt, pepper and thyme.
- Move the meat into a warm serving platter. Allow to sit for 10 minutes before cutting. Top with parsley. Serve along with the onions.

Nutrition Information

- Calories: 367 calories
- Sodium: 851mg sodium
- Fiber: 3g fiber)
- Total Carbohydrate: 15g carbohydrate (6g sugars
- Cholesterol: 91mg cholesterol
- Protein: 33g protein.
- Total Fat: 18g fat (5g saturated fat)

39. Beef Roast With Gravy

Serving: 8 servings. | Prep: 10mins | Ready in:

Ingredients

- 1 pound fresh baby carrots
- 1 can (4 ounces) mushroom stems and pieces, drained
- 1 beef rump roast or bottom round roast (3 pounds)
- 1/2 teaspoon garlic powder
- 1/4 teaspoon pepper
- 1 tablespoon canola oil
- 1 jar (12 ounces) beef gravy
- 1 can (10-3/4 ounces) condensed cream of mushroom soup, undiluted
- 1 cup water
- 1 envelope onion soup mix

Direction

- Place mushrooms and carrots in a 4- or 5-qt. slow cooker. Top the roast with pepper and garlic powder. Brown all sides of roast with oil in a large skillet. Move into the slow cooker.
- Combine the onion soup mix, water, mushroom soup and gravy; and pour over the roast. Cook with a cover for 6-8 hours on low, or until meat becomes tender. If necessary, remove fat from gravy; serve gravy along with beef.

Nutrition Information

- Calories: 314 calories
- Fiber: 2g fiber)
- Total Carbohydrate: 13g carbohydrate (3g sugars
- Cholesterol: 106mg cholesterol
- Protein: 36g protein.
- Total Fat: 12g fat (3g saturated fat)
- Sodium: 995mg sodium

40. Beef Stew For Two

Serving: 2 servings. | Prep: 30mins | Ready in:

Ingredients

- 1-1/2 cups dry red wine or beef broth, divided
- 3 tablespoons lemon juice
- 2 teaspoons reduced-sodium soy sauce
- 2 teaspoons Worcestershire sauce
- 1/2 pound beef stew meat, cut into 1-inch cubes
- 2 teaspoons olive oil
- 1 small onion, chopped
- 3 garlic cloves, minced
- 2-1/2 cups beef broth, divided
- 2 small potatoes, cut into 1-inch cubes
- 2 medium carrots, cut into 1-inch slices
- 1 cup sliced baby portobello mushrooms
- 2 fresh thyme sprigs
- 1/8 teaspoon cayenne pepper
- 2 teaspoons cornstarch

Direction

- Combine Worcestershire sauce, soy sauce, lemon juice, and 1 cup of wine in a big plastic resealable bag, then add the beef. Seal the bag, turning to coat, and refrigerate for 8 hours or overnight.
- Drain and throw out the marinade. Brown the beef with oil in a large saucepan then remove the meat and put aside. Using the same pan, sauté the onion until tender. Add garlic and cook for 1 more minute. Add the remaining wine and 2 cups of beef broth, then return the meat onto the pan.
- Allow the stew to boil. Decrease the heat and simmer, covered, for 30 minutes. Add cayenne, thyme, mushrooms, carrots, and potatoes, then allow to boil. Decrease the heat and simmer while covered until the beef and vegetables are tender, or for about 30 minutes. Throw away the thyme sprigs.
- Combine remaining beef broth and cornstarch in a small bowl until smooth, then stir into the stew gradually and allow to boil. Cook while stirring for 2 minutes or until thick.

Nutrition Information

- Calories: 466 calories
- Sodium: 697mg sodium
- Fiber: 5g fiber)
- Total Carbohydrate: 44g carbohydrate (10g sugars
- Cholesterol: 77mg cholesterol
- Protein: 29g protein.
- Total Fat: 13g fat (4g saturated fat)

41. Beef Tips On Rice

Serving: 75 servings (3/4 cup rice and 3/4 cup beef with sauce). | Prep: 45mins | Ready in:

Ingredients

- 20 pounds beef stew meat, cut into 1-inch cubes
- 2 tablespoons salt
- 5 teaspoons pepper
- 5 teaspoons dried thyme
- 15 cans (10-3/4 ounces each) condensed cream of mushroom soup, undiluted
- 4 cups water
- 4 cups chopped onion
- 2/3 cup chopped fresh parsley
- 2-1/2 teaspoons browning sauce, optional

- 6-1/2 to 7 pounds long grain rice, cooked

Direction

- Mix thyme, pepper, salt and beef well; put into 5 13x9-in. greased baking pans. Bake at 400°, with no cover, for 15 minutes; mix. Bake for 15 minutes; drain. Mix browning sauce (optional), parsley, onion, water and soup. Put on beef; stir well. Cover; bake for 1 1/2-2 hours at 350° till beef is tender. Serve on rice.

Nutrition Information

- Calories: 325 calories
- Total Fat: 9g fat (3g saturated fat)
- Sodium: 269mg sodium
- Fiber: 1g fiber)
- Total Carbohydrate: 33g carbohydrate (1g sugars
- Cholesterol: 75mg cholesterol
- Protein: 26g protein.

and turn to coat; keep cool in refrigerator for 8 hours or overnight.
- Drain. Remove marinade. Thread beef onto six soaked wooden or metal skewers. Moisten a paper towel with cooking oil using long-handled tongs, and coat the grill rack lightly. Cover and grill over medium heat or broil 4 in. from the heat, until meat achieves desired doneness, for 8-10 minutes, turning occasionally.

Nutrition Information

- Calories: 161 calories
- Sodium: 174mg sodium
- Fiber: 0 fiber)
- Total Carbohydrate: 3g carbohydrate (2g sugars
- Cholesterol: 64mg cholesterol
- Protein: 22g protein. Diabetic Exchanges: 3 lean meat.
- Total Fat: 6g fat (2g saturated fat)

42. Beef On A Stick

Serving: 6 kabobs. | Prep: 15mins | Ready in:

Ingredients

- 1/3 cup reduced-sodium soy sauce
- 3 tablespoons honey
- 2 tablespoons canola oil
- 2 tablespoons cider vinegar
- 2 tablespoons hoisin sauce
- 1 tablespoon brown sugar
- 1-1/2 teaspoons Worcestershire sauce
- 2 garlic cloves, minced
- 1 boneless beef top sirloin steak (1-1/2 pounds), cut into 1-inch cubes

Direction

- Mix the first eight ingredients in a large resealable plastic bag; add in beef. Close bag

43. Beef Or Venison Stew

Serving: 8-10 servings. | Prep: 10mins | Ready in:

Ingredients

- 2 tablespoons vegetable oil
- 2 pounds beef or venison stew meat
- 3 large onions, coarsely chopped
- 2 garlic cloves, crushed
- 1 tablespoon Worcestershire sauce
- 1 bay leaf
- 1 teaspoon dried oregano
- 1 tablespoon salt
- 1 teaspoon pepper
- 7 medium potatoes, peeled and quartered
- 1 pound carrots, cut into 1-inch pieces
- 1/4 cup all-purpose flour
- 1/4 cup cold water
- Browning sauce, optional

Direction

- Heat oil in a large Dutch oven. Cook meat until browned. Put in salt and pepper, oregano, bay leaf, Worcestershire sauce, garlic, onions. Simmer for 1-1/2 to 2 hours while covered, until meat is tender.
- Put in carrots and potatoes. Keep cooking about 30 to 45 minutes until veggies are tender. Stir water and flour; mix into stew. Cook and mix until bubbly and thick.
- Put browning sauce into gravy for more color (optional). Throw away bay leaf. Serve in a bowl.

Nutrition Information

- Calories: 323 calories
- Protein: 22g protein.
- Total Fat: 9g fat (3g saturated fat)
- Sodium: 788mg sodium
- Fiber: 5g fiber)
- Total Carbohydrate: 38g carbohydrate (8g sugars
- Cholesterol: 56mg cholesterol

44. Beefy Hash Brown Bake

Serving: 4 servings. | Prep: 15mins | Ready in:

Ingredients

- 4 cups frozen shredded hash brown potatoes
- 3 tablespoons canola oil
- 1/8 teaspoon pepper
- 1 pound ground beef
- 1 cup water
- 1 envelope brown gravy mix
- 1/2 teaspoon garlic salt
- 2 cups frozen mixed vegetables
- 1 can (2.8 ounces) french-fried onions, divided
- 1 cup shredded cheddar cheese, divided

Direction

- Mix pepper, oil and potatoes together in a large bowl. Press into a greased 8-in square baking dish. Bake with no cover at 350° until potatoes are thawed and set, about 15-20 minutes.
- In the meantime, cook the beef in a large saucepan over medium heat until not pink anymore; drain. Mix in garlic salt, gravy mix and water. Let it come to a boil; cook and stir for 2 minutes. Put in vegetables; cook and stir for 5 minutes. Stir in 1/2 of the cheese and onions.
- Spread over potatoes. Bake for 5-10 minutes. Sprinkle the remaining cheese and onions on top; bake until cheese is melted, about 5 more minutes.

Nutrition Information

- Calories: 682 calories
- Sodium: 1201mg sodium
- Fiber: 5g fiber)
- Total Carbohydrate: 39g carbohydrate (5g sugars
- Cholesterol: 105mg cholesterol
- Protein: 35g protein.
- Total Fat: 43g fat (16g saturated fat)

45. Berry Nice Brisket

Serving: 10-12 servings. | Prep: 15mins | Ready in:

Ingredients

- 1/4 cup all-purpose flour
- 1 can (14-1/2 ounces) beef broth
- 1 can (14 ounces) whole-berry cranberry sauce
- 1 cup cranberry juice
- 3 garlic cloves, minced
- 1 tablespoon minced fresh rosemary or 1 teaspoon dried rosemary, crushed
- 1 large onion, thinly sliced
- 1 fresh beef brisket (3 to 4 pounds)
- 1/2 teaspoon salt

- 1/4 teaspoon pepper

Direction

- In a big bowl, mix the broth and flour till smooth. Whisk in rosemary, garlic, cranberry juice and cranberry sauce. Add to a big roasting pan. Add the slices of onion on top.
- Use pepper and salt to season brisket. Position in pan with fat-side facing upward. Bake with cover at 350 degrees till the meat softens or for 3-3.5 hours, basting once in a while.
- Transfer the brisket to the serving platter and allow it to rest for 15 minutes. Thinly cut the meat across grain; serve along with the pan juices and onion.

Nutrition Information

- Calories: 219 calories
- Sodium: 298mg sodium
- Fiber: 1g fiber)
- Total Carbohydrate: 18g carbohydrate (11g sugars
- Cholesterol: 48mg cholesterol
- Protein: 24g protein. Diabetic Exchanges: 3 lean meat
- Total Fat: 5g fat (2g saturated fat)

46. Best Ever Roast Beef

Serving: 6 servings. | Prep: 15mins | Ready in:

Ingredients

- 1 boneless beef chuck roast (4 pounds), trimmed
- 1 large sweet onion, chopped
- 1-1/3 cups plus 3 tablespoons water, divided
- 1 can (10-1/2 ounces) condensed French onion soup
- 1 cup packed brown sugar
- 1/3 cup reduced-sodium soy sauce
- 1/4 cup cider vinegar
- 6 garlic cloves, minced
- 1 teaspoon ground ginger
- 1/4 teaspoon pepper
- 3 tablespoons cornstarch

Direction

- Take the roast and cut in half. Place in a 5-qt. slow cooker and add 1 1/3 cups of water and onion. Mix brown sugar, vinegar, pepper, soup, garlic, soy sauce, and ginger in a small bowl. Dump on top of roast and onion. Place cover and set cooker on low; cook until beef is tender, 7-8 hours. Take the meat out of the cooker and place on a platter; keep warm. Scrape the fat from the cooking juices and put the juices in a small pot. Heat the juices to a boil. In a separate bowl, mix the remaining water and cornstarch until not lumpy. Slowly stir into the pot. Heat to boiling. Stirring constantly cook until thick, 2 minutes. Serve the sauce with the roast beef.

Nutrition Information

- Calories: 718 calories
- Total Carbohydrate: 48g carbohydrate (40g sugars
- Cholesterol: 199mg cholesterol
- Protein: 62g protein.
- Total Fat: 29g fat (11g saturated fat)
- Sodium: 1056mg sodium
- Fiber: 1g fiber)

47. Biscuit Topped Beef Casserole

Serving: 2 servings. | Prep: 25mins | Ready in:

Ingredients

- 1/2 pound lean ground beef (90% lean)
- 1/4 cup chopped onion
- 1/2 cup water
- 1/2 cup tomato sauce

- 1/4 cup tomato paste
- 1/8 teaspoon pepper
- 1 cup frozen mixed vegetables, thawed
- 1/2 cup shredded part-skim mozzarella cheese, divided
- 1 tube (6 ounces) refrigerated flaky buttermilk biscuits
- 1 teaspoon butter, melted
- 1/4 teaspoon dried oregano

Direction

- Cook onion and beef in a small saucepan over moderate heat until meat is not pink anymore, drain. Stir in pepper, tomato paste, tomato sauce and water, then bring to a boil. Lower heat and simmer without a cover for 10 minutes.
- Take away from the heat and stir in 1/4 cup of cheese and vegetables. Transfer to a 1-quart baking dish coated with cooking spray (dish will be full).
- Split each biscuit in half horizontally and place around the edge of dish. Brush with butter and sprinkle oregano over. Sprinkle over beef filling with leftover cheese.
- Bake at 375 degrees without a cover until heated through and biscuits turn golden brown, about 18 to 22 minutes.

Nutrition Information

- Calories: 570 calories
- Sodium: 1289mg sodium
- Fiber: 7g fiber)
- Total Carbohydrate: 65g carbohydrate (11g sugars
- Cholesterol: 77mg cholesterol
- Protein: 40g protein.
- Total Fat: 17g fat (8g saturated fat)

48. Biscuit Topped Italian Casserole

Serving: 6-8 servings. | Prep: 20mins | Ready in:

Ingredients

- 1 pound ground beef
- 1 can (8 ounces) tomato sauce
- 3/4 cup water
- 1/4 teaspoon pepper
- 1 package (10 ounces) frozen mixed vegetables
- 2 cups shredded cheddar cheese, divided
- 1 tube (12 ounces) refrigerated buttermilk biscuits
- 1 tablespoon butter, melted
- 1/2 teaspoon dried oregano

Direction

- Cook beef in a big frying pan over medium heat until no pink remains; strain. Mix in pepper, water, and tomato sauce. Boil it. Lower the heat, put a cover on and simmer for 15 minutes. Take away from heat. Mix in 1 1/2 cups cheese and vegetables. Remove into a 13x9-inch baking dish coated with cooking spray.
- Separate each biscuit into two. Around the edge of the dish, arrange the biscuits, partially overlapping, use butter to brush and oregano to sprinkle. Sprinkle over the meat mixture with the leftover cheese. Bake without a cover at 375° until the biscuits turn golden brown, about 25-30 minutes.

Nutrition Information

- Calories: 354 calories
- Sodium: 718mg sodium
- Fiber: 2g fiber)
- Total Carbohydrate: 27g carbohydrate (2g sugars
- Cholesterol: 71mg cholesterol
- Protein: 22g protein.
- Total Fat: 17g fat (10g saturated fat)

49. Blue Cheese Burgers

Serving: 12 | Prep: 15mins | Ready in:

Ingredients

- 3 pounds lean ground beef
- 4 ounces blue cheese, crumbled
- 1/2 cup minced fresh chives
- 1/4 teaspoon hot pepper sauce
- 1 teaspoon Worcestershire sauce
- 1 teaspoon coarsely ground black pepper
- 1 1/2 teaspoons salt
- 1 teaspoon dry mustard
- 12 French rolls or hamburger buns

Direction

- Combine mustard, salt, black pepper, Worcestershire sauce, hot pepper sauce, chives, blue cheese, and ground beef together in a large bowl. Refrigerate, covered, for 2 hours.
- Heat grill for high heat beforehand. Shape the burger mixture gently into approximately 12 patties.
- Grease the grill grate with oil. Grill patties till well done, 5 minutes per side. Place onto rolls and serve.

Nutrition Information

- Calories: 348 calories;
- Total Fat: 20.5
- Sodium: 765
- Total Carbohydrate: 19.6
- Cholesterol: 81
- Protein: 27.2

50. Blue Cheese Flat Iron Steak

Serving: 4 servings. | Prep: 15mins | Ready in:

Ingredients

- 1/4 cup olive oil
- 2 tablespoons red wine vinegar
- 2 garlic cloves, minced
- 1 teaspoon dried oregano
- 1 teaspoon dried rosemary, crushed
- 1 teaspoon pepper
- 1/4 teaspoon salt
- 1-1/4 pounds beef flat iron steak or top sirloin steak (1 inch thick)
- BLUE CHEESE BUTTER:
- 1/4 cup crumbled blue cheese
- 3 tablespoons butter, softened
- 1 tablespoon minced fresh chives
- 1/8 teaspoon pepper

Direction

- Mix all the initial 7 ingredients together in a big Ziplock plastic bag. Put in the beef then seal the Ziplock bag and turn to coat the beef with the marinade. Keep in the fridge for 30 minutes.
- Combine the pepper, blue cheese, chives and butter together in a small bowl then put it aside. Drain the marinated beef and throw away the marinade mixture.
- Put the marinated beef on a grill over medium heat then cover and grill or put the marinated beef in a broiler and let it broil 4 inches away from the heat for 5 to 7 minutes on every side until the preferred meat doneness is achieved (a thermometer inserted on the meat should indicate 170°F for well-done, 160°F for medium and 145°F for medium-rare). Serve it with blue cheese butter on the side.

Nutrition Information

- Calories: 483 calories
- Cholesterol: 120mg cholesterol
- Protein: 29g protein.
- Total Fat: 39g fat (15g saturated fat)
- Sodium: 414mg sodium
- Fiber: 0 fiber)
- Total Carbohydrate: 2g carbohydrate (0 sugars

51. Blue Cheese Stroganoff

Serving: 2 servings. | Prep: 10mins | Ready in:

Ingredients

- 1 bacon strip, diced
- 1/2 pound boneless beef sirloin steak, cut into thin strips
- 1/4 teaspoon beef bouillon granules
- 1/4 cup hot water
- 3/4 cup frozen sugar snap peas
- 4 ounces cream cheese, softened
- 1/3 cup crumbled blue cheese
- 1 tablespoon all-purpose flour
- 1/8 teaspoon salt
- 1/8 teaspoon pepper
- 1/3 cup 2% milk
- Hot cooked egg noodles

Direction

- Cook bacon over medium heat in a small skillet until crispy. With a slotted spoon, remove to paper towel. Cook beef in the same skillet over medium heat until not pink anymore. Mix water and bouillon; blend into the skillet. Add in peas. Bring to a boil. Lower the heat; cover and simmer, about 10 minutes, or until tender.
- In the meantime, in a small bowl, whisk pepper, salt, flour, blue cheese, and cream cheese, until smooth. Whisk in milk. Gradually blend into the beef mixture. Cook and stir, until heated through, or for 2 to 3 minutes. Serve over noodles; dust with bacon.

Nutrition Information

- Calories: 475 calories
- Total Fat: 31g fat (17g saturated fat)
- Sodium: 890mg sodium
- Fiber: 2g fiber)

- Total Carbohydrate: 11g carbohydrate (6g sugars
- Cholesterol: 131mg cholesterol
- Protein: 36g protein.

52. Blue Cheese Stuffed Steaks For Two

Serving: 2 servings. | Prep: 20mins | Ready in:

Ingredients

- 5 garlic cloves, peeled
- 1 tablespoon canola oil
- 2 cups grape tomatoes
- 2 boneless beef top loin steaks (8 ounces each)
- 1/4 cup crumbled blue cheese
- 1/4 teaspoon salt
- 1/8 teaspoon pepper

Direction

- Sauté garlic in the oil in large pan, until tender. Cook, covered, over low heat until softened and golden, about 5 to 7 minutes. Put in tomatoes. Cook while stirring just until the tomatoes start to burst. Take away from pan. Put aside then keep warm.
- In thickest part of each steak, cut a pocket; fill with the blue cheese. Season with pepper and salt.
- Cook steaks in the same skillet over medium heat, until the meat reaches preferred doneness (a thermometer should register 145° for medium-rare; 160° for medium; well-done, 170°), about 4 to 5 minutes per side. Enjoy with the tomato mixture.

Nutrition Information

- Calories: 463 calories
- Total Fat: 23g fat (8g saturated fat)
- Sodium: 644mg sodium
- Fiber: 2g fiber)

- Total Carbohydrate: 10g carbohydrate (4g sugars
- Cholesterol: 113mg cholesterol
- Protein: 53g protein.

53. Brief Burritos

Serving: 8 servings. | Prep: 10mins | Ready in:

Ingredients

- 1 pound ground beef
- 1 can (16 ounces) refried beans
- 1 can (10 ounces) diced tomatoes and green chilies, drained
- 1/2 cup chili sauce
- 8 flour tortillas (10 inches), warmed
- 1/2 cup shredded cheddar cheese
- 1/2 cup sour cream

Direction

- Over medium heat, cook beef for 6 to 8 minutes or until no longer pink, breaking into crumbles, in a big skillet. Drain, then, stir chili sauce, tomatoes and beans in. Heat through.
- Near the center of each tortilla, put about 1/2 cup of meat mixture, then put sour cream and cheese on top. Fold sides and bottom of tortilla over filling. Roll up and immediately serve.

Nutrition Information

- Calories: 430 calories
- Protein: 21g protein.
- Total Fat: 14g fat (7g saturated fat)
- Sodium: 1022mg sodium
- Fiber: 9g fiber)
- Total Carbohydrate: 46g carbohydrate (5g sugars
- Cholesterol: 50mg cholesterol

54. Brisket With Cranberry Horseradish Gravy

Serving: 10 servings. | Prep: 15mins | Ready in:

Ingredients

- 1 teaspoon onion powder
- 1 teaspoon salt
- 1 teaspoon coarsely ground pepper
- 1/2 teaspoon ground allspice
- 1 fresh beef brisket (5 pounds)
- 1 can (14 ounces) whole-berry cranberry sauce
- 3/4 cup horseradish sauce
- 2 teaspoons lemon juice
- 1 bay leaf
- 3 tablespoons cornstarch
- 1/4 cup cold water

Direction

- Mix allspice, pepper, salt and onion powder; rub on brisket. Cut brisket in half; put in 5-qt. slow cooker.
- Mix bay leaf, lemon juice, horseradish and cranberry sauce; put on beef.
- Cover; cook till tender for 6-7 hours on low.
- Remove brisket; keep warm. Strain cooking juices and discard bay leaf. Put 3 cups cooking juices in small saucepan.
- Mix cold water and cornstarch till smooth; mix into juices. Boil; mix and cook till thick for 2 minutes. Across grain, thinly slice beef; serve with gravy.

Nutrition Information

- Calories: 426 calories
- Total Fat: 15g fat (4g saturated fat)
- Sodium: 446mg sodium
- Fiber: 1g fiber)
- Total Carbohydrate: 21g carbohydrate (13g sugars
- Cholesterol: 114mg cholesterol
- Protein: 46g protein.

55. Broccoli Primavera With Cheese Sauce

Serving: 8 servings. | Prep: 30mins | Ready in:

Ingredients

- 4 tablespoons olive oil
- 1 garlic clove, sliced
- 1 medium head of broccoli, cut into 2-inch x 1-inch pieces
- 1 small red pepper, diced
- 3/4 cup green onions, sliced
- 1 cup sliced fresh mushrooms
- 1/2 cup celery, diced
- 1 cup milk
- 5 ounces processed cheese spread, cubed
- 1/4 cup Parmesan cheese
- 1/2 teaspoon leaf oregano
- 1/2 pound ground beef or Johnsonville® Ground Mild Italian sausage, cooked and crumbled (optional)
- Cooked spaghetti

Direction

- Heat the oil in a large skillet. Cook the garlic until it is browned; then discard. Put celery, mushrooms, onion, red pepper, and broccoli; stir continuously and cook until crisp-tender.
- Add oregano, Parmesan cheese, cubed cheese, and milk, stir and cook until the cheese is melted. If desired, put in the meat. Place over the hot cooked pasta to serve.

Nutrition Information

- Calories:
- Protein:
- Total Fat:
- Sodium:
- Fiber:
- Total Carbohydrate:
- Cholesterol:

56. Broiled Pizza Burgers

Serving: 4 servings. | Prep: 5mins | Ready in:

Ingredients

- 1 pound ground beef
- 1 tablespoon chopped onion
- 2 teaspoons cornstarch
- 1 can (14-1/2 ounces) diced tomatoes, undrained
- 1 teaspoon dried oregano
- 1/4 teaspoon salt
- 1/4 teaspoon onion salt
- 10 slices process cheese (Velveeta), divided
- 4 hamburger buns, split

Direction

- Sauté onion and beef over medium heat in a large skillet until meat is no longer pink; drain well. Stir in cornstarch until well combined. Mix in onion salt, salt, oregano, and tomatoes cook without cover until slightly thickened, for 5 minutes. Add 6 cheese slices; cook, stir well until cheese is melted and combined.
- Place hamburger buns on an unoiled baking sheet, cut side up; ladle about 1/4 cup meat mixture onto each half of bun. Halve remainder of cheese slices diagonally; place atop meat mixture. Broil about 6 to 8 inches away from the heat until cheese melts, for 3 to 4 minutes.

Nutrition Information

- Calories: 560 calories
- Protein: 38g protein.
- Total Fat: 30g fat (16g saturated fat)
- Sodium: 1550mg sodium
- Fiber: 3g fiber)
- Total Carbohydrate: 33g carbohydrate (12g sugars
- Cholesterol: 101mg cholesterol

57. Broiled Sirloin

Serving: 10 servings. | Prep: 10mins | Ready in:

Ingredients

- 3 pounds beef top sirloin or round steaks (about 1 inch thick)
- 1 medium onion, chopped
- 1/2 cup lemon juice
- 1/4 cup canola oil
- 1 teaspoon garlic salt
- 1 teaspoon dried thyme
- 1 teaspoon dried oregano
- 1/2 teaspoon celery salt
- 1/2 teaspoon pepper
- 2 tablespoons butter, melted

Direction

- Pierce holes in both steak's sides with a meat fork. Put into a big resealable bag; add pepper, celery salt, oregano, thyme, garlic salt, oil, lemon juice and onion. Seal bag, turn till coated. Refrigerate it for 6 hours – overnight.
- Drain marinade; discard. Broil steaks for 8 minutes 6-in. from heat. Brush butter; flip. Broil for 6 minutes till meat gets desired doneness; 170° well done, 160° medium and 145° medium-rare on thermometer.

Nutrition Information

- Calories: 249 calories
- Sodium: 313mg sodium
- Fiber: 0 fiber)
- Total Carbohydrate: 3g carbohydrate (1g sugars
- Cholesterol: 61mg cholesterol
- Protein: 29g protein.
- Total Fat: 13g fat (4g saturated fat)

58. Bubbly Golden Mexican Beef Cobbler

Serving: 6 servings. | Prep: 20mins | Ready in:

Ingredients

- 1 pound ground beef
- 1 envelope reduced-sodium taco seasoning
- 3/4 cup water
- 1 jar (16 ounces) salsa
- 1 can (8-3/4 ounces) whole kernel corn, drained
- 2 cups shredded sharp cheddar cheese
- 3-1/3 cups biscuit/baking mix
- 1-1/3 cups 2% milk
- 1/8 teaspoon pepper

Direction

- Put a large skillet over medium heat setting and cook beef for about 6-8 minutes or until brown in color and starting to crumble then drain excess oil. Add in water and taco seasoning into the cooked beef. Cook the mixture bringing it to a boil until the liquid has reduced. Once done, transfer the mixture into an 11x7-inch baking dish and put corn, cheese and salsa on top.
- Put biscuit mix and milk together in a separate large bowl and mix thoroughly then put a couple tablespoonfuls of the mixture over cheese until the baking dish is fully filled. Season with pepper.
- Keep the baking dish uncovered then put into an oven at 350 degrees for about 35-45 minutes or until the topping is bubbling and golden brown in color.

Nutrition Information

- Calories: 646 calories
- Protein: 30g protein.
- Total Fat: 31g fat (14g saturated fat)
- Sodium: 1877mg sodium
- Fiber: 3g fiber)

- Total Carbohydrate: 59g carbohydrate (11g sugars
- Cholesterol: 90mg cholesterol

59. Burgers For A Bunch

Serving: 6-8 servings. | Prep: 45mins | Ready in:

Ingredients

- FILLING:
- 1 pound ground beef
- 1/2 cup chopped onion
- 1 teaspoon salt
- 1/4 teaspoon pepper
- 3/4 cup instant potato flakes
- 1 large egg, beaten
- 1/4 cup ketchup
- 1/4 cup hamburger relish
- 1 tablespoon prepared mustard
- 1/2 cup shredded cheddar cheese
- CRUST:
- 1/2 cup butter, divided
- 1/2 cup instant potato flakes, divided
- 2 cups all-purpose flour
- 1 tablespoon sugar
- 1 teaspoon cream of tartar
- 1 teaspoon baking soda
- 1/2 cup whole milk
- 1/4 cup mayonnaise
- Additional milk

Direction

- Cook the pepper, salt, onion, and beef in a large skillet over medium heat until the meat is not pink anymore; drain. Stir in mustard, relish, ketchup, egg, and potato flakes; then put aside.
- In a small saucepan, melt 2 tablespoons butter for the crust. Add 1/4 cup of potato flakes and stir; then put aside.
- Blend the remaining potato flakes, baking soda, cream of tartar, sugar, and flour in a bowl. Slice in the remaining butter; add mayonnaise and milk. Combine until forming a soft dough.
- Cut in half. Roll a portion of the dough out into a 10-inch circle on a floured surface. Arrange in a 9-inch pie plate. Spread the meat filling on top; dust with cheese. Roll the remaining dough out and put on top of the filling. Seal and flute the edges. Brush them with milk; dust with the saved buttered potato mixture.
- Bake at 375 degrees until golden brown, 20-25 minutes. To serve, slice into wedges.

Nutrition Information

- Calories: 464 calories
- Protein: 17g protein.
- Total Fat: 26g fat (12g saturated fat)
- Sodium: 915mg sodium
- Fiber: 2g fiber)
- Total Carbohydrate: 41g carbohydrate (7g sugars
- Cholesterol: 97mg cholesterol

60. Burrito Lasagna

Serving: 12 servings. | Prep: 35mins | Ready in:

Ingredients

- 2 pounds ground beef
- 2 cans (10 ounces each) enchilada sauce
- 1 envelope taco seasoning
- 1 tablespoon ground cumin
- 1 package (8.8 ounces) ready-to-serve Spanish rice
- 12 flour tortillas (8 inches), warmed
- 1 can (15 ounces) refried beans
- 4 cups shredded Mexican cheese blend
- Optional toppings: salsa, sliced avocado, shredded lettuce, taco sauce and/or sour cream

Direction

- Let oven heat up to 350°. Let beef cook on medium fire in a big skillet until brown, then drain. When beef is cooked, heat over cumin, taco seasoning, and enchilada sauce while stirring.
- Follow package instructions to cook rice. Even out 2 tablespoon of beans on each of the tortilla. In a 13x9 inches baking dish grease with oil, even out one cup of meat mixture. On top of it, make a layer of 4 tortillas, 1/3 of the rice, 1/3 of the cheese and 1/3 of the unused meat mixture. Duplicate layers. Finish the leftover tortillas, meat mixture, and rice until the dish is full.
- Let it bake with a cover for 20 minutes. Top with leftover cheese. Take off cover and let it bake for 10 to 15 minutes more until cheese melts. Wait for 10 minutes then serve. You may put toppings that you like.

Nutrition Information

- Calories: 515 calories
- Protein: 29g protein.
- Total Fat: 25g fat (12g saturated fat)
- Sodium: 1325mg sodium
- Fiber: 3g fiber)
- Total Carbohydrate: 44g carbohydrate (1g sugars
- Cholesterol: 83mg cholesterol

61. Cajun Meat Loaf

Serving: 175-200 servings. | Prep: 01hours45mins | Ready in:

Ingredients

- 40 bay leaves
- 1/2 cup salt
- 1/4 cup each pepper, white pepper, cayenne pepper, ground cumin and nutmeg
- 40 green onions, thinly sliced
- 15 medium onions, chopped
- 10 medium green peppers, chopped
- 40 garlic cloves, minced
- 4 cups butter
- 1 cup Worcestershire sauce
- 2/3 cup hot pepper sauce
- 6 cans (12 ounces each) evaporated milk
- 1 bottle (64 ounces) ketchup
- 8 packages (8 ounces each) dry bread crumbs (20 cups)
- 36 eggs, beaten
- 30 pounds lean ground beef (90% lean)
- 10 pounds ground pork

Direction

- Mix the seasonings together and put it aside. In a Dutch oven, sauté the green peppers, onions, and garlic until it's tender in butter. Add the hot pepper sauce, the reserved seasonings, and Worcestershire sauce. Stir and cook for about 8-10 minutes and get rid of the bay leaves. Take away from the heat, mix in the ketchup and milk and let cool.
- Add the eggs and breadcrumbs and mix well. In several big bowls, mix the pork, veggie mix, and beef and mix it well. Pat them into 11 baking pans that are greased and having size of 13 inches multiplied 9 inches.
- Bake them at 350 degrees Fahrenheit for about 65-75 minutes or until no longer pink and the thermometer says 160 degrees Fahrenheit then drain it.

Nutrition Information

- Calories: 222 calories
- Cholesterol: 97mg cholesterol
- Protein: 19g protein.
- Total Fat: 13g fat (6g saturated fat)
- Sodium: 526mg sodium
- Fiber: 1g fiber)
- Total Carbohydrate: 6g carbohydrate (2g sugars

62. California Tamale Pie

Serving: 5 servings. | Prep: 15mins | Ready in:

Ingredients

- 1 cup beef broth
- 3/4 cup cornmeal
- 1 pound ground beef
- 1 teaspoon chili powder
- 1/2 teaspoon ground cumin
- 1 jar (16 ounces) chunky salsa
- 1 can (15-1/4 ounces) whole kernel corn, drained
- 1 can (15 ounces) black beans, rinsed and drained
- 1/4 cup sliced ripe olives
- 1/2 cup shredded Monterey Jack cheese
- Optional toppings: sour cream and fresh jalapeno pepper slices, optional

Direction

- Mix cornmeal and broth together in a 3-quart slow cooker. Let sit for 5 minutes. Cook beef in a big skillet over medium heat until no pink remains; strain. Mix in cumin and chili powder. Remove to the slow cooker. Mix in olives, beans, corn, and salsa. Put the lid on and cook on low until fully heated, about 6-8 hours.
- Sprinkle cheese over. Put the lid on and cook until the cheese melts, about 5-10 minutes. If you want, put jalapeno slices and sour cream on top.

Nutrition Information

- Calories: 455 calories
- Protein: 27g protein.
- Total Fat: 16g fat (6g saturated fat)
- Sodium: 1112mg sodium
- Fiber: 7g fiber
- Total Carbohydrate: 45g carbohydrate (7g sugars
- Cholesterol: 66mg cholesterol

63. Camping Haystacks

Serving: 2 servings. | Prep: 10mins | Ready in:

Ingredients

- 1 can (15 ounces) chili with beans
- 2 packages (1 ounce each) corn chips
- 1/2 cup shredded cheddar cheese
- 1-1/2 cups chopped lettuce
- 1 small tomato, chopped
- 1/2 cup salsa
- 2 tablespoons sliced ripe olives
- 2 tablespoons sour cream

Direction

- Heat chili in a small saucepan. Split corn chips among 2 plates and put chili in top. Layer with sour cream, olives, salsa, tomato, lettuce and cheese. Serve promptly.

Nutrition Information

- Calories:
- Protein:
- Total Fat:
- Sodium:
- Fiber:
- Total Carbohydrate:
- Cholesterol:

64. Cheeseburger Skillet Dinner

Serving: 6 servings. | Prep: 10mins | Ready in:

Ingredients

- 1 package (7-1/4 ounces) macaroni and cheese
- 1 pound ground turkey or beef
- 1/2 cup chopped onion
- 1 package (16 ounces) frozen mixed vegetables
- 1/3 cup ketchup

- 1/4 cup water
- 1/2 teaspoon prepared mustard
- 1/4 teaspoon garlic powder
- 3/4 cup shredded cheddar cheese
- Salt and pepper to taste

Direction

- Cook macaroni and cheese based on the package directions.
- In the meantime, brown the beef or turkey with the onion in a big skillet then strain. Mix in the garlic powder, mustard, water, ketchup and vegetables. Cook for about 10 minutes until the vegetables are crisp-tender. Stir in cheddar cheese until dissolved. Stir in the macaroni and cheese. Add pepper and salt to taste.

Nutrition Information

- Calories: 436 calories
- Total Fat: 20g fat (10g saturated fat)
- Sodium: 679mg sodium
- Fiber: 4g fiber)
- Total Carbohydrate: 24g carbohydrate (10g sugars
- Cholesterol: 87mg cholesterol
- Protein: 25g protein.

65. Cheesy Lasagna

Serving: 12 servings. | Prep: 25mins | Ready in:

Ingredients

- 1 pound ground beef
- 1 large onion, chopped
- 1/2 cup chopped green pepper
- 3 cans (6 ounces each) tomato paste
- 3/4 cup water
- 2 tablespoons brown sugar
- 3 to 4 teaspoons dried oregano
- 1 tablespoon cider vinegar
- 1/4 teaspoon garlic powder
- 9 lasagna noodles, cooked and drained
- 2 cups shredded mozzarella cheese
- 2 cups shredded Monterey Jack cheese
- 8 ounces sliced provolone cheese
- 1/4 cup grated Parmesan cheese

Direction

- Sauté onions, beef, and green peppers in a big saucepan over medium heat until beef is not pink; drain grease. Pour garlic powder, water, brown sugar, vinegar, oregano and the tomato paste into the saucepan.
- Pour a cup of the meat sauce in a 9x13-inch greased baking pan. Layer 3 lasagna noodles, another cup of meat sauce, and mozzarella cheese. Repeat the layers 2 more times but substitute Monterey Jack cheese for the mozzarella the first time and Parmesan and provolone the second time.
- Place the uncovered dish in a 350°F oven until the cheese melts, 40 to 45 minutes. Let it cool for 10 minutes before slicing. Serve.

Nutrition Information

- Calories: 368 calories
- Total Carbohydrate: 22g carbohydrate (7g sugars
- Cholesterol: 71mg cholesterol
- Protein: 24g protein.
- Total Fat: 20g fat (11g saturated fat)
- Sodium: 398mg sodium
- Fiber: 2g fiber)

66. Cheesy Spinach Stuffed Meat Loaf

Serving: 6 servings. | Prep: 20mins | Ready in:

Ingredients

- 1-1/2 pounds ground round

- 3/4 cup soft bread crumbs
- 1/4 cup egg substitute
- 1 teaspoon salt
- 1/8 teaspoon pepper
- FILLING:
- 1 package (10 ounces) frozen chopped spinach, thawed and well drained
- 1/2 cup shredded part-skim mozzarella cheese
- 3 tablespoons grated Parmesan cheese
- 1 teaspoon Italian seasoning
- 1/8 teaspoon garlic powder
- TOPPING:
- 3 tablespoons ketchup
- 1/4 cup shredded low-fat mozzarella cheese

Direction

- Mix meatloaf ingredients lightly in a big bowl; pat into 14x10-in. rectangle on a waxed paper.
- Mix filling ingredients in a small bowl. Spread on rectangle; leave 3/4-in. around the edges. Roll up like a jellyroll fashion, starting at a short end. To seal, press the meat mixture over filling at both ends. Put loaf onto rack in the roasting pan, seam side down.
- Bake for 1 hour at 350°, uncovered. Spread with ketchup; bake it for 15 minutes more. Sprinkle cheese on top; allow to stand for several minutes then cut to 1-in. thick slices.

Nutrition Information

- Calories: 259 calories
- Protein: 30g protein. Diabetic Exchanges: 3 lean meat
- Total Fat: 9g fat (0 saturated fat)
- Sodium: 776mg sodium
- Fiber: 0 fiber
- Total Carbohydrate: 14g carbohydrate (0 sugars
- Cholesterol: 39mg cholesterol

67. Chicken Fried Steak Gravy

Serving: 4 | Prep: | Ready in:

Ingredients

- ¼ cup all-purpose flour
- 2 large egg whites, lightly beaten
- ¼ cup cornmeal
- ¼ cup whole-wheat flour
- ¼ cup plus 1 tablespoon cornstarch, divided
- 1 teaspoon paprika
- 1 pound cube steak, cut into 4 portions
- ¾ teaspoon kosher salt, divided
- ½ teaspoon freshly ground pepper
- 2 tablespoons canola oil, divided
- 1 14-ounce can reduced-sodium beef broth
- 1 tablespoon water
- ¼ cup half-and-half

Direction

- Preheat an oven to 350°F. Use cooking spray to coat the baking sheet.
- On a big plate, put all-purpose flour. In shallow dish, put egg whites. Whisk paprika, 1/4 cup cornstarch, whole-wheat flour and cornmeal in separate shallow dish. Use 1/2 tsp. each pepper and salt to season both sides of the steak. In flour, dredge steak; shake excess off. In egg whites, dip; dredge in cornmeal mixture.
- Heat 1 tbsp. oil in a big nonstick skillet on medium high heat. Lower heat to medium. Put 2 steak pieces in; cook for 3-5 minutes total, flipping once, till both sides are brown. Put steak onto prepped baking sheet; repeat using leftover 2 steak pieces and 1 tbsp. oil. Put baking sheet into oven; bake for 10 minutes till cooked through.
- Meanwhile, put broth in pan; boil on medium high heat for 3-5 minutes till reduced to 1 cup, mixing occasionally. Whisk leftover 1 tbsp. cornstarch and water till smooth. Take pan off heat; mix in cornstarch mixture. Put on heat; cook for 1-2 minutes till thick, mixing. Mix in half and half then season using leftover

pepper and 1/4 tsp. salt; serve with gravy over steak.

Nutrition Information

- Calories: 307 calories;
- Total Fat: 12
- Sodium: 502
- Fiber: 1
- Total Carbohydrate: 18
- Saturated Fat: 3
- Cholesterol: 83
- Sugar: 1
- Protein: 30

68. Chili Mac Cheese

Serving: 8 servings. | Prep: 30mins | Ready in:

Ingredients

- 2 packages (7-1/4 ounces each) macaroni and cheese dinner mix
- 2 pounds ground beef
- 1 small onion, chopped
- 1 can (14-1/2 ounces) diced tomatoes, undrained
- 1 can (10 ounces) diced tomatoes and green chilies, undrained
- 1 can (8 ounces) tomato sauce
- 2 tablespoons chili powder
- 1 teaspoon garlic salt
- 1/2 teaspoon ground cumin
- 1/4 teaspoon crushed red pepper flakes
- 1/4 teaspoon pepper
- 2 cups (16 ounces) sour cream
- 1-1/2 cups shredded Mexican cheese blend, divided

Direction

- Set the oven at 350° to preheat. Put the cheese packets aside from the dinner mixes. Boil 2 quarts water in a large saucepan. Put in macaroni, then cook until softened, 8-10 minutes.
- Meanwhile, over medium heat, cook while stirring onion and beef in a Dutch oven until the beef is no longer pink, for 8-10 minutes; let drain. Stir in seasonings, tomato sauce, green chilies, and tomatoes. Allow the macaroni to drain; then put into the beef mixture. Stir in 1 cup cheese, sour cream, and the contents of cheese packets.
- Transfer to an oiled 13x9-in. baking dish; lay remaining cheese on top. Uncover and bake until bubbly, for 20-25 minutes.

Nutrition Information

- Calories: 631 calories
- Total Fat: 35g fat (17g saturated fat)
- Sodium: 1286mg sodium
- Fiber: 3g fiber)
- Total Carbohydrate: 22g carbohydrate (10g sugars
- Cholesterol: 105mg cholesterol
- Protein: 35g protein.

69. Chili Sauce Meat Loaf

Serving: 6 servings. | Prep: 20mins | Ready in:

Ingredients

- 1/3 cup plus 2 tablespoons chili sauce, divided
- 1 egg white
- 1 tablespoon Worcestershire sauce
- 3/4 cup quick-cooking oats
- 3/4 cup finely chopped onion
- 2 garlic cloves, minced
- 1 teaspoon dried thyme
- 1/2 teaspoon salt
- 1/2 teaspoon pepper
- 1-1/2 pounds lean ground beef (90% lean)

Direction

- Mix pepper, salt, thyme, garlic, onion, oats, Worcestershire sauce, egg white and 1/3 cup of chili sauce in a large bowl. Put crumbled beef over mixture and stir well.
- Form into a 9x4-in. loaf then put in an 11x7-in. baking dish greased with cooking spray.
- Bake without a cover for 50 minutes at 350°. Brush with the rest of chili sauce. Then bake for 5-10 more minutes, until no pink remains, and a thermometer shows 160°. Allow to stand for 10 minutes before cutting.

Nutrition Information

- Calories: 244 calories
- Fiber: 2g fiber)
- Total Carbohydrate: 14g carbohydrate (5g sugars
- Cholesterol: 69mg cholesterol
- Protein: 24g protein. Diabetic Exchanges: 3 lean meat
- Total Fat: 10g fat (4g saturated fat)
- Sodium: 565mg sodium

70. Chilies Rellenos Casserole

Serving: 6 servings. | Prep: 15mins | Ready in:

Ingredients

- 1 can (7 ounces) whole green chilies
- 1-1/2 cups shredded Colby-Monterey Jack cheese
- 3/4 pound ground beef
- 1/4 cup chopped onion
- 1 cup whole milk
- 4 large eggs
- 1/4 cup all-purpose flour
- 1/4 teaspoon salt
- 1/8 teaspoon pepper

Direction

- Chop chilies and remove seeds; dry over paper towels. Arrange chilies onto the bottom of a greased 2-qt. baking dish. Add cheese on top. Cook onion and beef on medium heat in a skillet till meat is not pink anymore; drain. Scoop on top of the cheese.
- Whip pepper, salt, flour, eggs and milk in a bowl till becoming smooth; add on top of beef mixture. Bake, while uncovered, at 350 degrees for 45 to 50 minutes or until a knife inserted in the middle comes out clean. Allow to rest for 5 minutes prior to serving.

Nutrition Information

- Calories: 321 calories
- Cholesterol: 212mg cholesterol
- Protein: 24g protein.
- Total Fat: 20g fat (11g saturated fat)
- Sodium: 406mg sodium
- Fiber: 0 fiber)
- Total Carbohydrate: 9g carbohydrate (3g sugars

71. Chipotle Rubbed Beef Tenderloin

Serving: 8 servings. | Prep: 10mins | Ready in:

Ingredients

- 1 beef tenderloin roast (2 pounds)
- 2 teaspoons canola oil
- 3 teaspoons coarsely ground pepper
- 3 garlic cloves, minced
- 2-1/2 teaspoons brown sugar
- 1 teaspoon salt
- 1 teaspoon ground coriander
- 1/2 teaspoon ground chipotle pepper
- 1/4 teaspoon cayenne pepper

Direction

- Brush oil on beef. Mix leftover ingredients; rub on meat. Cover; refrigerate it for 2 hours.
- Put on a rack coated in cooking spray in shallow roasting pan and bake at 400°, with no cover, for 45-55 minutes till meat reaches preferred doneness (a thermometer should read 170° for well-done, 160° for medium and 145° for medium-rare. Stand before slicing about 10 minutes.

Nutrition Information

- Calories: 195 calories
- Total Carbohydrate: 2g carbohydrate (1g sugars
- Cholesterol: 71mg cholesterol
- Protein: 24g protein. Diabetic Exchanges: 3 lean meat.
- Total Fat: 9g fat (3g saturated fat)
- Sodium: 351mg sodium
- Fiber: 0 fiber)

72. Chunky Pasta Sauce

Serving: 8 servings. | Prep: 25mins | Ready in:

Ingredients

- 1 pound ground beef
- 1/2 pound ground pork
- 2 cans (28 ounces each) diced tomatoes, undrained
- 1/2 to 1 cup water
- 1 can (6 ounces) tomato paste
- 1 cup chopped carrots
- 1 medium onion, cut into wedges
- 1 medium sweet red pepper, cut into 1-inch pieces
- 2 tablespoons sugar
- 2 teaspoons minced garlic
- 1 teaspoon salt
- 1 teaspoon dried basil
- 1 teaspoon dried oregano
- 1 teaspoon pepper
- Hot cooked bow tie pasta

Direction

- Cook beef and pork in a large skillet over medium heat until no longer pink; drain.
- Transfer to a 3-qt. slow cooker. Then stir in the water, tomatoes, vegetables, tomato paste, seasonings, garlic and sugar. Cook with a cover on low for 6-8 hours, until vegetables are softened. Serve along with pasta.

Nutrition Information

- Calories:
- Fiber:
- Total Carbohydrate:
- Cholesterol:
- Protein:
- Total Fat:
- Sodium:

73. Church Supper Hot Dish

Serving: 8 servings. | Prep: 40mins | Ready in:

Ingredients

- 1 pound ground beef
- 2 cups sliced peeled potatoes
- 2 cups finely chopped celery
- 3/4 cup finely chopped carrots
- 1/4 cup finely chopped green pepper
- 1/4 cup finely chopped onion
- 2 tablespoons butter
- 1 cup water
- 2 cans (10-3/4 ounces each) condensed cream of mushroom soup, undiluted
- 1 can (5 ounces) chow mein noodles, divided
- 1 cup shredded cheddar cheese

Direction

- Preheat oven to 350°. In a big frying pan over medium heat, cook beef till not pink anymore; let drain and set it aside.
- Sauté onion, green pepper, carrots, celery and potatoes in butter in the same pan for 5 minutes. Put in water; simmer, covered, for 10 minutes or until vegetables becomes softened. Mix in cooked ground beef and soup until blended.
- In a greased shallow 2-quart baking dish, add half of the chow mein noodles. Spread meat mixture over noodles. Bake, covered, for 20 minutes. Top with the leftover noodles and cheese. Bake while uncovered for 10 more minutes or until heated through.

Nutrition Information

- Calories: 339 calories
- Sodium: 537mg sodium
- Fiber: 3g fiber)
- Total Carbohydrate: 25g carbohydrate (2g sugars
- Cholesterol: 53mg cholesterol
- Protein: 16g protein.
- Total Fat: 20g fat (9g saturated fat)

74. Cider Beef Stew

Serving: 4 servings. | Prep: 20mins | Ready in:

Ingredients

- 3 tablespoons all-purpose flour
- 1 teaspoon salt
- 1/2 teaspoon pepper
- 1 pound beef stew meat, cut into 1-inch pieces
- 2 tablespoons canola oil
- 1 cup apple cider
- 1/2 cup water
- 1 tablespoon cider vinegar
- 1/2 teaspoon dried thyme
- 2 large carrots, cut into 1-inch pieces
- 1 celery rib, cut into 1-inch pieces
- 1 large potato, peeled and cubed
- 1 medium onion, sliced

Direction

- Mix pepper, salt, and flour together in a big resealable plastic bag. Add beef, several pieces each time, and shake to cover. Put beef in a big saucepan with oil to brown; strain. Mix in thyme, vinegar, water, and cider; boil it. Lower the heat, simmer with a cover until the meat is soft, about 105 minutes.
- Add onion, potato, celery, and carrots; boil again. Lower the heat, simmer with a cover until the vegetables are soft, about 45 minutes.

Nutrition Information

- Calories: 381 calories
- Fiber: 4g fiber)
- Total Carbohydrate: 37g carbohydrate (13g sugars
- Cholesterol: 70mg cholesterol
- Protein: 25g protein.
- Total Fat: 15g fat (4g saturated fat)
- Sodium: 671mg sodium

75. Classic Cashew Beef For Two

Serving: 2 servings. | Prep: 15mins | Ready in:

Ingredients

- 2 teaspoons cornstarch
- 2 teaspoons soy sauce
- 1/2 teaspoon sesame oil
- 1/2 teaspoon oyster sauce
- 1/8 teaspoon ground ginger
- Dash cayenne pepper
- 1/4 cup cold water
- 1/2 pound beef top sirloin steak, cut into 1/2-in pieces
- 1 tablespoon canola oil, divided
- 4 green onions, cut into 1-in. lengths

- 1/3 cup lightly salted cashews
- 1 garlic clove, minced
- Hot cooked rice

Direction

- Mix initial 7 ingredients till smooth in a small bowl; put aside.
- Stir-fry beef in 1/2 tbsp. oil till not pink in a big skillet/wok. Remove; keep warm. Stir-fry garlic, cashews and onions for 1 minute in leftover oil.
- Mix cornstarch mixture; put in pan. Boil; mix and cook till thick for 2 minutes. Add beef then heat through; serve it with rice.

Nutrition Information

- Calories: 379 calories
- Fiber: 2g fiber)
- Total Carbohydrate: 11g carbohydrate (1g sugars
- Cholesterol: 46mg cholesterol
- Protein: 30g protein.
- Total Fat: 24g fat (5g saturated fat)
- Sodium: 462mg sodium

76. Classic Lasagna

Serving: 10 | Prep: 15mins | Ready in:

Ingredients

- 9 lasagna noodles
- 1 tablespoon olive oil
- 1 pound ground beef
- 1 pound bulk Italian sausage
- 1 (16 ounce) can sliced mushrooms, drained
- 1 teaspoon garlic salt
- 1 teaspoon dried oregano
- 1/2 teaspoon dried thyme
- 1/4 teaspoon dried basil
- 4 (15 ounce) cans tomato sauce
- salt and pepper to taste
- 1 (15 ounce) container ricotta cheese
- 3 eggs, beaten
- 1/3 cup grated Parmesan cheese
- 1 pound shredded mozzarella cheese

Direction

- Turn oven to 175°C (350°F).
- Boil slightly salted water in a big pot. Place lasagna pasta and olive oil in the pot until al dente, about 8-10 minutes. Drain water.
- Cook sausage and ground beef in a big pot on medium heat. Add in the garlic salt, mushrooms, oregano, thyme, tomato sauce and basil. Season with pepper and salt. Let it simmer 30 minutes.
- Combine eggs, parmesan cheese and ricotta cheese in a bowl.
- Cover bottom of 13in.x9in. pan with a thin layer of meat sauce. Place a layer of three noodles. Pour 1/4 of ricotta cheese mixture over. Layer with 1/3 of mozzarella cheese and 1/3 of meat sauce. Repeat layers twice; put a 1/4 pound mozzarella cheese on top.
- Bake in oven for 1 1/2 hours. Let it set for 10-15 minutes then serve.

Nutrition Information

- Calories: 647 calories;
- Sodium: 2012
- Total Carbohydrate: 31.2
- Cholesterol: 174
- Protein: 38.8
- Total Fat: 41.4

77. Coffee Roast Beef

Serving: 6 servings plus leftovers. | Prep: 20mins | Ready in:

Ingredients

- 1 boneless beef chuck roast (5 pounds)

- 2 tablespoons olive oil
- 1 medium onion, chopped
- 1 garlic clove, minced
- 1 teaspoon dried oregano
- 1 teaspoon dried basil
- 1/2 teaspoon pepper
- 3/4 teaspoon salt
- 1 cup strong brewed coffee
- 3/4 cup plus 1/3 cup water, divided
- 3/4 cup beef stock
- 3 tablespoons all-purpose flour

Direction

- In the Dutch oven, brown the roast on all sides in oil. Take out and put aside. Put the onion into pan; sauté till soften. Put in the seasonings and garlic; cook for 60 seconds more.
- Pour in stock, three quarters cup of the water and coffee; bring the roast back to the pan. Boil. Bake with cover at 325 degrees till the meat softens or for 2.25-2.75 hours.
- Transfer the beef to serving platter; keep it warm. Mix the rest of water and flour till smooth. Whisk into the pan. Boil; cook and whisk till thicken or for 2 minutes.
- Put aside 2 cups of the shredded cooked Coffee Roast Beef for Mini Beef Chimichangas and half pound cooked cubed beef for the Spinach Beef Stew. Cut the rest of the roast and serve along with the gravy.

Nutrition Information

- Calories:
- Fiber:
- Total Carbohydrate:
- Cholesterol:
- Protein:
- Total Fat:
- Sodium:

78. Coffee Braised Roast Beef

Serving: 10 servings. | Prep: 10mins | Ready in:

Ingredients

- 1 cup cider vinegar
- 4 garlic cloves, crushed, divided
- 1 boneless beef chuck roast (4 to 5 pounds), trimmed
- 2 teaspoons salt
- 1 teaspoon pepper
- 1 cup strong brewed coffee
- 1 cup beef broth
- 1 medium onion, sliced
- 3 tablespoons cornstarch
- 1/4 cup cold water
- Mashed potatoes

Direction

- Mix 2 garlic cloves and vinegar together in a big resealable plastic bag. Put in the roast, close the bag and flip to coat. Chill overnight, flipping sometimes.
- Strain and dispose of the marinade. Pat dry the roast, sprinkle pepper and salt over. In a 5- or 6-quart slow cooker, put the roast; add the leftover garlic, broth, onion and coffee. Cover and cook on low for 6-7 hours, or until the meat is soft.
- Take the roast out and keep warm. Drain the cooking juices, disposing of the garlic and onion; remove the fat. Stir cold water and cornstarch together until smooth in a small bowl; slowly mix into the slow cooker. Cover and cook on high for 30 minutes, or until the gravy is thick. Cut the roast, serve together with the gravy and mashed potatoes.

Nutrition Information

- Calories: 324 calories
- Total Carbohydrate: 3g carbohydrate (0 sugars
- Cholesterol: 118mg cholesterol
- Protein: 36g protein.
- Total Fat: 17g fat (7g saturated fat)

- Sodium: 636mg sodium
- Fiber: 0 fiber)

79. Coffee Braised Short Ribs

Serving: 8 servings. | Prep: 25mins | Ready in:

Ingredients

- 4 pounds bone-in beef short ribs
- 1-1/2 teaspoons salt, divided
- 1 teaspoon ground coriander
- 1/2 teaspoon pepper
- 2 tablespoons olive oil
- 1-1/2 pounds small red potatoes, cut in half
- 1 medium onion, chopped
- 1 cup reduced-sodium beef broth
- 1 whole garlic bulb, cloves separated, peeled and slightly crushed
- 4 cups strong brewed coffee
- 2 teaspoons red wine vinegar
- 3 tablespoons butter

Direction

- Scatter pepper, coriander and 1 teaspoon salt on ribs. Brown ribs in oil in batches in a big skillet. Move ribs to a 6-quart slow cooker using tongs. Put in onion and potatoes.
- Put broth to the skillet, stir to loosen browned bits. Take to a boil; cook until liquid is decreased by half. Toss in leftover salt and garlic; place to the slow cooker. Pour coffee on top. Cover and cook for 6-8 hours at low, until meat is soft.
- Transfer potatoes and ribs to a serving plate; keep warm. In a small saucepan, strain cooking juices; skim the fat. Take to a boil; cook till liquid is decreased by half. Mix in vinegar. Take off from heat; stir in butter. Enjoy with ribs and potatoes.

Nutrition Information

- Calories: 320 calories
- Fiber: 2g fiber)
- Total Carbohydrate: 17g carbohydrate (2g sugars
- Cholesterol: 66mg cholesterol
- Protein: 21g protein.
- Total Fat: 18g fat (8g saturated fat)
- Sodium: 569mg sodium

80. Colorful Beef Stir Fry

Serving: 4 cups. | Prep: 35mins | Ready in:

Ingredients

- 1/4 cup reduced-sodium soy sauce
- 1 tablespoon honey
- 2 teaspoons sesame oil
- 3 garlic cloves, minced
- 1/8 teaspoon ground ginger
- 1/2 pound boneless beef sirloin steak, thinly sliced
- 4-1/2 teaspoons cornstarch
- 1/2 cup reduced-sodium beef broth
- 1-1/2 teaspoons canola oil, divided
- 1 small green pepper, cut into chunks
- 1 small onion, cut into chunks
- 1 medium carrot, julienned
- 1/4 cup sliced celery
- 1 small zucchini, julienned
- 1/2 cup fresh snow peas
- 1/2 cup canned bean sprouts, rinsed and drained
- Hot cooked rice or linguine, optional

Direction

- Combine the first 5 ingredients in a small mixing bowl. Put beef into a large resealable plastic bag; pour in 1/2 marinade. Seal the bag and shake to coat well; chill beef and marinade for at least 2 hours. Chill the remaining marinade, covered, in the fridge.
- Whisk together cornstarch and broth in a small mixing bowl until no lumps remain. Mix in the

reserved marinade; put aside. Drain marinated beef and discard marinade. Cook beef in 1 teaspoon oil in a wok or large nonstick skillet coated with cooking spray until no longer pink; drain. Take the cooked beef out and keep warm.

- Sauté onion and green pepper in the remaining oil for 2 minutes in the same skillet. Add celery and carrot, sauté for 2 to 3 minutes more. Add snow peas and zucchini; sauté for 1 minute. Mix in bean sprouts and cook until thoroughly heated.
- Stir broth mixture and pour over the vegetable mixture in the skillet, mix. Bring to a boil; cook, stirring, until thickened for 1 to 2 minutes. Add cooked beef; cook through. Enjoy with linguine or over rice.

Nutrition Information

- Calories: 318 calories
- Sodium: 542mg sodium
- Fiber: 4g fiber)
- Total Carbohydrate: 41g carbohydrate (8g sugars
- Cholesterol: 43mg cholesterol
- Protein: 21g protein. Diabetic Exchanges: 2 lean meat
- Total Fat: 8g fat (2g saturated fat)

81. Colossal Cornburger

Serving: 6 servings. | Prep: 20mins | Ready in:

Ingredients

- 1 large egg, lightly beaten
- 1 cup cooked whole kernel corn
- 1/2 cup coarsely crushed cheese crackers
- 1/4 cup sliced green onions
- 1/4 cup chopped fresh parsley
- 1 teaspoon Worcestershire sauce
- 2 pounds ground beef
- 1 teaspoon salt
- 1/2 teaspoon pepper
- 1/2 teaspoon ground sage

Direction

- Mix Worcestershire sauce, parsley, green onions, crackers, corn and egg in a medium sized bowl; reserve. Mix seasonings and ground beef in a big bowl.
- Pat the mixture of beef, 1/2 at a time, on waxed paper sheets into an 8-1/2-inch round. Onto a round of meat, scoop the corn mixture, leaving an inch border. Put another round of meat on top; peel off top waxed paper sheet and enclose the edges. Flip to one thoroughly-greased wire grill basket; remove waxed paper.
- Grill with cover for 12 to 15 minutes per side, over moderate heat, or until juices run clear and thermometer registers 160°. For oven procedure, on baking pan, put the burger. Bake for 40 to 45 minutes at 350° or till juices run clear and thermometer registers 160°. Slice into wedges and serve.

Nutrition Information

- Calories: 364 calories
- Sodium: 551mg sodium
- Fiber: 1g fiber)
- Total Carbohydrate: 9g carbohydrate (2g sugars
- Cholesterol: 136mg cholesterol
- Protein: 33g protein.
- Total Fat: 21g fat (8g saturated fat)

82. Company Pot Roast

Serving: 6 servings. | Prep: 20mins | Ready in:

Ingredients

- 1 boneless beef chuck roast (3 to 4 pounds)
- 2 tablespoons olive oil
- 1 cup sherry or beef broth

- 1/2 cup reduced-sodium soy sauce
- 1/4 cup sugar
- 2 teaspoons beef bouillon granules
- 1 cinnamon stick (3 inches)
- 8 medium carrots, cut into 2-inch pieces
- 6 medium potatoes, peeled and cut into 1-1/2-inch pieces
- 1 medium onion, sliced
- 2 tablespoons cornstarch
- 2 tablespoons cold water

Direction

- Cook all sides of roast to brown with oil in a Dutch oven; then drain. Mix the cinnamon stick, bouillon, sugar, soy sauce and sherry; pour over the roast.
- Bake with a cover for 2-3/4 to 3-1/4 hours at 325°, or until vegetables and meat become tender, putting in the onion, potatoes and carrots in the last half an hour of the cooking time.
- Transfer vegetables and roast to a serving platter; and keep warm. Mix cornstarch and water until smooth. Transfer into pan and bring to boil; cook while stirring for 2 minutes, or until thickened. Serve along with roast and vegetables.

Nutrition Information

- Calories: 713 calories
- Protein: 49g protein.
- Total Fat: 26g fat (9g saturated fat)
- Sodium: 1437mg sodium
- Fiber: 5g fiber)
- Total Carbohydrate: 56g carbohydrate (17g sugars
- Cholesterol: 148mg cholesterol

83. Confetti Casserole

Serving: 6 servings. | Prep: 20mins | Ready in:

Ingredients

- 1 pound ground beef
- 1 medium onion, finely chopped
- 1 teaspoon garlic powder
- 4 medium potatoes, peeled and quartered
- 3 medium carrots, cut into 1-inch chunks
- 1 package (9 ounces) frozen cut green beans
- 1 package (10 ounces) frozen corn
- 1 can (14-1/2 ounces) Italian diced tomatoes, undrained

Direction

- Cook garlic powder, onion, and beef in a large skillet over medium heat until the meat is not pink anymore; then drain.
- Layer potatoes, carrots, beans and corn in a 3-quart slow cooker. Put the beef mixture on top. Top with the tomatoes. Put on a cover and cook on low until the potatoes become tender, 8-10 hours.

Nutrition Information

- Calories:
- Cholesterol:
- Protein:
- Total Fat:
- Sodium:
- Fiber:
- Total Carbohydrate:

84. Confetti Meat Loaf

Serving: 8 servings. | Prep: 20mins | Ready in:

Ingredients

- 2 eggs
- 1 tablespoon cider vinegar
- 1/3 cup dry bread crumbs
- 5 bacon strips, cooked and crumbled
- 1/3 cup shredded peeled tart apple
- 1/3 cup grated carrots

- 1/3 cup each chopped celery, onion, green pepper and sweet red pepper
- 3 garlic cloves, minced
- 3 tablespoons dried parsley flakes
- 1-1/4 teaspoons salt
- 1 teaspoon pepper
- 2 pounds ground beef

Direction

- Combine the parsley, salt, pepper, garlic, vegetables, apple, bacon, breadcrumbs, vinegar and eggs in a bowl. Put crumbled beef over the mixture and mix thoroughly.
- Pat and shape into a well-greased 9x5-in. loaf pan. Bake without a cover for 1 hour at 350°, until no pink remains, and a thermometer reaches 160°; drain. Allow to sit for 10 minutes before cutting.

Nutrition Information

- Calories:
- Sodium:
- Fiber:
- Total Carbohydrate:
- Cholesterol:
- Protein:
- Total Fat:

85. Coriander Crusted Beef With Spicy Cranberry Relish

Serving: 8 servings (6 cups relish) | Prep: 25mins | Ready in:

Ingredients

- 1-1/2 cups orange juice
- 6 cups fresh or frozen cranberries
- 1-1/2 cups sugar
- 1/2 cup olive oil
- 1 to 2 jalapeno peppers, seeded and finely chopped
- 5 garlic cloves, minced
- 1 tablespoon red wine vinegar
- 1/2 teaspoon ground cumin
- 1/4 teaspoon salt
- RUB:
- 4 shallots, finely chopped
- 3/4 cup kosher salt
- 6 tablespoons packed brown sugar
- 1/4 cup coriander seeds, ground
- 1/4 cup whole peppercorns, ground
- 4 garlic cloves, minced
- 1 beef ribeye roast (3 to 4 pounds)

Direction

- Heat orange juice to a boil in a small saucepan. Cook for about 15 minutes until half of the liquid reduces. Process cranberries and sugar in a food processor until coarsely chopped; place to a bowl.
- Heat oil on medium heat in a large skillet. Put in jalapeno; sauté until softened, 1 to 2 minutes. Add in garlic; cook for an extra 1 minute. Blend in salt, cumin, vinegar, orange juice, and cranberry mixture.
- To make rub, combine garlic, peppercorns, coriander seeds, brown sugar, kosher salt, and shallots; rub on the roast. Place to a shallow dish. Put in the refrigerator, covered, for 8 hours or overnight.
- Start preheating the oven at 350°. Take out and discard rub from roast; arrange roast on a rack in a shallow roasting pan, with the fat side up. Roast until meat achieves the desired doneness (for medium-rare, a thermometer should register 145°; medium, 160°; well-done, 170°), 1 3/4 to 2 1/4 hours. Take the roast out of oven; tent with foil. Allow to stand for 15 minutes before cutting. Cut the roast; use with relish.

Nutrition Information

- Calories:
- Sodium:
- Fiber:
- Total Carbohydrate:

- Cholesterol:
- Protein:
- Total Fat:

86. Corn 'n' Beef Pasta Bake

Serving: 6-8 servings. | Prep: 15mins | Ready in:

Ingredients

- 1 pound ground beef
- 1 medium onion, chopped
- 1 medium green or sweet red pepper, chopped
- 2 garlic cloves, minced
- 2 cups frozen corn, thawed
- 1 can (14-1/2 ounces) diced tomatoes, undrained
- 1-1/2 cups uncooked bow tie pasta
- 1 cup buttermilk
- 3 ounces cream cheese, cubed
- 1 to 2 teaspoons chili powder
- Salt and pepper to taste
- 1 cup shredded Monterey Jack cheese

Direction

- Cook garlic, green pepper, onion, and beef in a large skillet on medium heat until the beef is not pink anymore; then drain. Stir in pepper, salt, chili powder, cream cheese, buttermilk, pasta, tomatoes, and corn.
- Place into a 2 1/2-quart baking dish coated with cooking spray; dust with cheese. Put a cover on and bake for 40 minutes at 375 degrees. Remove the cover and bake until the pasta becomes tender, or for 25-30 more minutes.

Nutrition Information

- Calories: 0

87. Corned Beef Dinner

Serving: 8 servings. | Prep: 25mins | Ready in:

Ingredients

- 4 to 5 medium red potatoes, quartered
- 2 cups fresh baby carrots, halved lengthwise
- 3 cups chopped cabbage
- 1 corned beef brisket with spice packet (3-1/2 pounds)
- 3 cups water
- 1 tablespoon caraway seeds

Direction

- Add cabbage, carrots and potatoes into a 5-quart slow cooker. Halve the brisket; add on top of the vegetables. Put in the contents of the spice packet, caraway seeds and water. Cook with cover on low till the veggies and meat soften or for 8 to 10 hours.

Nutrition Information

- Calories:
- Total Fat:
- Sodium:
- Fiber:
- Total Carbohydrate:
- Cholesterol:
- Protein:

88. Corned Beef Potato Dinner

Serving: 4 servings. | Prep: 30mins | Ready in:

Ingredients

- 1 pound red potatoes, cut into small wedges
- 1-1/2 cups water
- 1 large onion, thinly sliced and separated into rings
- 4 cups coleslaw mix

- 8 ounces thinly sliced deli corned beef, cut into 1/4-inch strips
- 1 tablespoon canola oil
- 1/3 cup red wine vinegar
- 4 teaspoons spicy brown mustard
- 1 teaspoon sugar
- 1 teaspoon caraway seeds
- 1/2 teaspoon garlic powder
- 1/2 teaspoon salt
- 1/2 teaspoon pepper

Direction

- Add the water and potatoes into a 3-quart microwavable bowl. Microwave on high setting with cover till the potatoes become tender-crisp or for 4 to 5 minutes. Put in onion; cook with cover till the onions soften or for 1 to 2 minutes. Whisk in coleslaw mix. Cook with cover till the potatoes soften or for 2 to 3 more minutes; drain off.
- In the big skillet, sauté the corned beef in oil for 3 to 4 minutes; drain off. Whisk in the rest ingredients. Cook and whisk till fully heated or for 60 seconds. Put into potato mixture; toss to blend. Microwave with cover till completely heated or for 1 to 2 minutes.

Nutrition Information

- Calories: 216 calories
- Sodium: 1040mg sodium
- Fiber: 4g fiber)
- Total Carbohydrate: 28g carbohydrate (6g sugars
- Cholesterol: 32mg cholesterol
- Protein: 12g protein.
- Total Fat: 6g fat (2g saturated fat)

89. Cream Cheese And Swiss Lasagna

Serving: 12 servings. | Prep: 40mins | Ready in:

Ingredients

- 1-1/2 pounds lean ground beef (90% lean)
- 1 pound Johnsonville® Ground Mild Italian sausage
- 1 medium onion, finely chopped
- 3 garlic cloves, minced
- 2 cans (15 ounces each) tomato sauce
- 1 can (14-1/2 ounces) Italian diced tomatoes, undrained
- 1 can (6 ounces) tomato paste
- 2 teaspoons dried oregano
- 1 teaspoon dried basil
- 1 teaspoon Italian seasoning
- 1/2 teaspoon sugar
- 1/2 teaspoon salt
- 1/4 teaspoon pepper
- 9 no-cook lasagna noodles
- 12 ounces cream cheese, softened
- 2 cups shredded part-skim mozzarella cheese, divided
- 2 cups shredded Parmesan cheese
- 2 cups shredded Swiss cheese

Direction

- Cook the sausage, onion and beef in a Dutch oven on medium heat until meat is not pink. Put in garlic; cook 1 more minute and drain. Add in the tomatoes, tomato sauce, tomato paste, basil, oregano, Italian seasoning, pepper, sugar and salt. Let it boil. Lower the heat and let it simmer, without lid, 30 minutes.
- Grease 13x 9-inch baking tray, pour in 1 cup sauce. Layer with 3 pasta noodles, 1/3 of cream cheese by teaspoonfuls, 1/2 cup of mozzarella, 2/3 cup Parmesan, 2/3 cup Swiss cheese, and 1/3 of remaining sauce. Repeat the layers twice more (pan should be filled). Put the pan on a cookie sheet.
- Cover pan and bake at 350°, 45 minutes. Drizzle with left mozzarella. Return to the oven without cover, 10 to 15 minutes longer until bubbling and cheese melts. Let it sit for 15 minutes before slicing.

Nutrition Information

- Calories: 522 calories
- Protein: 35g protein.
- Total Fat: 31g fat (17g saturated fat)
- Sodium: 1196mg sodium
- Fiber: 3g fiber)
- Total Carbohydrate: 24g carbohydrate (8g sugars
- Cholesterol: 118mg cholesterol

90. Creamy Beef Lasagna

Serving: 12 servings. | Prep: 20mins | Ready in:

Ingredients

- 1-1/2 pounds ground beef
- 2 cans (15 ounces each) tomato sauce
- 1/4 cup chopped onion
- 2 teaspoons sugar
- 2 teaspoons salt
- 2 teaspoons Worcestershire sauce
- 1/2 teaspoon garlic salt
- 2 packages (8 ounces each) cream cheese, softened
- 1 cup sour cream
- 1/4 cup milk
- 18 lasagna noodles, cooked and drained
- 1 cup shredded cheddar cheese
- Minced fresh parsley, optional

Direction

- Cook beef until not pink on medium heat in a frying pan. Drain excess grease. Mix in sugar, garlic salt, onion, Worcestershire sauce, tomato sauce, and salt. Beat milk, cream cheese, and sour cream until smooth in a different bowl. Take a 13x9-in. greased pan and add a fourth of the meat sauce. Layer with six noodles and a third of cream cheese mixture. Starting with meat sauce, repeat the layers twice. Put remaining meat sauce on top. Cover; bake in a 350-degree oven for 40 minutes. Remove cover and sprinkle on cheddar cheese. Bake until cheese melts, 5 minutes. Let it cool for 15 minutes before cutting. Sprinkle parsley on top.

Nutrition Information

- Calories: 403 calories
- Cholesterol: 82mg cholesterol
- Protein: 21g protein.
- Total Fat: 20g fat (11g saturated fat)
- Sodium: 795mg sodium
- Fiber: 2g fiber)
- Total Carbohydrate: 33g carbohydrate (4g sugars

91. Creamy Reuben Casserole

Serving: 4 servings. | Prep: 10mins | Ready in:

Ingredients

- 1 can (14 ounces) sauerkraut, rinsed and well drained
- 1-1/4 cups chopped cooked corned beef
- 1 cup (8 ounces) sour cream
- 1 small onion, chopped
- 1 garlic clove, minced
- 1 cup shredded Swiss cheese
- 2 slices rye bread, cubed
- 2 tablespoons butter, melted

Direction

- In a big bowl, mix the garlic, onion, sour cream, corned beef, and sauerkraut.
- Move to a greased 11x7-inch baking dish. Scatter bread and cheese over; trickle with butter. Bake with no cover at 350° for about 25-30 minutes, or up to heated through.

Nutrition Information

- Calories: 0

92. Crescent Topped Casserole

Serving: 6-8 servings. | Prep: 15mins | Ready in:

Ingredients

- 2 pounds ground beef
- 1/4 cup chopped onion
- 2 cans (8 ounces each) tomato sauce
- 1 envelope spaghetti sauce mix
- 3/4 cup sour cream
- 2 cups shredded part-skim mozzarella cheese
- 1 tube (8 ounces) refrigerated crescent rolls
- 2 tablespoons butter, melted
- 1/3 cup grated Parmesan cheese

Direction

- In a large skillet over the medium heat, cook onion and beef till meat is no longer pink; drain. Mix in spaghetti sauce mix and tomato sauce. Lower the heat; let it simmer with no cover, for 5 minutes. Take away from heat; mix in sour cream. Place into a greased baking dish of 13x9 inches. Sprinkle mozzarella cheese on top.
- Unroll crescent dough into a rectangle; seal seams and perforations. Add on top of the mozzarella cheese. Brush with butter and sprinkle Parmesan cheese on top.
- Bake with no cover, at 375° until golden brown, about 25-30 minutes.

Nutrition Information

- Calories:
- Fiber:
- Total Carbohydrate:
- Cholesterol:
- Protein:
- Total Fat:
- Sodium:

93. Crunchy Beef Bake

Serving: 4-6 servings. | Prep: 15mins | Ready in:

Ingredients

- 2 cups uncooked spiral pasta
- 1 pound ground beef
- 3/4 cup chopped green pepper
- 1 garlic clove, minced
- 1 can (14-1/2 ounces) diced tomatoes, undrained
- 1 can (10-3/4 ounces) condensed cream of mushroom soup, undiluted
- 3/4 cup shredded cheddar cheese
- 3/4 teaspoon seasoned salt
- 1 can (2.8 ounces) french-fried onions

Direction

- Cook pasta following package instructions. In the meantime, in a Dutch oven over medium heat, cook garlic, green pepper and beef until green pepper is tender and the beef is no longer pink; drain.
- Drain pasta; put into the beef mixture along with salt, cheese, soup and tomatoes.
- Place into a greased 2-quart baking dish. Cover and bake at 350° for 30-40 minutes. Remove the cover; sprinkle onions on top and return to the oven for 5 more minutes.

Nutrition Information

- Calories: 417 calories
- Total Carbohydrate: 36g carbohydrate (4g sugars
- Cholesterol: 54mg cholesterol
- Protein: 21g protein.
- Total Fat: 20g fat (9g saturated fat)
- Sodium: 884mg sodium
- Fiber: 3g fiber)

94. Curly Noodle Dinner

Serving: 4-6 servings. | Prep: 5mins | Ready in:

Ingredients

- 1 pound ground beef
- 1 package (3 ounces) beef ramen noodles
- 1 can (14-1/2 ounces) stewed tomatoes
- 1 can (8-1/2 ounces) whole kernel corn, drained

Direction

- Brown beef in a frying pan and drain. Mix in corn, tomatoes and noodles with the contents of accompanying seasoning packet. Boil the mixture. Lower the heat, simmer while covered until the noodles get tender, about 10 minutes.

Nutrition Information

- Calories: 228 calories
- Protein: 16g protein.
- Total Fat: 9g fat (4g saturated fat)
- Sodium: 587mg sodium
- Fiber: 2g fiber)
- Total Carbohydrate: 19g carbohydrate (6g sugars
- Cholesterol: 37mg cholesterol

95. Deviled Baked Steak

Serving: 6-8 servings. | Prep: 15mins | Ready in:

Ingredients

- 2 pound beef top round steak (1 inch thick)
- 3/4 cup all-purpose flour
- 1 teaspoon ground mustard
- 1 teaspoon salt
- 1/2 teaspoon pepper
- 2 to 3 tablespoons canola oil
- 1 medium onion, sliced
- 1 can (14-1/2 ounces) diced tomatoes, undrained
- 1 medium carrot, diced
- 1 teaspoon brown sugar
- 2 teaspoons Worcestershire sauce
- Cooked noodles or mashed potatoes

Direction

- From steak, trim extra fat; cut to serving-size pieces. Mix pepper, salt, mustard and flour; pound into steak.
- In batches, brown steak in oil in a skillet. Put meat into big baking dish; put onion over. Mix Worcestershire sauce, brown sugar, carrot and tomatoes; put on meat.
- Cover; bake till meat is tender for 1 1/2-2 hours at 325°. Put meat onto serving platter. Simmer onion-tomato mixture till reduced to thick gravy if desired; serve gravy and meat with noodles/mashed tomatoes.

Nutrition Information

- Calories:
- Sodium:
- Fiber:
- Total Carbohydrate:
- Cholesterol:
- Protein:
- Total Fat:

96. Deviled Swiss Steak

Serving: 8 servings. | Prep: 20mins | Ready in:

Ingredients

- 1/2 cup all-purpose flour
- 1 tablespoon ground mustard
- 1/2 teaspoon salt
- 1/8 teaspoon pepper
- 2 beef flank steaks (1 pound each), halved
- 2 tablespoons butter

- 1 cup thinly sliced onion
- 1 can (28 ounces) stewed tomatoes
- 2 tablespoons Worcestershire sauce
- 1 tablespoon brown sugar

Direction

- Mix pepper, salt, mustard and flour together in a large resealable plastic bag. Put in steaks; shake to coat well. Heat butter in a large non-stick skillet; brown the steaks on both sides. Remove into a 5-qt. slow cooker. Sprinkle onion on top. Combine brown sugar, Worcestershire sauce and tomatoes together in a bowl; transfer over the onion and the meat. Cook with a cover on low till the meat is tender, 6-8 hours.

Nutrition Information

- Calories: 286 calories
- Protein: 26g protein. Diabetic Exchanges: 3 lean meat
- Total Fat: 12g fat (6g saturated fat)
- Sodium: 575mg sodium
- Fiber: 2g fiber)
- Total Carbohydrate: 17g carbohydrate (0 sugars
- Cholesterol: 66mg cholesterol

97. Double Duty Layered Enchilada Casserole

Serving: 12 servings. | Prep: 15mins | Ready in:

Ingredients

- 5 cups reserved Double-Duty Hearty Chili without Beans or any thick chili without beans
- 1-1/2 cups frozen corn (about 8 ounces)
- 1 can (15 ounces) black beans, rinsed and drained
- 1 can (15 ounces) pinto beans, rinsed and drained
- 6 flour tortillas (10 inches)
- 3 cups shredded Mexican cheese blend, divided
- 1 can (10 ounces) enchilada sauce
- Shredded lettuce and chopped fresh tomatoes, optional

Direction

- Set oven to 375° to preheat. Stir beans, corn and reserved chili in a large bowl. Distribute a cup chili mixture evenly into a greased 13x9 inch baking pan. Put layers of 2 tortillas, 2 cups chili mixture, 1 cup cheese, and 1/2 cup enchilada sauce over the mixture in the baking pan. Repeat layering. Put leftover tortillas and chili mixture on top.
- Bake for 20-25 minutes while covered, until heated through. Scatter leftover cheese on top. Bake for 10 to 15 more minutes while uncovered, until cheese is melted. Let sit for 10 minutes before slicing. Serve together with tomatoes and lettuce (optional). Freeze option: Freeze uncooked casserole while covered. Before using, defrost partly in the fridge overnight. Take out of the fridge half an hour before baking. Set oven to 375° to preheat. Cover with foil; bake following directions, rising covered time until a thermometer inserted in the middle registers 165°, about 40 to 45 minutes. Serve following directions.

Nutrition Information

- Calories: 409 calories
- Total Fat: 17g fat (7g saturated fat)
- Sodium: 1031mg sodium
- Fiber: 6g fiber)
- Total Carbohydrate: 41g carbohydrate (5g sugars
- Cholesterol: 60mg cholesterol
- Protein: 25g protein.

98. Dressed Up Meatballs

Serving: 8 servings. | Prep: 10mins | Ready in:

Ingredients

- 2 pounds frozen fully cooked homestyle meatballs, thawed
- 2 medium carrots, julienned
- 1 small onion, halved and sliced
- 1 small green pepper, julienned
- 1 garlic clove, minced
- 1 jar (10 ounces) sweet-and-sour sauce
- 4-1/2 teaspoons soy sauce
- Hot cooked rice

Direction

- In a 3-quart microwave-safe dish, add meatballs; top with garlic, pepper, onion, and carrots. In a small bowl, combine soy sauce and sweet-and-sour sauce; put over meatballs.
- Microwave, covered, stirring twice, on High for about 6-8 minutes or until vegetables become soft and meatballs are heated through. Use with rice.

Nutrition Information

- Calories: 294 calories
- Cholesterol: 94mg cholesterol
- Protein: 20g protein.
- Total Fat: 15g fat (5g saturated fat)
- Sodium: 516mg sodium
- Fiber: 1g fiber)
- Total Carbohydrate: 20g carbohydrate (9g sugars

99. Easy Grilled Flank Steak

Serving: 4 servings. | Prep: 20mins | Ready in:

Ingredients

- 1 small onion, chopped
- 1/2 cup dry red wine or reduced-sodium beef broth
- 2 tablespoons olive oil
- 2 garlic cloves, minced
- 1 teaspoon brown sugar
- 1/4 teaspoon pepper
- 2 fresh sage leaves, thinly sliced or 3/4 teaspoon dried sage leaves
- 1/2 teaspoon salt
- 1/2 teaspoon minced fresh gingerroot
- 1 beef flank steak (1 pound)

Direction

- Put the initial nine ingredients together in a big resealable plastic bag. Create diamond shapes by scoring the steak surface into 1/4-in. deep cuts and insert into bag. Seal the bag up and turn to coat the meat before refrigerating for a minimum of 8 hours or through the night. Drain the meat and get rid of the marinade. Drip cooking oil onto a paper towel to moisten it then use long-handled tongs to coat the grill with it lightly. Over medium heat, broil the steak 4-in. from heat or grill it with a cover on until the meat is at desired level of doneness. Grill each side of the meat for about 6 to 8 minutes. For medium-rare meat, a thermometer should register at 145°F and for medium, it should be 160°F. For well-done meat, it should read 170°F. Leave it to stand for 5 minutes before cutting across the grain into thin slices.

Nutrition Information

- Calories: 205 calories
- Total Carbohydrate: 2g carbohydrate (1g sugars
- Cholesterol: 54mg cholesterol
- Protein: 22g protein. Diabetic Exchanges: 3 lean meat
- Total Fat: 11g fat (4g saturated fat)
- Sodium: 179mg sodium
- Fiber: 0 fiber)

100. Easy Lasagna

Serving: 12 servings. | Prep: 5mins | Ready in:

Ingredients

- 1-1/2 cups 4% cottage cheese
- 1 large egg
- 1/4 cup grated Parmesan cheese
- 1 tablespoon minced fresh parsley or 1 teaspoon dried parsley flakes
- 1/2 teaspoon dried oregano
- 1/4 teaspoon dried basil
- 9 lasagna noodles, cooked, rinsed and drained
- 4 cups Three-Meat Sauce
- 2 cups shredded part-skim mozzarella cheese

Direction

- Mix the following ingredients in a large bowl: egg, parsley, basil, cottage cheese, oregano, and Parmesan cheese. Grease your 13x9-inch baking pan and arrange a layer of 1/3 of noodles, sauce, cottage cheese mixture, and mozzarella. Repeat same steps and layers twice.
- Seal with cover and bake it at 350°F for about half an hour. Remove the cover and bake again for another 15-20 minutes until bubbling. Set aside for 15 minutes before you start to cut.

Nutrition Information

- Calories: 282 calories
- Sodium: 665mg sodium
- Fiber: 1g fiber)
- Total Carbohydrate: 20g carbohydrate (3g sugars
- Cholesterol: 67mg cholesterol
- Protein: 20g protein.
- Total Fat: 13g fat (6g saturated fat)

101. Easy Spaghetti

Serving: 2 servings. | Prep: 30mins | Ready in:

Ingredients

- 1/2 pound lean ground beef (90% lean)
- 1/4 cup chopped onion
- 2 cups meatless spaghetti sauce
- 1 cup water
- 3 ounces uncooked spaghetti, broken
- 1/4 pound reduced-fat process cheese (Velveeta), cubed
- 2 teaspoons grated Parmesan cheese

Direction

- Cook onion and beef together in a nonstick skillet on moderate heat until meat is not pink anymore, then drain. Stir in spaghetti, water and spaghetti sauce, then bring the mixture to a boil. Lower heat and simmer, covered, until spaghetti is softened, about 20 minutes. Put in process cheese and stir until it is melted. Use Parmesan cheese to sprinkle over top.

Nutrition Information

- Calories: 570 calories
- Total Fat: 15g fat (8g saturated fat)
- Sodium: 2115mg sodium
- Fiber: 5g fiber)
- Total Carbohydrate: 63g carbohydrate (24g sugars
- Cholesterol: 81mg cholesterol
- Protein: 43g protein.

102. Enchilada Casser Ole!

Serving: 8 servings. | Prep: 25mins | Ready in:

Ingredients

- 1 pound lean ground beef (90% lean)
- 1 large onion, chopped

- 2 cups salsa
- 1 can (15 ounces) black beans, rinsed and drained
- 1/4 cup reduced-fat Italian salad dressing
- 2 tablespoons reduced-sodium taco seasoning
- 1/4 teaspoon ground cumin
- 6 flour tortillas (8 inches)
- 3/4 cup reduced-fat sour cream
- 1 cup shredded reduced-fat Mexican cheese blend
- 1 cup shredded lettuce
- 1 medium tomato, chopped
- 1/4 cup minced fresh cilantro

Direction

- Place onion and beef in a large frying pan, cook on medium heat until beef is not pink. Drain the excess grease. Mix in cumin, dressing, beans, and taco seasoning. Line the bottom of a greased 11x7-in. baking dish with three tortillas. Place half of the meat and bean mixture, then one layer each of sour cream and cheese. Repeat the layers. Bake in a 400-degree oven covered for 25 minutes. Remove cover and return to oven until heated through about 5-10 minutes. Remove from oven and let cool for 5 minutes. Serve by topping with cilantro, lettuce and tomato.

Nutrition Information

- Calories: 357 calories
- Sodium: 864mg sodium
- Fiber: 3g fiber)
- Total Carbohydrate: 37g carbohydrate (6g sugars
- Cholesterol: 45mg cholesterol
- Protein: 23g protein. Diabetic Exchanges: 3 lean meat
- Total Fat: 12g fat (5g saturated fat)

103. Fabulous Fajitas

Serving: 10 | Prep: 15mins | Ready in:

Ingredients

- 2 green bell peppers, sliced
- 1 red bell pepper, sliced
- 1 onion, thinly sliced
- 1 cup fresh sliced mushrooms
- 2 cups diced, cooked chicken meat
- 1 (.7 ounce) package dry Italian-style salad dressing mix
- 10 (12 inch) flour tortillas

Direction

- Slice onion and peppers into thin slices. Do not dice; keep the slices thin and long.
- Sauté onion and peppers with a little oil until soft. Add chicken and mushrooms. Keep cooking over low heat until fully heated. Mix in dry salad dressing mix and mix well.
- Warm the tortillas and roll the mixture inside. Put shredded cheddar cheese, diced tomato and shredded lettuce on top if you want.

Nutrition Information

- Calories: 427 calories;
- Total Fat: 10.3
- Sodium: 1078
- Total Carbohydrate: 64.2
- Cholesterol: 21
- Protein: 18

104. Fajita Skillet

Serving: 4 servings. | Prep: 20mins | Ready in:

Ingredients

- 2 flour tortillas (10 inches), cut into 1/2-inch strips
- 3 tablespoons olive oil, divided

- 1/2 pound boneless skinless chicken breasts, cut into strips
- 1/2 pound beef top sirloin steak, cut into thin strips
- 1 medium green pepper, sliced
- 1 small onion, sliced
- 2 tablespoons soy sauce
- 2 teaspoons brown sugar
- 1/2 teaspoon chili powder
- 1/2 teaspoon ground cumin
- 1/4 teaspoon pepper
- 1 teaspoon cornstarch
- 2 tablespoons lime juice
- 1 cup cubed fresh pineapple
- 1 medium tomato, coarsely chopped

Direction

- Fry tortilla strips on both sides with oil in a big skillet until turning golden brown, or for 1 minute. Put on paper towels to drain.
- Cook pepper, cumin, chili powder, brown sugar, soy sauce, onion, green pepper, beef, and chicken with the leftover oil in the same skillet until the chicken is not pink anymore, or for 3-4 minutes.
- Mix together lime juice and cornstarch in a small bowl until smooth; pour into the pan. Boil it, stir and cook until thickened, or for 1 minute. Mix in tomato and pineapple, thoroughly heat. Enjoy with tortilla strips.

Nutrition Information

- Calories: 390 calories
- Protein: 27g protein. Diabetic Exchanges: 3 lean meat
- Total Fat: 17g fat (3g saturated fat)
- Sodium: 717mg sodium
- Fiber: 5g fiber)
- Total Carbohydrate: 29g carbohydrate (10g sugars
- Cholesterol: 63mg cholesterol

105. Family Style Meat Loaf Dinner

Serving: 6 servings. | Prep: 35mins | Ready in:

Ingredients

- 2 eggs
- 1 cup crushed saltines
- 1 medium onion, chopped
- 1/2 cup old-fashioned oats
- 1/2 cup heavy whipping cream
- 2 tablespoons Worcestershire sauce
- 2-1/2 teaspoons Montreal steak seasoning
- 1/2 teaspoon coarse ground pepper
- 2-1/2 pounds ground beef
- 4 medium potatoes, peeled and cubed
- 2 cups fresh baby carrots
- 1/3 cup finely chopped onion
- 2 cans (10-3/4 ounces each) condensed cream of mushroom soup, undiluted
- 2 cans (4 ounces each) mushroom stems and pieces, drained
- 1 envelope pork gravy mix

Direction

- Slice three 25x3-inch strips from a heavy-duty foil; form into crisscrosses that look like spokes of a wheel. Arrange the strips up the sides and on the bottom of a 6-quart slow cooker. Grease the strips.
- Blend pepper, steak seasoning, Worcestershire sauce, cream, oats, onion, cracker crumbs, and eggs in a large bowl. Crumble the beef over the mixture, then combine thoroughly. Form into a loaf; arrange in the center of the strips. Put onion, carrots, and potatoes around the meat.
- Blend gravy mix, mushrooms, and soup in a small bowl; place the mixture over the vegetables and meat. Put a cover on and cook on low heat until no longer pink and a thermometer registers 160 degrees, 5-6 hours. Place gravy and vegetables in a serving bowl. Transfer the meatloaf to a platter with foil

strips as handles; then divide the meat into 12 slices.

Nutrition Information

- Calories: 726 calories
- Fiber: 6g fiber)
- Total Carbohydrate: 52g carbohydrate (9g sugars
- Cholesterol: 219mg cholesterol
- Protein: 42g protein.
- Total Fat: 38g fat (15g saturated fat)
- Sodium: 1775mg sodium

106. Fancy Skillet Steaks

Serving: 2 servings. | Prep: 15mins | Ready in:

Ingredients

- 2 beef top sirloin steaks (6 ounces each)
- 3 teaspoons olive oil, divided
- 1/4 cup chopped onion
- 1/4 cup oil-packed sun-dried tomatoes, chopped
- 2 tablespoons balsamic vinegar
- 1 teaspoon sugar
- 1 garlic clove, minced
- 1/2 teaspoon lemon-pepper seasoning

Direction

- Cook steaks in 1 tsp. oil in a big skillet on medium high heat for about 4-5 minutes per side till meat gets desired doneness; 170° well-done, 160° medium and 145° for medium rare on a thermometer. Remove; keep warm.
- Put leftover oil, lemon-pepper, garlic, sugar, vinegar, tomatoes and onion in skillet; mix and cook till onion is tender for 4-5 minutes; put on steaks.

Nutrition Information

- Calories: 331 calories
- Sodium: 226mg sodium
- Fiber: 1g fiber)
- Total Carbohydrate: 10g carbohydrate (6g sugars
- Cholesterol: 94mg cholesterol
- Protein: 33g protein.
- Total Fat: 17g fat (4g saturated fat)

107. Fast Philly Cheesesteak Pizza

Serving: 6 slices. | Prep: 20mins | Ready in:

Ingredients

- 1 tube (13.8 ounces) refrigerated pizza crust
- 2 cups frozen pepper and onion stir-fry blend
- 2 tablespoons Dijon-mayonnaise blend
- 1/2 pound thinly sliced deli roast beef, cut into wide strips
- 1-1/2 cups shredded cheddar cheese

Direction

- Preheat the oven to 425°. Cover a pizza pan of 12 inch with cooking spray. Unroll and push dough to fit the prepared pan. For a rim, pinch the edge. Bake for 8 to 10 minutes, until edge is lightly browned.
- Meanwhile, position a big greased non-stick skillet over medium - high heat. Put in stir-fry blend; cook and mix until heated through, about 3 to 5 minutes.
- Distribute mayonnaise mixture over crust; top with vegetables and roast beef. Dust with cheese. Bake for 10 to 15 minutes, until cheese is melted.

Nutrition Information

- Calories: 330 calories
- Total Carbohydrate: 34g carbohydrate (6g sugars

- Cholesterol: 51mg cholesterol
- Protein: 20g protein.
- Total Fat: 13g fat (7g saturated fat)
- Sodium: 983mg sodium
- Fiber: 1g fiber)

108. Fiesta Beef Bowls

Serving: 6 servings. | Prep: 25mins | Ready in:

Ingredients

- 1-1/2 pounds boneless beef top round steak
- 1 can (10 ounces) diced tomatoes and green chilies
- 1 medium onion, chopped
- 2 garlic cloves, minced
- 1 teaspoon dried oregano
- 1 teaspoon chili powder
- 1 teaspoon ground cumin
- 1/4 teaspoon salt
- 1/4 teaspoon pepper
- 2 cans (15 ounces each) pinto beans, rinsed and drained
- 3 cups hot cooked rice
- 1/2 cup shredded cheddar cheese
- 6 tablespoons sliced ripe olives
- 6 tablespoons thinly sliced green onions
- 6 tablespoons guacamole

Direction

- In 3-qt. slow cooker, put round steak. Mix seasonings, garlic, onion and tomatoes in a small bowl; put on steak. Cover; cook till meat is tender for 8-9 hours on low.
- Take meat from slow cooker. Put beans in tomato mixture; cover. Cook for 30 minutes on high heat till beans heat through. Slice meat when cool to handle. Layer bean mixture, meat and rice in individual bowls; top with guacamole, onions, olives and cheese.

Nutrition Information

- Calories: 460 calories
- Total Fat: 11g fat (4g saturated fat)
- Sodium: 720mg sodium
- Fiber: 9g fiber)
- Total Carbohydrate: 52g carbohydrate (4g sugars
- Cholesterol: 74mg cholesterol
- Protein: 38g protein.

109. Fiesta Grilled Flank Steak

Serving: 4 servings. | Prep: 20mins | Ready in:

Ingredients

- 1/2 cup unsweetened pineapple juice
- 1 tablespoon lime juice
- 1/2 teaspoon garlic salt
- 1/2 teaspoon ground cumin
- 1 beef flank steak (1 pound)
- 1 cup cubed fresh pineapple
- 1/2 cup salsa verde
- 1 medium ripe avocado, peeled and cubed
- 1 green onion, finely chopped
- 1 tablespoon minced fresh cilantro

Direction

- Mix the cumin, garlic salt, lime juice and pineapple juice together in a big ziplock plastic bag. Cut 1/4-inch deep diamond shapes on the surface of the beef then put it in the ziplock bag. Seal the ziplock bag and turn to coat the beef with the marinade; keep in the fridge for 8 hours or overnight.
- Mix the avocado, pineapple, cilantro, salsa and green onion together in a small bowl. Cover the bowl and keep in the fridge until it's time to serve.
- Drain the marinated beef and throw away the marinade mixture. Use tongs to lightly rub an oiled paper towel on the grill rack. Put the marinated beef on a grill over medium heat then cover and grill or put the beef on a broiler and let it broil 4 inches away from the heat for

6-8 minutes on both sides until the preferred meat doneness is achieved (a thermometer inserted in the meat should indicate 160°F for medium, 170°F for well-done and 145°F for medium-rare).
- Allow the beef to sit for 5 minutes before cutting it into thin slices across the grain. Serve it with the prepared salsa on the side.

Nutrition Information

- Calories: 274 calories
- Protein: 24g protein. Diabetic Exchanges: 3 lean meat
- Total Fat: 15g fat (4g saturated fat)
- Sodium: 322mg sodium
- Fiber: 4g fiber)
- Total Carbohydrate: 12g carbohydrate (5g sugars
- Cholesterol: 54mg cholesterol

110. Flank Steak With Cilantro Salsa Verde

Serving: 4 servings. | Prep: 15mins | Ready in:

Ingredients

- 1 beef flank steak or top sirloin steak, 1 inch thick (about 1-1/4 pounds)
- 1/4 teaspoon salt
- 1/4 teaspoon pepper
- 1 cup salsa verde
- 1/2 cup fresh cilantro leaves
- 1 medium ripe avocado, peeled and diced
- 1 medium tomato, seeded and diced

Direction

- Season steak with pepper and salt. On medium heat, grill steak while covered or broil four inches from the heat until it reaches the preferred doneness (an inserted thermometer in the steak should register 170° Fahrenheit for well-done, 160 degrees F for medium done, and 145° Fahrenheit for medium rare). Set aside for 5 minutes.
- In a food processor, pulse cilantro and salsa until well combined. Thinly cut the steak across the grain. Serve steak slices with tomato, avocado, and salsa mix.

Nutrition Information

- Calories: 263 calories
- Total Fat: 15g fat (4g saturated fat)
- Sodium: 571mg sodium
- Fiber: 4g fiber)
- Total Carbohydrate: 8g carbohydrate (2g sugars
- Cholesterol: 54mg cholesterol
- Protein: 24g protein. Diabetic Exchanges: 3 lean meat

111. Flank Steak With Couscous

Serving: 4 servings. | Prep: 10mins | Ready in:

Ingredients

- 1 garlic clove, minced
- 1 teaspoon olive oil
- 1/2 teaspoon Italian seasoning
- 1/4 teaspoon pepper
- 1/8 teaspoon salt
- 1 beef flank steak (1 pound)
- 2 packages (5.8 ounces each) roasted garlic and olive oil couscous
- 3/4 cup diced roasted sweet red pepper, drained
- 1/2 cup Italian salad dressing

Direction

- Preheat broiler. Mix initial 5 ingredients; rub on steak. Put onto broiler pan.

- Broil it 2-3-in. from heat for 6-8 minutes per side till meat gets desired doneness; thermometer should register 135° for medium-rare. Stand for 5 minutes.
- Meanwhile, follow package directions to cook couscous; mix in red pepper. Thinly slice steak across grain; drizzle dressing then serve with couscous.

Nutrition Information

- Calories: 587 calories
- Total Carbohydrate: 61g carbohydrate (5g sugars
- Cholesterol: 54mg cholesterol
- Protein: 34g protein.
- Total Fat: 21g fat (5g saturated fat)
- Sodium: 1445mg sodium
- Fiber: 3g fiber)

112. Flank Steak With Horseradish Sauce

Serving: 4 servings. | Prep: 10mins | Ready in:

Ingredients

- 1 beef flank steak (1 pound)
- 3 tablespoons lemon juice
- 2 tablespoons Dijon mustard
- 2 tablespoons Worcestershire sauce
- 2 garlic cloves, minced
- 1/8 teaspoon hot pepper sauce
- HORSERADISH SAUCE:
- 1/4 cup fat-free mayonnaise
- 1/4 cup reduced-fat sour cream
- 1 tablespoon Dijon mustard
- 2 green onions, finely chopped
- 2 teaspoons prepared horseradish

Direction

- Score the surface of the steak using a sharp knife to make diamond shapes with shallow diagonal cuts at 1-in. intervals. Repeat the process on other side.
- Mix the next five ingredients in a large resealable plastic bag; put the steak. Close bag and turn to coat; keep in refrigerator for 8 hours or overnight. In a small bowl, mix the sauce; covered, and keep cool in refrigerator.
- Drain and remove marinade. Grill the steak over medium-hot heat, with cover, until achieves desired doneness (a thermometer should read 145deg for medium-rare; 160deg for medium; and 170deg for well-done), for 7-9 minutes on each side. Cut steak thinly across the grain; best served with sauce.

Nutrition Information

- Calories: 225 calories
- Sodium: 353mg sodium
- Fiber: 0 fiber)
- Total Carbohydrate: 5g carbohydrate (0 sugars
- Cholesterol: 51mg cholesterol
- Protein: 26g protein. Diabetic Exchanges: 4 lean meat.
- Total Fat: 10g fat (5g saturated fat)

113. Flavorful Italian Pot Roast

Serving: 8-10 servings. | Prep: 20mins | Ready in:

Ingredients

- 1 beef rump roast or bottom round roast (4 to 5 pounds)
- 1 to 2 teaspoons salt
- 2 tablespoons vegetable oil
- 2 garlic cloves, minced
- 1/2 teaspoon dried parsley flakes
- 1/2 teaspoon pepper
- 2 carrots, sliced
- 1 whole onion, studded with 2 whole cloves
- 1 can (15 ounces) tomato puree
- 1/2 cup water or red wine

- 1/2 teaspoon beef bouillon granules
- Cooked egg noodles

Direction

- Rub the roast with salt. In the Dutch oven, brown the roast in oil. Put in all of the rest of the ingredients excluding noodles. Boil; lower the heat and let simmer with cover till meat softens or for roughly 2 to 3 hours.
- Get rid of the onion. Take the roast out; chop into slices. Serve on top of the noodles along with gravy.

Nutrition Information

- Calories: 283 calories
- Total Fat: 11g fat (3g saturated fat)
- Sodium: 348mg sodium
- Fiber: 1g fiber)
- Total Carbohydrate: 4g carbohydrate (2g sugars
- Cholesterol: 109mg cholesterol
- Protein: 37g protein.

114. Flavorful Meat Loaf

Serving: 4 servings. | Prep: 10mins | Ready in:

Ingredients

- 1 medium carrot, shredded
- 1/4 cup chopped onion
- 2 tablespoons soy sauce
- 1 teaspoon tomato paste
- 2 garlic cloves, minced
- 1/4 teaspoon ground ginger
- 1/8 teaspoon crushed red pepper flakes
- Pepper to taste
- 1/2 pound ground beef
- 1/2 pound ground pork

Direction

- Mix the first 8 ingredients in a bowl then add the pork and beef in, mixing thoroughly. Form the mixture into a loaf in a shallow, ungreased baking pan. Bake at 350°F until the meat isn't pink for 45 to 50 minutes. It is ready when the thermometer says 160°F. Drain.

Nutrition Information

- Calories:
- Sodium:
- Fiber:
- Total Carbohydrate:
- Cholesterol:
- Protein:
- Total Fat:

115. Florentine Meatballs

Serving: 4 servings plus 16 cooked meatballs. | Prep: 20mins | Ready in:

Ingredients

- 2 packages (10 ounces each) frozen chopped spinach, thawed and squeezed dry
- 1/2 cup seasoned bread crumbs
- 1/4 cup grated Parmesan cheese
- 4 garlic cloves, minced
- 2 teaspoons dried oregano
- 2 eggs, lightly beaten
- 2 pounds lean ground beef (90% lean)
- 1 jar (26 ounces) spaghetti sauce
- Hot cooked spaghetti

Direction

- Combine the initial 6 ingredients in a big bowl. Crumble beef and add to the mixture, combine nicely. Form into 32 balls.
- Arrange meatballs on an oiled rack placed in a shallow baking pan. Bake at 400 degrees without cover until not pink anymore, about 24-28 minutes. Place on paper towels to drain.

- Save 1/2 of meatballs for other purposes or Italian Stroganoff. Heat spaghetti sauce in a big saucepan; add the rest of meatballs. Serve along with spaghetti.

Nutrition Information

- Calories: 403 calories
- Total Fat: 19g fat (6g saturated fat)
- Sodium: 1197mg sodium
- Fiber: 6g fiber)
- Total Carbohydrate: 27g carbohydrate (12g sugars
- Cholesterol: 130mg cholesterol
- Protein: 32g protein.

116. Fourth Of July Bean Casserole

Serving: 12 servings. | Prep: 20mins | Ready in:

Ingredients

- 1/2 pound bacon strips, diced
- 1/2 pound ground beef
- 1 cup chopped onion
- 1 can (28 ounces) pork and beans
- 1 can (16 ounces) kidney beans, rinsed and drained
- 1 can (15-1/4 ounces) lima beans, rinsed and drained
- 1/2 cup barbecue sauce
- 1/2 cup ketchup
- 1/2 cup sugar
- 1/2 cup packed brown sugar
- 2 tablespoons prepared mustard
- 2 tablespoons molasses
- 1 teaspoon salt
- 1/2 teaspoon chili powder

Direction

- Cook onion, beef, and bacon over medium heat in a large skillet until meat is no longer pink; drain off grease.
- Pour mixture into an oiled 2 1/2-quart baking dish. Mix in all of the beans; stir well. Combine the remaining ingredients in a small bowl; mix into bean and beef mixture.
- Bake, covered for 45 minutes at 350°; remove cover, and bake for 15 more minutes.

Nutrition Information

- Calories: 278 calories
- Protein: 12g protein.
- Total Fat: 6g fat (2g saturated fat)
- Sodium: 933mg sodium
- Fiber: 7g fiber)
- Total Carbohydrate: 47g carbohydrate (26g sugars
- Cholesterol: 15mg cholesterol

117. French Beef Stew

Serving: 8 | Prep: | Ready in:

Ingredients

- 1 1/2 pounds cubed beef stew meat
- 1/4 cup all-purpose flour
- 2 tablespoons vegetable oil
- 2 (14.5 ounce) cans Italian-style diced tomatoes
- 1 (14 ounce) can beef broth
- 4 carrots, chopped
- 2 potatoes, peeled and chopped
- 3/4 teaspoon dried thyme
- 2 tablespoons Dijon-style prepared mustard
- salt and pepper to taste

Direction

- In a large plastic food storage bag, mix flour and meat together; toss to evenly coat.

- In a 6-quart saucepan with hot vegetable oil, cook in meat until fully browned. Taste with pepper and salt to your preference.
- Include in thyme, potatoes, carrots, beef broth and diced tomatoes. Bring to a boil; lower the heat to medium-low; simmer with a cover until the beef is tender, or for 1 hour.

Nutrition Information

- Calories: 343 calories;
- Protein: 18.7
- Total Fat: 20.1
- Sodium: 491
- Total Carbohydrate: 20
- Cholesterol: 57

118. French Onion Shepherd's Pie

Serving: 4 servings. | Prep: 45mins | Ready in:

Ingredients

- 2 large onions, halved and thinly sliced
- 1 tablespoon canola oil
- 1 pound ground beef
- 2 tablespoons all-purpose flour
- 1/2 teaspoon salt
- 1 can (14-1/2 ounces) reduced-sodium beef broth
- 2 tablespoons brandy or additional reduced-sodium beef broth
- 1 tablespoon Worcestershire sauce
- 1 tablespoon stone-ground mustard
- 3 cups mashed potatoes
- 1 cup shredded Swiss cheese

Direction

- Add onions to oil in a big frying pan, sauté until they get soft. Lower to medium-low heat, cook until they turn deep golden brown, about 35 to 40 minutes, stirring periodically.
- In the meantime, add beef to a big saucepan, cook over medium heat until it is not pink any longer; drain. Mix in salt and flour until well combined, cook for 60 seconds longer. Blend the mustard, Worcestershire sauce, brandy and broth together. Mix into the pan little by little. Boil the mixture, cook and stir until it gets thick, about 2 minutes. Mix in onion and heat through.
- Move the beef mixture to an 8-inch square baking dish coated with cooking spray. Add tomatoes on top and spread out, dredge cheese over top. Set oven at 375°, bake while uncovered until it bubbles and the cheese melts, about 30 to 35 minutes.

Nutrition Information

- Calories: 563 calories
- Fiber: 2g fiber)
- Total Carbohydrate: 42g carbohydrate (5g sugars
- Cholesterol: 101mg cholesterol
- Protein: 34g protein.
- Total Fat: 27g fat (11g saturated fat)
- Sodium: 1150mg sodium

119. Gala Beef Tenderloin Filets

Serving: 6 servings. | Prep: 10mins | Ready in:

Ingredients

- 6 beef tenderloin steaks (1-1/2 to 2 inches thick and 6 ounces each)
- 1/4 teaspoon salt
- 1/8 teaspoon pepper
- 2 tablespoons butter, divided
- 1 tablespoon olive oil
- 2 tablespoons finely chopped onion
- 2 garlic cloves, minced
- 1/3 cup dry red wine or beef broth
- 2 tablespoons minced fresh parsley

- 1/2 teaspoon browning sauce, optional

Direction

- Season steaks using pepper and salt. Heat oil and 1 tbsp. butter in a big skillet on medium high heat; cook the steaks for 5-8 minutes per side till meat gets desired doneness; 170° well done, 160° medium and 145° for medium-rare on a thermometer. Remove; keep warm.
- Sauté garlic and onion in leftover butter for a minute in same skillet. Add broth/wine; mix and cook for a minute. Mix in browning sauce (optional) and parsley; drizzle on beef.

Nutrition Information

- Calories:
- Total Carbohydrate:
- Cholesterol:
- Protein:
- Total Fat:
- Sodium:
- Fiber:

120. Garlic Beef Enchiladas

Serving: 5 servings. | Prep: 30mins | Ready in:

Ingredients

- 1 pound ground beef
- 1 medium onion, chopped
- 2 tablespoons all-purpose flour
- 1 tablespoon chili powder
- 1 teaspoon salt
- 1 teaspoon garlic powder
- 1/2 teaspoon ground cumin
- 1/4 teaspoon rubbed sage
- 1 can (14-1/2 ounces) stewed tomatoes, cut up
- SAUCE:
- 1/3 cup butter
- 4 to 6 garlic cloves, minced
- 1/2 cup all-purpose flour
- 1 can (14-1/2 ounces) beef broth
- 1 can (15 ounces) tomato sauce
- 1 to 2 tablespoons chili powder
- 1 to 2 teaspoons ground cumin
- 1 to 2 teaspoons rubbed sage
- 1/2 teaspoon salt
- 10 flour tortillas (6 inches), warmed
- 2 cups shredded Colby-Monterey Jack cheese, divided
- Optional toppings: halved grape tomatoes, minced fresh cilantro, sliced jalapeno peppers and medium red onion, chopped or sliced

Direction

- Set an oven to 350 degrees and start preheating. Cook the onion and beef over medium heat in a large skillet for 6-8 minutes until the beef is not pink anymore, breaking the meat into crumbles; then drain the beef. Stir in seasonings and flour. Put in tomatoes; then boil. Turn down the heat; put on a cover and simmer for 15 minutes.
- Heat the butter over medium-high heat in a saucepan. Put in garlic; stir and cook until it becomes tender, about a minute. Add flour and stir until combined; beat in the broth gradually. Then boil; stir and cook until thick, 2 minutes. Stir in the seasonings and tomato sauce; heat through.
- Add 1 1/2 cups of sauce to an ungreased 13x9-inch baking dish. Top each tortilla with approximately 1/4 cup of the beef mixture, but not in the center. Put 1-2 tablespoons of cheese on top. Roll and place over the sauce with seam side down. Place the remaining sauce on top.
- Put on a cover and bake for 30-35 minutes until heated through. Dust with the remaining cheese. Remove the cover and bake for 10-15 more minutes until the cheese melts. If desired, serve together with toppings of your choice.

Nutrition Information

- Calories: 751 calories

- Total Carbohydrate: 56g carbohydrate (8g sugars
- Cholesterol: 128mg cholesterol
- Protein: 38g protein.
- Total Fat: 43g fat (21g saturated fat)
- Sodium: 2536mg sodium
- Fiber: 4g fiber)

121. Garlic Beef Stroganoff

Serving: 6-8 servings. | Prep: 20mins | Ready in:

Ingredients

- 2 teaspoons beef bouillon granules
- 1 cup boiling water
- 1 can (10-3/4 ounces) condensed cream of mushroom soup, undiluted
- 2 jars (4-1/2 ounces each) sliced mushrooms, drained
- 1 large onion, chopped
- 3 garlic cloves, minced
- 1 tablespoon Worcestershire sauce
- 1-1/2 to 2 pounds beef top round steak, cut into thin strips
- 2 tablespoons canola oil
- 1 package (8 ounces) cream cheese, cubed
- Hot cooked noodles

Direction

- Dissolve bouillon in water in a 3-quart slow cooker. Put in Worcestershire sauce, garlic, onion, mushrooms and soup. Brown beef in oil in a skillet.
- Move to the slow cooker. Cover and cook for 7 to 8 hours at low, until the meat is soft. Mix in cream cheese until smooth. Enjoy with noodles.

Nutrition Information

- Calories: 281 calories
- Sodium: 661mg sodium

- Fiber: 1g fiber)
- Total Carbohydrate: 7g carbohydrate (2g sugars
- Cholesterol: 81mg cholesterol
- Protein: 23g protein.
- Total Fat: 18g fat (8g saturated fat)

122. Garlic Lover's Beef Stew

Serving: 10 servings. | Prep: 30mins | Ready in:

Ingredients

- 1 boneless beef chuck roast (3 pounds), cut into 2-inch pieces
- 1-1/4 teaspoons salt
- 3/4 teaspoon coarsely ground pepper
- 1/2 cup all-purpose flour
- 2 tablespoons olive oil
- 12 garlic cloves, minced
- 1 cup dry red wine or reduced-sodium beef broth
- 2 cans (14-1/2 ounces each) diced tomatoes, undrained
- 1 can (14-1/2 ounces) reduced-sodium beef broth
- 6 medium carrots, thinly sliced
- 2 medium onions, chopped
- 2 tablespoons tomato paste
- 2 teaspoons minced fresh rosemary or 1/2 teaspoon dried rosemary, crushed
- 2 teaspoons minced fresh thyme or 1/2 teaspoon dried thyme
- 2 bay leaves
- Dash ground cloves
- Hot mashed potatoes

Direction

- Drizzle the beef with flour, pepper, and salt; toss to coat.
- Heat the oil on medium high heat in the big skillet. Brown the beef in batches. Transfer using the slotted spoon. Lower the heat to

- medium. Put in garlic; cook and stir for 60 seconds.
- Pour wine into the skillet, mixing to loosen browned bits in the pan. Move into a 5- or 6-quart slow cooker. Mix in beef, cloves, bay leaves, thyme, rosemary, tomato paste, onions, carrots, broth, and tomatoes.
- Cook while covered over low heat till beef becomes tender for 8 to 10 hours. Take out the bay leaves. Serve along with the mashed potatoes.

Nutrition Information

- Calories: 330 calories
- Fiber: 3g fiber)
- Total Carbohydrate: 17g carbohydrate (6g sugars
- Cholesterol: 89mg cholesterol
- Protein: 29g protein. Diabetic Exchanges: 4 lean meat
- Total Fat: 16g fat (5g saturated fat)
- Sodium: 586mg sodium

123. Garlic Mushroom French Beef Stew

Serving: 20 servings (1 cup each). | Prep: 40mins | Ready in:

Ingredients

- 5 pounds beef sirloin tip roast, cut into 1-inch cubes
- 1-1/2 teaspoons salt
- 1/2 teaspoon pepper
- 3 tablespoons olive oil
- 2 large sweet onions, chopped
- 3 medium carrots, sliced
- 5 tablespoons butter, divided
- 6 garlic cloves, minced
- 2 pounds assorted fresh mushrooms, such as portobello, shiitake and/or oyster), sliced
- 4 large Yukon Gold potatoes, cubed
- 1 carton (32 ounces) beef broth
- 1 cup dry red wine or additional beef broth
- 1 tablespoon minced fresh basil or 1 teaspoon dried basil
- 3 tablespoons all-purpose flour
- 1 cup heavy whipping cream
- 2/3 cup crumbled blue cheese

Direction

- With pepper and salt, season the beef. Put oil in stockpot and brown beef in batches. Remove the beef and keep warm. Add 2 tablespoons butter to the same stockpot and sauté carrots and onions for 4 minutes. Mix in the garlic and cook for 2 more minutes. Mix in potatoes, beef, mushrooms, basil, wine, and broth. Heat to boiling. Cover, decrease heat, and gently boil for 1 1/4 hours. Remove cover and simmer until meat is tender, 20-30 minutes. Melt the rest of the butter in a small pan. Mix in flour until not lumpy. Slowly add the cream. Heat to boiling; stir constantly and cook until thick, about 2 minutes. Mix into stockpot with stew and cook until entirely heat. Sprinkle cheese on top.

Nutrition Information

- Calories: 336 calories
- Cholesterol: 100mg cholesterol
- Protein: 27g protein.
- Total Fat: 16g fat (8g saturated fat)
- Sodium: 517mg sodium
- Fiber: 2g fiber)
- Total Carbohydrate: 18g carbohydrate (4g sugars

124. Garlic Pepper Tenderloin Steaks

Serving: 4 servings. | Prep: 5mins | Ready in:

Ingredients

- 1-1/2 teaspoons minced garlic
- 1 teaspoon ground mustard
- 1 teaspoon paprika
- 1 teaspoon chili powder
- 1 teaspoon pepper
- 1/2 teaspoon salt
- 1/2 teaspoon dried thyme
- 1/4 to 1/2 teaspoon cayenne pepper
- 4 beef tenderloin steaks (4 ounces each)
- 2 teaspoons olive oil

Direction

- Mix all the seasonings in a small bowl. Coat the steaks with oil and the seasoning mixture. Place it inside the refrigerator, covered, for 60 minutes.
- Wet the paper towel with cooking oil and wipe it into the grill rack using the long-handled tongs. Place the steak in the greased rack and grill it uncovered over medium heat. You can also broil the steak 4-inches away from heat source until the steak meets its desired doneness, about 7-10 minutes per side. For a medium-rare cooked steak, the thermometer should read 145°F, 160°F for the moderate cooked steak, and 170°F for the well-done steak.

Nutrition Information

- Calories: 209 calories
- Sodium: 353mg sodium
- Fiber: 1g fiber)
- Total Carbohydrate: 2g carbohydrate (0 sugars
- Cholesterol: 70mg cholesterol
- Protein: 24g protein. Diabetic Exchanges: 3 lean meat
- Total Fat: 11g fat (3g saturated fat)

125. German Style Beef Roast

Serving: 10 servings. | Prep: 10mins | Ready in:

Ingredients

- 1 boneless beef chuck roast (4 pounds), trimmed
- 1 teaspoon pepper
- 1 large onion, thinly sliced
- 1 bottle (12 ounces) beer or nonalcoholic beer
- 1 cup ketchup
- 1/4 cup packed brown sugar
- 1/4 cup all-purpose flour
- 1/4 cup cold water

Direction

- Divide roast into 2 equal portions; season with pepper. Arrange roast and onion in a 5-quart slow cooker. Combine brown sugar, ketchup, and beer in a small bowl; pour over onion and roast in the cooker. Cook, covered for 8 to 10 hours on low setting until meat is tender.
- Transfer roast to a serving platter and keep warm. Ladle fat off the cooking liquid; pour liquid into a small saucepan, and bring to a boil.
- Stir together water and flour until smooth; slowly mix into the pan. Bring to a boil; cook for 2 minutes until gravy thickens, stirring well while cooking. Serve roast with gravy.

Nutrition Information

- Calories: 376 calories
- Total Carbohydrate: 16g carbohydrate (13g sugars
- Cholesterol: 118mg cholesterol
- Protein: 36g protein.
- Total Fat: 17g fat (7g saturated fat)
- Sodium: 382mg sodium
- Fiber: 0 fiber)

126. Gorgonzola Beef Wellingtons

Serving: 8 servings. | Prep: 40mins | Ready in:

Ingredients

- 8 beef tenderloin steaks (6 to 8 ounces each)
- 1/2 teaspoon plus 1/8 teaspoon salt, divided
- 1/2 teaspoon plus 1/8 teaspoon pepper, divided
- 4 tablespoons butter, divided
- 1 pound fresh mushrooms, thinly sliced
- 2 shallots, finely chopped
- 6 garlic cloves, minced
- 1 package (17.3 ounces) frozen puff pastry, thawed
- 1 cup crumbled Gorgonzola cheese
- 2 large eggs, beaten
- 4 cups reduced-sodium beef broth
- 1/2 cup Madeira wine or additional reduced-sodium beef broth
- 2 tablespoons tomato paste
- 1 teaspoon dried thyme

Direction

- Season the steaks with half a teaspoon each of pepper and salt. Place the steaks in a big skillet, cook them in 2 tablespoons of butter in batches until browned. Take them out of the skillet; allow to cool slightly and place them in the fridge until cooled.
- Using the same skillet, cook and stir the shallots and mushrooms in the remaining butter until softened. Stir in the garlic and the rest of the pepper and salt; allow to cook for additional 1 minute.
- Roll each puff pastry sheet, forming a 14-in square, on a lightly floured surface. Slice them into four 6-1/2-in. squares (make use of the scraps to create decorative cutouts if preferred).
- Put 2 tablespoons of cheese in the middle of each square and top it off with 3 tablespoons mushroom mixture and a steak. Gently brush the pastry edges using the egg. Gather opposite corners of pastry over steak, pinching the seams to tightly seal.
- Arrange on a greased 15x10x1-in. baking pan with the seam side facing down. Slash four small slits on top of the pastry. Place the cutouts over tops if preferred. Brush with egg. Let bake for about 25-30 minutes at 425° or until pastry turns golden brown and the meat achieves the desired doneness (for medium-rare, a thermometer should reach 135°; medium - 140°; medium-well - 145°).
- In the meantime, combine wine and broth in a big saucepan. Let the mixture boil; allow to cook for roughly half an hour until the liquid is lessened by half. Mix in thyme and tomato paste. Serve alongside the beef Wellingtons.

Nutrition Information

- Calories: 707 calories
- Protein: 49g protein.
- Total Fat: 38g fat (15g saturated fat)
- Sodium: 863mg sodium
- Fiber: 6g fiber)
- Total Carbohydrate: 42g carbohydrate (2g sugars
- Cholesterol: 158mg cholesterol

127. Grandma Schwartz's Rouladen

Serving: 6 servings. | Prep: 35mins | Ready in:

Ingredients

- 3 bacon strips, chopped
- 1-1/2 pounds beef top round steak
- 2 tablespoons Dijon mustard
- 3 medium carrots, quartered lengthwise
- 6 dill pickle spears
- 1/4 cup finely chopped onion
- 1 cup sliced fresh mushrooms
- 1 small parsnip, peeled and chopped
- 1 celery rib, chopped
- 1 can (10-3/4 ounces) condensed golden cream of mushroom soup, undiluted
- 1/3 cup dry red wine
- 2 tablespoons Worcestershire sauce
- 2 tablespoons minced fresh parsley

Direction

- In a big skillet, cook the bacon on medium heat till crisp. Take out the paper towels using a slotted spoon; drain, save the drippings.
- At the same time, slice the steak into 6 serving-sized pieces; pound using a meat mallet to a-quarter-inch in thickness. Spread over the tops with the mustard. Add 2 carrot pieces and 1 pickle spear on top of each; drizzle with the onion. Roll up from a short side and use the toothpicks to secure.
- In a big skillet, brown the roll-ups in the bacon drippings on medium high heat. Add the roll-ups into the 4-quart slow cooker. Add the cooked bacon, celery, parsnip and mushrooms on top.
- In a small-sized bowl, stir Worcestershire sauce, wine and soup. Add onto the top. Keep covered and cook over low heat till the beef softens or for 6 to 8 hours. Drizzle with the parsley.

Nutrition Information

- Calories: 288 calories
- Protein: 28g protein.
- Total Fat: 11g fat (3g saturated fat)
- Sodium: 1030mg sodium
- Fiber: 3g fiber)
- Total Carbohydrate: 14g carbohydrate (4g sugars
- Cholesterol: 74mg cholesterol

128. Grandma's Beef Stew

Serving: 2 servings. | Prep: 10mins | Ready in:

Ingredients

- 1/2 pound lean ground beef (90% lean)
- 1/2 medium onion, chopped
- 3 tablespoons chopped green pepper
- 1 can (8-3/4 ounces) whole kernel corn, drained
- 2/3 cup condensed tomato soup, undiluted
- 1-1/2 teaspoons Worcestershire sauce
- 1 teaspoon sugar
- 3/4 teaspoon salt

Direction

- Cook the green pepper, onion, and beef in a large saucepan on medium heat until the meat is no longer pink, then drain. Add in the remaining ingredients, and boil. Decrease the heat and simmer while covered for 30 minutes.

Nutrition Information

- Calories: 341 calories
- Protein: 26g protein.
- Total Fat: 9g fat (3g saturated fat)
- Sodium: 1826mg sodium
- Fiber: 4g fiber)
- Total Carbohydrate: 33g carbohydrate (16g sugars
- Cholesterol: 56mg cholesterol

129. Greek Pasta And Beef

Serving: 12 servings. | Prep: 30mins | Ready in:

Ingredients

- 1 package (16 ounces) elbow macaroni
- 1 pound ground beef
- 1 large onion, chopped
- 1 garlic clove, minced
- 1 can (8 ounces) tomato sauce
- 1/2 cup water
- 1 teaspoon salt
- 1/2 teaspoon ground cinnamon
- 1/4 teaspoon ground nutmeg
- 1/4 teaspoon pepper
- 1 large egg, lightly beaten
- 1/2 cup grated Parmesan cheese

- SAUCE:
- 1/4 cup butter
- 1/4 cup all-purpose flour
- 1/4 teaspoon ground cinnamon
- 3 cups 2% milk
- 2 large eggs, lightly beaten
- 1/3 cup grated Parmesan cheese

Direction

- Follow the instruction on package to cook the macaroni. In a big skillet, cook the onion and beef on medium heat till the meat is not pink anymore. Put in the garlic; cook for 60 seconds more. Drain off. Whisk in seasonings, water and tomato sauce. Let simmer with cover for 10 minutes, whisk once in a while.
- Drain the macaroni and add into a big bowl. Whisk in the cheese and egg; put aside.
- For the sauce, in a big saucepan, melt the butter; whisk in the cinnamon and flour till smooth. Slowly pour in the milk. Boil on medium heat; cook and whisk till it thickens a bit or for 2 minutes. Take out of heat. Whisk a bit of the hot mixture into the eggs; bring all of them back to the pan, whisk continuously. Whisk in the cheese.
- In the greased 3-quart baking dish, spread 1/2 macaroni mixture. Add the leftover macaroni mixture and beef mixture on top. Add the sauce on top. Bake, with no cover, at 350 degrees till the thermometer reaches 160 degrees or for 45 to 50 minutes. Allow it to rest for 5 minutes prior to serving.

Nutrition Information

- Calories: 330 calories
- Sodium: 467mg sodium
- Fiber: 2g fiber)
- Total Carbohydrate: 35g carbohydrate (5g sugars
- Cholesterol: 96mg cholesterol
- Protein: 18g protein.
- Total Fat: 13g fat (6g saturated fat)

130. Grilled Beef Tenderloins

Serving: 2 servings. | Prep: 10mins | Ready in:

Ingredients

- 1/4 cup dry red wine
- 1/4 cup reduced-sodium soy sauce
- 1/2 teaspoon garlic powder
- 1/2 teaspoon dried oregano
- 1/4 teaspoon ground cumin
- 1/4 teaspoon ground ancho chili pepper
- 1/4 teaspoon pepper
- 2 beef tenderloin steaks (6 ounces each)

Direction

- Mix all the initial 7 ingredients together in a big Ziplock plastic bag. Put in the steaks then seal the Ziplock bag and turn to coat the steaks with the marinade. Keep in the fridge for a maximum of 4 hours.
- Drain the marinated steaks and throw away the marinade mixture. Use tongs to lightly rub an oiled paper towel on the grill rack. Put the marinated steaks on a grill over medium heat then cover and grill or put the marinated steaks in a broiler and let it broil 4 inches away from heat for 4 to 6 minutes on every side until the preferred meat doneness is achieved (a thermometer inserted on the meat should indicate 170°F for well-done, 160°F for medium and 145°F for medium-rare).

Nutrition Information

- Calories: 263 calories
- Protein: 37g protein. Diabetic Exchanges: 5 lean meat.
- Total Fat: 10g fat (4g saturated fat)
- Sodium: 402mg sodium
- Fiber: 0 fiber)
- Total Carbohydrate: 1g carbohydrate (0 sugars
- Cholesterol: 75mg cholesterol

131. Grilled Ribeyes With Herb Butter

Serving: 4 servings. | Prep: 25mins | Ready in:

Ingredients

- 1/4 cup olive oil
- 1/4 cup dry red wine
- 1 tablespoon minced fresh rosemary or 1 teaspoon dried rosemary, crushed
- 1 tablespoon red wine vinegar
- 1 tablespoon Dijon mustard
- 1 teaspoon coarsely ground pepper
- 1 teaspoon Worcestershire sauce
- 2 garlic cloves, minced
- 4 beef ribeye steaks (3/4 pound each)
- STEAK SEASONINGS:
- 2 teaspoons kosher salt
- 1 teaspoon sugar
- 1 teaspoon herbes de Provence
- 1 teaspoon coarsely ground pepper
- HERB BUTTER:
- 1/4 cup butter, softened
- 1 tablespoon minced fresh parsley
- 1 teaspoon prepared horseradish

Direction

- Mix the first 8 ingredients together in a big ziplock bag; put in steaks. Seal and flip the bag to coat steaks with marinade. Place the bag in the refrigerator overnight.
- Drain steaks and get rid of the marinade. Mix the steak seasoning together and spread over steaks.
- On medium heat, grill steaks or broil three-four inches from heat for 5-7mins per side until it reaches the preferred doneness (an inserted thermometer in the steak should register 170° Fahrenheit for well-done, 160 degrees F for medium done, and 145° Fahrenheit for medium rare).
- Make the herb butter by mixing horseradish, parsley, and butter together in a bowl. Spread a tablespoon herb butter on each steak.

Nutrition Information

- Calories: 976 calories
- Protein: 61g protein.
- Total Fat: 77g fat (31g saturated fat)
- Sodium: 1271mg sodium
- Fiber: 1g fiber)
- Total Carbohydrate: 5g carbohydrate (1g sugars
- Cholesterol: 232mg cholesterol

132. Grilled Steaks With Marinated Tomatoes

Serving: 6 servings. | Prep: 25mins | Ready in:

Ingredients

- 1/4 cup light beer
- 3 tablespoons raspberry vinaigrette
- 3 tablespoons olive oil
- 1 tablespoon torn fresh basil
- 1 tablespoon cider vinegar
- 2 teaspoons garlic powder
- 2 teaspoons coriander seeds, crushed
- 1-1/2 teaspoons minced fresh oregano
- 1 teaspoon sugar
- 1/2 teaspoon salt
- 1/2 teaspoon pepper
- 3 large tomatoes, sliced
- RUB:
- 2 teaspoons Montreal steak seasoning
- 2 teaspoons chili powder
- 1 teaspoon salt
- 1 teaspoon celery seed
- 1 teaspoon smoked paprika
- 1/2 teaspoon pepper
- 2 beef top sirloin steaks (1 inch thick and 1 pound each)

Direction

- Mix the initial 11 ingredients together in a bowl until well combined. In a 13-in x 9-in dish, arrange tomatoes and add the beer mixture on; cover. Let it chill in the refrigerator for at least an hour.
- Combine the rub seasonings together and massage over steaks. On medium heat, grill steaks while covered or broil four inches from heat for 8-10 minutes per side until it reaches the preferred doneness (an inserted thermometer in the steak should register 170 degrees F for well-done, 160 degrees F for medium, and 145 degrees F for medium rare). Set aside for 5 minutes; slice into thirds.
- Arrange the sliced steaks on a dish and add tomatoes on top. Drizzle with the leftover beer mixture.

Nutrition Information

- Calories: 321 calories
- Total Fat: 17g fat (4g saturated fat)
- Sodium: 962mg sodium
- Fiber: 2g fiber
- Total Carbohydrate: 7g carbohydrate (3g sugars
- Cholesterol: 61mg cholesterol
- Protein: 34g protein.

133. Ground Beef Spiral Bake

Serving: 2 casseroles (8 servings each). | Prep: 40mins | Ready in:

Ingredients

- 1 package (16 ounces) spiral pasta
- 2 pounds ground beef
- 2/3 cup chopped onion
- 1 teaspoon minced garlic
- 2 jars (26 ounces each) spaghetti sauce
- 2 tablespoons tomato paste
- 1 teaspoon dried basil
- 1 teaspoon dried oregano
- 4 cups shredded part-skim mozzarella cheese

Direction

- Based on the instruction on package, cook the pasta; drain off. At the same time, in a Dutch oven, cook the onion and beef on medium heat till the meat is not pink anymore. Put in the garlic; cook for 60 seconds more. Drain off. Whisk in oregano, basil, tomato paste and spaghetti sauce. Boil. Lower the heat; let simmer without a cover for 5 to 10 minutes.
- Whisk the pasta into the meat mixture. Move into two greased 13x9-inch baking plates. Scatter each with 2 cups of the cheese. Put a cover on and freeze one casserole for no more than 3 months.
- Bake leftover casserole without a cover at 350 degrees till thoroughly heated, about 25 to 30 minutes.
- To use the freeze casserole: Thaw in fridge overnight. Bake without a cover at 350 degrees till thoroughly heated, about 35 to 40 minutes.

Nutrition Information

- Calories: 359 calories
- Total Fat: 15g fat (6g saturated fat)
- Sodium: 627mg sodium
- Fiber: 3g fiber)
- Total Carbohydrate: 32g carbohydrate (8g sugars
- Cholesterol: 54mg cholesterol
- Protein: 23g protein.

134. Guinness Corned Beef And Cabbage

Serving: 9 servings. | Prep: 20mins | Ready in:

Ingredients

- 2 pounds red potatoes, quartered
- 1 pound carrots, cut into 3-inch pieces
- 2 celery ribs, cut into 3-inch pieces
- 1 small onion, quartered
- 1 corned beef brisket with spice packet (3 to 3-1/2 pounds)
- 8 whole cloves
- 6 whole peppercorns
- 1 bay leaf
- 1 bottle (12 ounces) Guinness stout or reduced-sodium beef broth
- 1/2 small head cabbage, thinly sliced
- Prepared horseradish

Direction

- Mix onion, celery, carrots and potatoes in 6-qt. slow cooker. Add corned beef; throw/keep spice packet for another use.
- On double thickness of cheesecloth, put bay leaf, peppercorns and cloves; gather cloth corners to enclose seasonings. Use string to tie securely; put in slow cooker. Put stout on top.
- Cook for 8-10 hours on low, covered, till veggies and meat a retender; add cabbage during final hour of cooking. Throw spice bag.
- Diagonally cut beef across grain to thin slices; serve the beef with horseradish and veggies.

Nutrition Information

- Calories: 374 calories
- Total Fat: 20g fat (7g saturated fat)
- Sodium: 1256mg sodium
- Fiber: 4g fiber
- Total Carbohydrate: 25g carbohydrate (5g sugars
- Cholesterol: 104mg cholesterol
- Protein: 22g protein.

135. Hamburger Rice Skillet

Serving: 4 servings. | Prep: 5mins | Ready in:

Ingredients

- 1 pound ground beef
- 3 cups water
- 2 medium carrots, cut into 1/4-inch slices
- 1 celery rib, chopped
- 1 envelope onion soup mix
- 2 cups uncooked instant rice

Direction

- Add beef to a big frying pan, cook over medium heat until it is not pink any longer; drain. Mix in the soup mix, celery, carrots and water. Boil the mixture. Lower the heat, simmer while covered until vegetables get tender, about 8 minutes.
- Boil the mixture once more. Add rice and cover. Take away from the heat, let rest until the rice gets tender, about 5 minutes.

Nutrition Information

- Calories:
- Total Fat:
- Sodium:
- Fiber:
- Total Carbohydrate:
- Cholesterol:
- Protein:

136. Hash Brown Beef Pie

Serving: 6-8 servings. | Prep: 15mins | Ready in:

Ingredients

- 1 pound ground beef
- 1 medium onion, chopped
- 1 garlic clove, minced
- 1 can (14-1/2 ounces) diced tomatoes, drained
- 1 teaspoon chili powder
- 1 teaspoon dried oregano
- 1/2 teaspoon salt
- 1/4 teaspoon pepper

- 1-1/2 cups frozen mixed vegetables
- TOPPING:
- 3 cups frozen shredded hash brown potatoes, thawed and drained
- 1 cup shredded cheddar cheese
- 1 large egg
- 1/8 teaspoon salt
- 1/8 teaspoon pepper

Direction

- Cook garlic, onion, and beef in a large skillet until the beef is not pink anymore; then drain. Stir in pepper, salt, oregano, chili powder, and tomatoes; boil. Turn down the heat; remove the cover and bring to a simmer for 10 minutes. Add in the vegetables and stir.
- Add into a 9-inch pie plate coated with cooking spray. Blend the topping ingredients; evenly spread on the meat mixture. Remove the cover and bake for half an hour at 400 degrees.

Nutrition Information

- Calories: 233 calories
- Total Fat: 12g fat (6g saturated fat)
- Sodium: 389mg sodium
- Fiber: 3g fiber)
- Total Carbohydrate: 15g carbohydrate (4g sugars
- Cholesterol: 79mg cholesterol
- Protein: 18g protein.

137. Hawaiian Beef Dish

Serving: 2 servings. | Prep: 15mins | Ready in:

Ingredients

- 1/2 pound lean ground beef (90% lean)
- 1 medium onion, halved and sliced
- 1/3 cup sliced celery
- 1/3 cup chopped green pepper
- 1 garlic clove, minced
- 2 teaspoons butter
- 1 can (8 ounces) unsweetened pineapple chunks
- 1/4 cup packed brown sugar
- 1 tablespoon all-purpose flour
- 1 tablespoon white wine vinegar
- 1/4 teaspoon salt
- 1 cup hot cooked rice

Direction

- Cook beef in a small skillet on moderate heat until not pink anymore, then drain and set aside. Sauté garlic, green pepper, celery and onion in butter in the same skillet until tender-crisp, about 5 minutes.
- Drain pineapple and save juice; put the pineapple aside. Pour in sufficient water into the juice to measure 1/2 cup. Mix pineapple juice mixture, salt, vinegar, flour and brown sugar till smooth in a bowl. Put into skillet and bring to a boil. Cook and stir on moderate heat about 2 minutes then stir in pineapple and beef. Heat through; serve along with rice.

Nutrition Information

- Calories: 515 calories
- Total Fat: 12g fat (6g saturated fat)
- Sodium: 440mg sodium
- Fiber: 4g fiber)
- Total Carbohydrate: 75g carbohydrate (44g sugars
- Cholesterol: 66mg cholesterol
- Protein: 26g protein.

138. Haystack Supper

Serving: 2 casseroles (6 servings each). | Prep: 25mins | Ready in:

Ingredients

- 1-3/4 cups crushed saltines (about 40 crackers)
- 2 cups cooked rice
- 3 pounds ground beef
- 1 large onion, chopped
- 1-1/2 cups tomato juice
- 3/4 cup water
- 3 tablespoons taco seasoning
- Seasoned salt, salt and pepper to taste
- 1/2 cup butter, cubed
- 1/2 cup all-purpose flour
- 4 cups milk
- 1 pound process cheese (Velveeta), cubed
- 4 cups shredded lettuce
- 3 cups shredded sharp cheddar cheese
- 3 medium tomatoes, diced
- 1 jar (10 ounces) pimiento-stuffed olives
- 1 package (14-1/2 ounces) tortilla chips

Direction

- Portion the crackers between 2 unoiled baking dishes, about 13x9 inches. Add rice over top of each.
- Cook onion and beef in large skillet until the meat is no longer pink, then drain. Put in seasonings, water and tomato juice; simmer about 15 to 20 mins. Add over rice.
- Melt butter in large saucepan. Stir in the flour until they become smooth. Put in milk gradually. Boil. Cook while stirring until thickened, about 2 mins.
- Lower the heat; mix in the Velveeta cheese until it is melted. Add over the beef mixture. Place the lettuce, the cheddar cheese, the tomatoes, and the olives on top. Enjoy with the chips. Place any leftovers in refrigerator.

Nutrition Information

- Calories: 888 calories
- Total Fat: 55g fat (24g saturated fat)
- Sodium: 1746mg sodium
- Fiber: 3g fiber)
- Total Carbohydrate: 57g carbohydrate (9g sugars
- Cholesterol: 164mg cholesterol
- Protein: 41g protein.

139. Healthy Italian Pot Roast

Serving: 12 servings. | Prep: 15mins | Ready in:

Ingredients

- 1 beef rump roast or bottom round roast (3 pounds)
- 1-1/2 cups water
- 6 garlic cloves, minced
- 2 bay leaves
- 2 tablespoons dried basil
- 4-1/2 teaspoons dried oregano
- 1-1/2 teaspoons salt
- 1/2 teaspoon crushed red pepper flakes
- 1/2 teaspoon garlic powder
- 1 tablespoon cornstarch
- 3 tablespoons cold water

Direction

- Brown roast on all sides in a greased Dutch oven; drain excess grease. Mix seasonings, water, and garlic; pour over the roast. Heat to a boil. Cover, decrease heat, and simmer until roast is tender, 2 3/4 to 3 1/4 hours.
- Throw out bay leaves. Put roast on a serving plate; let it sit for 10 minutes. In the meantime, for the gravy, dump loosened brown bits and pan drippings into a measuring cup; skim fat and discard. Move to a small pot. Mix cold water and cornstarch until smooth; slowly whisk into drippings. Heat to a boil; stir and cook until thick, 2 minutes. Slice roast; eat with gravy.

Nutrition Information

- Calories: 183 calories
- Total Fat: 7g fat (2g saturated fat)
- Sodium: 398mg sodium
- Fiber: 1g fiber)

- Total Carbohydrate: 2g carbohydrate (0 sugars
- Cholesterol: 82mg cholesterol
- Protein: 27g protein. Diabetic Exchanges: 3 lean meat

140. Hearty Burritos

Serving: 8 burritos. | Prep: 20mins | Ready in:

Ingredients

- 1/2 pound ground beef
- 1 large green pepper, chopped
- 1 medium onion, chopped
- 1 package (16 ounces) frozen cubed hash brown potatoes, thawed
- 1 can (15 ounces) black beans, rinsed and drained
- 1 can (14-1/2 ounces) Mexican diced tomatoes, undrained
- 1 cup frozen corn, thawed
- 1/2 cup salsa
- 1/2 cup cooked rice
- 2 teaspoons chili powder
- 1/2 teaspoon salt
- 2 cups shredded cheddar cheese
- 8 flour tortillas (10 inches), warmed
- Sour cream, chopped tomatoes, guacamole, additional shredded cheddar cheese and salsa, optional

Direction

- Over medium heat, cook the onion, green pepper and beef until meat is no longer pink in a big skillet. Drain. Put salt, chili powder, rice, salsa, corn, tomatoes, beans and potatoes. On each tortilla, sprinkle 1/4 cup of chees off center. Put about 1 cup of beef mixture on top. Fold ends and sides over filling.
- Individually wrap burritos in foil for up to 3 months, let it freeze. Or on a baking sheet, put burritos seam side down.
- For 25 minutes, bake until heated through at 350°. If desired, serve with salsa, additional cheese, guacamole, tomatoes and sour cream.
- To use frozen burritos: Thaw in refrigerator overnight, then, as directed, bake and serve.

Nutrition Information

- Calories:
- Sodium:
- Fiber:
- Total Carbohydrate:
- Cholesterol:
- Protein:
- Total Fat:

141. Hearty Cheese Tortellini

Serving: 6 servings. | Prep: 30mins | Ready in:

Ingredients

- 1/2 pound Johnsonville® Ground Mild Italian sausage
- 1/2 pound lean ground beef (90% lean)
- 1 jar (24 ounces) marinara sauce
- 1 can (14-1/2 ounces) Italian diced tomatoes
- 1 cup sliced fresh mushrooms
- 1 package (9 ounces) refrigerated cheese tortellini
- 1 cup shredded part-skim mozzarella cheese

Direction

- Place a small skillet on medium heat; cook the beef and sausage till no longer pink; drain. Move to a 3-quart slow cooker. Mix in mushrooms, tomatoes and marinara sauce. Cook with a cover on low till heated through, about 6-7 hours.
- Follow the package instructions to prepare tortellini; mix into the meat mixture. Top with cheese. Cook with a cover till the cheese is melted, for 15 minutes.

Nutrition Information

- Calories: 388 calories
- Fiber: 3g fiber)
- Total Carbohydrate: 40g carbohydrate (15g sugars
- Cholesterol: 63mg cholesterol
- Protein: 24g protein.
- Total Fat: 14g fat (7g saturated fat)
- Sodium: 908mg sodium

142. Hearty Green Chili Stew

Serving: 8 servings. | Prep: 10mins | Ready in:

Ingredients

- 2 pounds beef stew meat, cut into 1-inch cubes
- 2 medium onions, chopped
- 2 tablespoons canola oil
- 1 can (15 ounces) pinto beans, rinsed and drained
- 1 can (14-1/2 ounces) diced tomatoes, undrained
- 2 cans (4 ounces each) chopped green chilies
- 1 cup water
- 3 beef bouillon cubes
- 1 garlic clove, minced
- 1 teaspoon sugar
- 1/2 teaspoon salt, optional
- 1/4 teaspoon pepper
- Shredded cheddar or Monterey Jack cheese, optional

Direction

- Brown beef and onions in oil in a large skillet; drain. Transfer to a slow cooker (5 qt).
- Combine the beans, garlic, sugar, tomatoes, bouillon, water, salt, pepper, and chilies; pour over beef. Cover and cook until beef is tender on low setting for 6-8 hours. Sprinkle with cheese if desired.

Nutrition Information

- Calories: 259 calories
- Fiber: 0 fiber)
- Total Carbohydrate: 12g carbohydrate (0 sugars
- Cholesterol: 70mg cholesterol
- Protein: 25g protein. Diabetic Exchanges: 2-1/2 meat
- Total Fat: 12g fat (0 saturated fat)
- Sodium: 363mg sodium

143. Hearty Lasagna

Serving: 12 servings. | Prep: 01hours45mins | Ready in:

Ingredients

- 1-1/2 pounds ground beef
- 1 medium onion, chopped
- 1 garlic clove, minced
- 3 tablespoons olive oil
- 1 can (28 ounces) Italian diced tomatoes, undrained
- 1 can (8 ounces) tomato sauce
- 1 can (6 ounces) tomato paste
- 1 teaspoon dried oregano
- 1 teaspoon sugar
- 1 teaspoon salt
- 1/4 teaspoon pepper
- 2 carrots, halved
- 2 celery ribs, halved
- 12 ounces lasagna noodles
- 1 carton (15 ounces) ricotta cheese
- 2 cups shredded part-skim mozzarella cheese
- 1/2 cup grated Parmesan cheese

Direction

- Cook garlic, onion, and beef in oil using a large skillet, until the onion is tenderized, and the meat turns brown. Strain. Add tomato paste, tomato sauce, tomatoes, oregano, salt, pepper, and sugar and mix evenly. Add in celery and carrots into the sauce. Simmer without covering for 1-1/2 hours, periodically stirring the sauce. In the meantime, follow package instructions to prepare the lasagna noodles. Strain and run under cold water. Dispose celery and carrots. Grease a 13x9-inch baking tray and layer as follows; 1/3 of noodles, 1/3 of meat sauce, 1/3 ricotta cheese, 1/3 mozzarella cheese, and 1/3 Parmesan cheese. Repeat the arrangement again. Cover with excess noodles and meat sauce. Cut a piece of aluminum foil into a heart and place at the center of the sauce. Distribute remainder of ricotta around the heart. Scatter remaining Parmesan and mozzarella. Bake while uncovered for 45 minutes at 350 degrees. Dispose the heart-shaped foil. Let the dish sit for 10-15 minutes before slicing.

Nutrition Information

- Calories: 391 calories
- Protein: 25g protein.
- Total Fat: 16g fat (8g saturated fat)
- Sodium: 790mg sodium
- Fiber: 3g fiber)
- Total Carbohydrate: 36g carbohydrate (12g sugars
- Cholesterol: 56mg cholesterol

144. Hearty Shepherd's Pie

Serving: 6 servings. | Prep: 35mins | Ready in:

Ingredients

- 1 pound lean ground beef (90% lean)
- 1 medium onion, chopped
- 1 can (10-3/4 ounces) condensed cream of celery soup, undiluted
- 1 can (8-1/2 ounces) peas and carrots, drained
- 1 jar (4-1/2 ounces) sliced mushrooms, drained
- 1/4 cup water
- 1 tablespoon minced fresh rosemary or 1 teaspoon dried rosemary, crushed
- 1 teaspoon garlic powder, divided
- 1/2 teaspoon salt
- 1/4 teaspoon pepper
- 2 cups prepared instant mashed potatoes
- 3 ounces cream cheese, softened and cubed
- 1/4 cup sour cream
- 1/4 cup grated Parmesan cheese

Direction

- Cook ground beef and onion in a frying pan on medium heat until not pink. Drain excess grease. Mix in peas, soup, mushrooms, carrots, rosemary, salt, water, pepper, and 1/2 teaspoon garlic powder. Heat until the whole mixture is hot. Place in a deep-dish 9-in. greased pie pan. In a separate bowl, beat sour cream, rest of the garlic powder, mashed potatoes and cream cheese until combined. Evenly spread on top of beef mixture. Take the Parmesan cheese and sprinkle on top. Do not cover; bake in a 350-degree oven until heated and potatoes are light brown, 20-25 minutes.

Nutrition Information

- Calories: 419 calories
- Cholesterol: 91mg cholesterol
- Protein: 23g protein.
- Total Fat: 22g fat (12g saturated fat)
- Sodium: 985mg sodium
- Fiber: 4g fiber)
- Total Carbohydrate: 31g carbohydrate (5g sugars

145. Hearty Skillet Stew

Serving: 2 servings. | Prep: 20mins | Ready in:

Ingredients

- 1/2 pound beef top round steak, cut into 1/2-inch cubes
- 1/3 cup chopped onion
- 2 cups chopped cabbage
- 2 medium carrots, chopped
- 1 medium potato, cut into 1/2-inch chunks
- 3/4 cup water
- 1/3 cup reduced-sodium soy sauce
- 2 to 3 tablespoons sugar
- 1/2 teaspoon cornstarch
- 1 teaspoon cold water

Direction

- Coat a large nonstick skillet using cooking spray then brown the steak with onion. Stir in sugar, soy sauce, water, potato, carrots, and cabbage, then allow to boil. Decrease the heat and simmer while covered for 25 minutes or until the meat becomes tender.
- In a small bowl, combine cold water and cornstarch until smooth, then stir this into the beef mixture. Set to a boil, then cook while stirring for 1 - 2 minutes or until thick.

Nutrition Information

- Calories: 371 calories
- Protein: 32g protein.
- Total Fat: 4g fat (1g saturated fat)
- Sodium: 1689mg sodium
- Fiber: 6g fiber)
- Total Carbohydrate: 51g carbohydrate (21g sugars
- Cholesterol: 64mg cholesterol

146. Hearty Slow Cooker Lasagna

Serving: 8 servings. | Prep: 25mins | Ready in:

Ingredients

- 1 pound ground beef
- 1 tablespoon olive oil
- 1/2 cup chopped onion
- 1/2 cup chopped zucchini
- 1/2 cup chopped carrot
- 1 jar (24 ounces) marinara sauce
- 2 teaspoons Italian seasoning
- 1/2 teaspoon crushed red pepper flakes, optional
- 2 cartons (15 ounces each) part-skim ricotta cheese
- 1 cup grated Parmesan cheese
- 4 large eggs
- 1/2 cup loosely packed basil leaves, chopped
- 12 no-cook lasagna noodles
- 3 cups shredded part-skim mozzarella cheese
- Quartered grape tomatoes and additional chopped fresh basil, optional

Direction

- Using strips of durable foil cut it by 25x3 inches into crisscross until they look like wheel rods. Settle these cut strips on the bottom and up sides of the 5 qt. slow cooker. Use cooking spray to coat the strips.
- Let the beef cook until there's no visible pink on medium heat for 6 to 8 minutes. Drain excess water and set-side.
- Heat the same pot with oil on medium high fire. Cook and stir onion, zucchini, and carrot for 2 to 3 minutes. If it becomes tender, stir marinara sauce, Italian seasoning and beef mixture; crushed red pepper can also be added if you want. Mix parmesan egg, ricotta, and basil in a big bowl.
- At the bottom of the slow cooker, spread half cup meat sauce. Arrange 4 noodles on top of it, break if necessarily to fit. Level with 1 to 2/3 cups cheese mixture, one cup mozzarella cheese, and 1 to one and a half cups meat mixture. Do this process twice to form layers. Place cover and let it cook on low heat for four hours. Once noodles are tender, let it stand for half an hour. You may garnish it with additional basil and grape tomatoes if you want.

Nutrition Information

- Calories: 631 calories
- Protein: 43g protein.
- Total Fat: 32g fat (15g saturated fat)
- Sodium: 1074mg sodium
- Fiber: 3g fiber)
- Total Carbohydrate: 40g carbohydrate (8g sugars
- Cholesterol: 199mg cholesterol

147. Hearty Stuffed Green Peppers

Serving: 4 servings. | Prep: 20mins | Ready in:

Ingredients

- 6 medium fresh tomatoes, peeled, seeded and chopped
- 1 medium onion, chopped
- 3 celery ribs, diced
- 1 can (8 ounces) tomato sauce
- 1 cup water
- 2 teaspoons salt, divided
- 1/2 teaspoon pepper, divided
- 4 medium green peppers
- 1 pound lean ground beef (90% lean)
- 1 cup instant rice, cooked
- 1 teaspoon dried basil

Direction

- In the Dutch oven or the big sauce pan, mix a quarter tsp. of the pepper, 1 tsp. of the salt, water, tomato sauce, celery, onion, and tomatoes. Boil. Lower the heat and let simmer for 10 to 15 minutes.
- At the same time, chop the tops off of the green peppers and discard the seeds; put aside. In the bowl, mix the rest of pepper and salt, basil, rice and ground beef; combine them well. Fill the peppers with the beef mixture. Gently add the peppers into the tomato sauce. Scoop some of the sauce on the tops of the peppers.
- Keep covered and let simmer till the peppers soften and the beef is cooked or for 40 to 45 minutes.

Nutrition Information

- Calories: 373 calories
- Total Fat: 9g fat (4g saturated fat)
- Sodium: 1565mg sodium
- Fiber: 7g fiber)
- Total Carbohydrate: 46g carbohydrate (13g sugars
- Cholesterol: 56mg cholesterol
- Protein: 28g protein.

148. Hearty Vegetable Beef Ragout

Serving: 8 servings. | Prep: 15mins | Ready in:

Ingredients

- 4 cups uncooked whole wheat spiral pasta
- 1 pound lean ground beef (90% lean)
- 1 large onion, chopped
- 3 garlic cloves, minced
- 2 cans (14-1/2 ounces each) Italian diced tomatoes, undrained
- 1 jar (24 ounces) meatless spaghetti sauce
- 2 cups finely chopped fresh kale
- 1 package (9 ounces) frozen peas, thawed
- 3/4 teaspoon garlic powder
- 1/4 teaspoon pepper
- Grated Parmesan cheese, optional

Direction

- Follow the package instructions to prepare pasta and drain. In the meantime, add garlic, onion and beef to a Dutch oven, cook over medium heat until the beef is not pink any

longer, about 6 to 8 minutes, crumbling the beef; drain.
- Mix in the pepper, garlic powder, peas, kale, spaghetti sauce and tomatoes. Boil the mixture. Lower the heat, simmer while uncovered until the kale gets tender, about 8 to 10 minutes. Mix the pasta into the sauce. Add cheese to serve if preferred.

Nutrition Information

- Calories: 302 calories
- Total Fat: 5g fat (2g saturated fat)
- Sodium: 837mg sodium
- Fiber: 7g fiber)
- Total Carbohydrate: 43g carbohydrate (15g sugars
- Cholesterol: 35mg cholesterol
- Protein: 20g protein. Diabetic Exchanges: 2 starch

149. Herb Stuffed Red Peppers

Serving: 2 servings. | Prep: 25mins | Ready in:

Ingredients

- 2 large sweet red peppers
- 2 tablespoons water
- 1/2 pound ground beef
- 1/2 cup chopped onion
- 1-1/2 cups cooked brown rice
- 1 tablespoon dried parsley flakes
- 3/4 teaspoon salt
- 1/8 to 1/4 teaspoon cayenne pepper
- 1/8 teaspoon ground allspice
- 1 can (8 ounces) tomato sauce
- 1/4 cup chicken broth
- 2 teaspoons balsamic vinegar
- 1-1/2 teaspoons dried basil
- 4 tablespoons grated Parmesan or Romano cheese, divided

Direction

- Remove the peppers' tops and seeds. Add the water and pepper to a microwave-safe bowl. Microwave while covered on high setting until the peppers reach crisp-tender stage, about 2 to 3 minutes and set aside.
- Add onion and beef to a small frying pan, cook over medium heat until the meat is not pink any longer then drain. Take away from the heat, mix in the allspice, cayenne, salt, parsley and rice.
- Boil the broth and tomato sauce in a small saucepan. Mix in 3 tablespoons of Parmesan cheese, basil and vinegar then mix the rice mixture with about half a cup of sauce. Fill the mixture into the peppers. Lay them on a cooking-spray-coated 1 quart baking dish.
- Set oven at 350°, bake while covered for half an hour. Dredge the rest of Parmesan cheese over top. Uncover and bake for 5 to 10 more minutes until the peppers get tender. Add the rest of sauce and serve.

Nutrition Information

- Calories: 482 calories
- Total Fat: 15g fat (7g saturated fat)
- Sodium: 1798mg sodium
- Fiber: 8g fiber)
- Total Carbohydrate: 55g carbohydrate (10g sugars
- Cholesterol: 63mg cholesterol
- Protein: 32g protein.

150. Herbed Roast Beef

Serving: 10-12 servings. | Prep: 10mins | Ready in:

Ingredients

- 2 teaspoons fennel seed, crushed
- 2 teaspoons dried rosemary, crushed

- 2 teaspoons each dried basil, marjoram, savory and thyme
- 2 teaspoons rubbed sage
- 1-1/2 teaspoons salt
- 2 bone-in beef rib roasts (4 to 6 pounds each)
- 2 medium onions, sliced
- 6 fresh rosemary sprigs
- HORSERADISH SAUCE:
- 1-1/2 cups (12 ounces) sour cream
- 1/4 cup prepared horseradish
- 3 tablespoons lemon juice
- 2 tablespoons minced chives

Direction

- In the small-sized bowl, mix salt, sage, thyme, savory, marjoram, basil, rosemary and fennel seed; rub on the roasts. Put the roasts with the fat-side facing upward onto the rack in a roasting pan. Add the rosemary sprigs and onions on top.
- Bake, with no cover, at 350 degrees till the meat has the doneness that you wish (for the medium-rare, the thermometer should reach 145 degrees; medium, 160 degrees; well-done, 170 degrees) or for 2.5-3.5 hours.
- Get rid of rosemary and onions. Allow the roasts to rest for 10 to 15 minutes prior to slicing. At the same time, in the small-sized bowl, mix the sauce ingredients. Serve along with the beef.

Nutrition Information

- Calories:
- Fiber:
- Total Carbohydrate:
- Cholesterol:
- Protein:
- Total Fat:
- Sodium:

151. Herbed Sirloin Tip

Serving: 6-8 servings. | Prep: 15mins | Ready in:

Ingredients

- 2 teaspoons salt
- 1/2 teaspoon garlic salt
- 1/2 teaspoon celery salt
- 1/2 teaspoon dried rosemary, crushed
- 1/4 teaspoon onion powder
- 1/4 teaspoon paprika
- 1/4 teaspoon pepper
- 1/8 teaspoon dill weed
- 1/8 teaspoon rubbed sage
- 1 beef sirloin tip roast (2 pounds)

Direction

- Mix seasonings together; rub all over the roast. Put on cover and refrigerate for the minimum of 2 hours.
- Set oven to 425° to preheat. In a large shallow roasting pan, put roast on a rack. Bake without a cover for 40-60 minutes, or until the meat's doneness reaches desired level (for medium-rare meat, a thermometer should show 145°; 160° for medium; 170° for well-done). Allow to sit for 10-15 minutes before cutting.

Nutrition Information

- Calories: 139 calories
- Sodium: 844mg sodium
- Fiber: 0 fiber)
- Total Carbohydrate: 0 carbohydrate (0 sugars
- Cholesterol: 60mg cholesterol
- Protein: 21g protein.
- Total Fat: 5g fat (2g saturated fat)

152. Hobo Knapsacks

Serving: 6 servings. | Prep: 15mins | Ready in:

Ingredients

- 2 medium potatoes, peeled and thinly sliced
- 2 large tomatoes, chopped
- 1 large onion, chopped
- 1 package (10 ounces) frozen mixed vegetables, thawed
- 1 can (4 ounces) mushroom stems and pieces, drained
- 1 large egg, beaten
- 1/2 cup tomato juice
- 1/2 cup old-fashioned oats
- 1 tablespoon finely chopped onion
- 1 teaspoon salt
- 1/4 teaspoon pepper
- 1 pound lean ground beef (90% lean)
- Additional salt and pepper, optional

Direction

- Combine mushrooms, mixed vegetables, onion, tomatoes and potatoes in a large bowl; put aside.
- In another large bowl, mix pepper, salt, onion, oats, tomato juice and egg together; crumble beef over the mixture; stir well. Separate the meat mixture into six portions; crumble each portion onto a foil piece of 18x12 inches.
- Place vegetable mixture on top; add in additional pepper and salt for seasoning if desired. Gather the edges of foil together; crimp to seal, creating a packet. Arrange on baking sheets.
- Bake at 350° until a thermometer reads 160° and no more pink color, about 50-60 minutes.

Nutrition Information

- Calories: 252 calories
- Sodium: 603mg sodium
- Fiber: 5g fiber)
- Total Carbohydrate: 27g carbohydrate (7g sugars
- Cholesterol: 82mg cholesterol
- Protein: 20g protein.
- Total Fat: 8g fat (3g saturated fat)

153. Home Style Meat Loaf

Serving: 5 meat loaves (12 servings each). | Prep: 45mins | Ready in:

Ingredients

- 6 eggs, lightly beaten
- 4 cups 2% milk
- 4 cups dry bread crumbs
- 2-1/2 cups shredded carrots
- 1-1/4 cups chopped onions
- 5 teaspoons salt
- 4 teaspoons pepper
- 10 pounds ground beef
- 5 pounds ground pork

Direction

- Mix the first 7 ingredients in two very big bowls. Crumble meat over the top and combine well.
- Form into 5 loaves; put each in an ungreased 13x9-in. baking pan. Bake without a cover at 350° until no longer pink and a thermometer reads 160 degrees, 75 to 85 minutes. Drain.

Nutrition Information

- Calories: 276 calories
- Cholesterol: 95mg cholesterol
- Protein: 24g protein.
- Total Fat: 16g fat (6g saturated fat)
- Sodium: 329mg sodium
- Fiber: 0 fiber)
- Total Carbohydrate: 7g carbohydrate (1g sugars

154. Home Style Roast Beef

Serving: 25-30 servings. | Prep: 10mins | Ready in:

Ingredients

- 1 beef rump roast or bottom round roast (10 to 12 pounds)
- 1 can (14-1/2 ounces) chicken broth
- 1 can (10-1/4 ounces) beef gravy
- 1 can (10-3/4 ounces) condensed cream of celery soup, undiluted
- 1/4 cup water
- 1/4 cup Worcestershire sauce
- 1/4 cup soy sauce
- 3 tablespoons dried parsley flakes
- 3 tablespoons dill weed
- 2 tablespoons dried thyme
- 4-1/2 teaspoons garlic powder
- 1 teaspoon celery salt
- Pepper to taste
- 1 large onion, sliced 1/4 inch thick
- 8 bacon strips
- 1/4 cup butter, cubed

Direction

- Put roast with fat side up in a large roasting pan. Combine the soy sauce, Worcestershire sauce, water, soup, gravy and broth in a small bowl; and pour over roast. Drizzle with seasonings. Top the roast with onion slices. Put bacon strips over onion diagonally. Sprinkle butter over top.
- Bake without a cover for 2-1/2 to 3-1/2 hours at 325°, until the meat's doneness reaches desired level (a thermometer should show 145° for medium-rare; 160° for medium; 170° for well-done). Allow to sit for 15 minutes before cutting.

Nutrition Information

- Calories: 259 calories
- Total Fat: 13g fat (5g saturated fat)
- Sodium: 487mg sodium
- Fiber: 0 fiber)
- Total Carbohydrate: 3g carbohydrate (1g sugars
- Cholesterol: 100mg cholesterol
- Protein: 31g protein.

155. Homemade Apple Cider Beef Stew

Serving: 8 servings. | Prep: 30mins | Ready in:

Ingredients

- 2 pounds beef stew meat, cut into 1-inch cubes
- 2 tablespoons canola oil
- 3 cups apple cider or juice
- 2 tablespoons cider vinegar
- 2 teaspoons salt, optional
- 1/4 to 1/2 teaspoon dried thyme
- 1/4 teaspoon pepper
- 3 medium potatoes, peeled and cubed
- 4 medium carrots, cut into 3/4-inch pieces
- 3 celery ribs, cut into 3/4-inch pieces
- 2 medium onions, cut into wedges
- 1/4 cup all-purpose flour
- 1/4 cup water

Direction

- Cook beef in oil over medium-high heat in a Dutch oven until all sides are nicely browned; drain. Add pepper, thyme, salt if desired, vinegar, and cider; bring to a boil. Lower heat; simmer, covered for 1 hour and 15 minutes.
- Add onions, celery, carrots, and potatoes; bring back to a boil. Lower heat; simmer, covered until beef and vegetables are softened, about 30 to 35 minutes.
- Stir flour with water until smooth; mix into the stew. Bring to a boil; cook for 2 minutes until thickened, stir well while cooking.

Nutrition Information

- Calories: 315 calories
- Protein: 24g protein. Diabetic Exchanges: 3 lean meat
- Total Fat: 12g fat (0 saturated fat)
- Sodium: 238mg sodium
- Fiber: 0 fiber)

- Total Carbohydrate: 29g carbohydrate (0 sugars
- Cholesterol: 70mg cholesterol

156. Homemade Pizza

Serving: 2 pizzas (3 servings each). | Prep: 25mins | Ready in:

Ingredients

- 1 package (1/4 ounce) active dry yeast
- 1 teaspoon sugar
- 1-1/4 cups warm water (110° to 115°)
- 1/4 cup canola oil
- 1 teaspoon salt
- 3-1/2 cups all-purpose flour
- 1/2 pound ground beef
- 1 small onion, chopped
- 1 can (15 ounces) tomato sauce
- 3 teaspoons dried oregano
- 1 teaspoon dried basil
- 1 medium green pepper, diced
- 2 cups shredded part-skim mozzarella cheese

Direction

- Dissolve sugar and yeast in water in a large bowl; allow them to stand for 5 minutes. Add salt and oil. Mix in flour, 1 cup at a time, until it forms a soft dough.
- Transfer onto a floured surface; knead for about 2-3 minutes until elastic and smooth. Transfer to a greased bowl, flipping once to grease the top. Allow it to rise for about 45 minutes, with cover, in a warm place until twice the size. In the meantime, cook onion and beef over medium heat until not pink anymore; drain.
- Punch the dough down; split in half. Force every dough to a greased 12-inch pizza pan. Mix the basil, oregano, and tomato sauce; smear over each crust. Place cheese, green pepper, and beef mixture on top.
- Bake for 25-30 minutes at 400 degrees or until crust turn light brown.

Nutrition Information

- Calories: 537 calories
- Total Fat: 19g fat (7g saturated fat)
- Sodium: 922mg sodium
- Fiber: 4g fiber)
- Total Carbohydrate: 64g carbohydrate (5g sugars
- Cholesterol: 40mg cholesterol
- Protein: 25g protein.

157. Homemade Ragu Bolognese

Serving: 10 servings (7-1/2 cups). | Prep: 25mins | Ready in:

Ingredients

- 1 pound ground beef
- 1/2 pound ground pork
- 1/4 pound bacon strips, diced
- 2 medium onions, chopped
- 2 celery ribs, chopped
- 2 small carrots, chopped
- 4 garlic cloves, minced
- 1 cup dry red wine or beef broth
- 1 can (28 ounces) crushed tomatoes
- 1 can (15 ounces) tomato sauce
- 2 tablespoons tomato paste
- 2 bay leaves
- 2 teaspoons sugar
- 1 teaspoon salt
- 1/2 teaspoon dried thyme
- 1/2 teaspoon dried oregano
- 1/2 teaspoon each ground cumin, nutmeg and pepper
- 1/2 cup heavy whipping cream
- 2 tablespoons butter
- 2 tablespoons minced fresh parsley

- 1/2 cup grated Parmesan cheese
- Hot cooked pasta

Direction

- In the Dutch oven, cook carrots, celery, onion, bacon, pork, and beef on medium heat till the meat is not pink anymore; drain off. Put in the garlic; cook for 2 minutes more. Put in the wine; cook till the liquid is decreased by half or for 4 to 5 minutes.
- Whisk in seasonings, sugar, bay leaves, tomato paste, tomato sauce and tomatoes. Boil. Lower the heat; let simmer, with no cover, till thicken or for 1.5-2 hours, whisking from time to time.
- Get rid of the bay leaves. Put in the parsley, butter and cream; cook for 2 minutes more. Whisk in the cheese. Serve with the pasta.

Nutrition Information

- Calories: 309 calories
- Protein: 18g protein.
- Total Fat: 18g fat (9g saturated fat)
- Sodium: 746mg sodium
- Fiber: 3g fiber)
- Total Carbohydrate: 15g carbohydrate (5g sugars
- Cholesterol: 73mg cholesterol

158. Honey Garlic Meatballs

Serving: 10-12 servings. | Prep: 5mins | Ready in:

Ingredients

- 2 pounds ground beef
- 1 cup dry bread crumbs
- 2 large eggs
- 1 teaspoon salt
- 1 tablespoon butter
- 6 garlic cloves, minced
- 3/4 cup ketchup
- 1/2 cup honey

- 1/4 cup soy sauce
- Cooked rice

Direction

- Mix the salt, eggs, breadcrumbs and ground beef; combine them well. Form into 48 balls, roughly 1.5 inch diameter. Add the meatballs onto the greased rack in the shallow baking pan. Bake at 500 degrees for 12 to 15 minutes, flip frequently; drain off. Melt butter in the big skillet; sauté the garlic till becoming soft. Mix the soy sauce, honey, and ketchup; put into the skillet. Boil. Lower the heat and let simmer, keep covered, roughly 5 minutes. Put in the meatballs. Let simmer, while uncovered, till meatballs become glazed a bit and sauce becomes thick. Serve on the rice.

Nutrition Information

- Calories:
- Total Fat:
- Sodium:
- Fiber:
- Total Carbohydrate:
- Cholesterol:
- Protein:

159. Horseradish Encrusted Beef Tenderloin

Serving: 8 servings. | Prep: 30mins | Ready in:

Ingredients

- 1 whole garlic bulb
- 1 teaspoon olive oil
- 1/3 cup prepared horseradish
- 1/4 teaspoon salt
- 1/4 teaspoon dried basil
- 1/4 teaspoon dried thyme
- 1/4 teaspoon pepper
- 1/3 cup soft bread crumbs

- 1 beef tenderloin roast (3 pounds)

Direction

- Get rid of the papery outer skin of garlic (no peeling or separating cloves). Trim top of the garlic bulb; brush oil over the garlic. Wrap garlic in heavy-duty foil. Bake for 30 to 35 minutes at 425° in the oven, or until tender. Allow to cool for 10 to 15 minutes.
- Squeeze to remove softened garlic to a small bowl; mix in pepper, thyme, basil, salt, and horseradish. Add bread crumbs; stir until evenly coated. Distribute all over the top of tenderloin. Arrange tenderloin on a rack in a large shallow roasting pan.
- Bake for 45 to 55 minutes at 400° or until desired doneness of meat is reached (a thermometer should reach 145° for medium-rare, 160° for medium, and 170° for well-done). Allow to cool for 10 minutes before cutting to serve.

Nutrition Information

- Calories: 268 calories
- Cholesterol: 75mg cholesterol
- Protein: 37g protein. Diabetic Exchanges: 5 lean meat.
- Total Fat: 11g fat (4g saturated fat)
- Sodium: 119mg sodium
- Fiber: 1g fiber)
- Total Carbohydrate: 4g carbohydrate (1g sugars

160. Hot Tamale Casserole

Serving: 6 servings. | Prep: 35mins | Ready in:

Ingredients

- 2 cups water
- 1/4 teaspoon salt
- 1/8 teaspoon cayenne pepper
- 1/2 cup cornmeal
- 1-1/2 pounds lean ground beef (90% lean)
- 1 large onion, chopped
- 1 medium green pepper, chopped
- 2 garlic cloves, minced
- 1 can (16 ounces) kidney beans, rinsed and drained
- 1 can (10 ounces) enchilada sauce
- 1 can (4 ounces) chopped green chilies
- 1 can (2-1/4 ounces) sliced ripe olives, drained
- 2 teaspoons chili powder
- 2 teaspoons minced fresh cilantro
- 3/4 cup shredded cheddar cheese

Direction

- Heat cayenne, water, and salt to a boil in a small heavy pot. Decrease heat to a gentle boil; gradually stir in cornmeal. Stir constantly with a wooden spoon; cook until polenta cleanly pulls away from the sides of the pot and is thick, 15-20 minutes.
- In the meantime, cook garlic, onion, beef, and green pepper in a big frying pan on medium heat until beef is not pink. Mix in the chili powder, chilies, beans, cilantro, enchilada sauce, and olives; cook through.
- Spread the polenta in the bottom of a square 8-in. greased pan. Put meat mixture on top. Cover; bake in a 350-degree oven for 25 minutes. Sprinkle on cheese. Do not cover; bake until cheese melts and filling is bubbling, 2-5 minutes.

Nutrition Information

- Calories: 369 calories
- Total Carbohydrate: 30g carbohydrate (4g sugars
- Cholesterol: 86mg cholesterol
- Protein: 32g protein.
- Total Fat: 15g fat (7g saturated fat)
- Sodium: 837mg sodium
- Fiber: 7g fiber)

161. Hungarian Stuffed Cabbage

Serving: 4-6 servings. | Prep: 20mins | Ready in:

Ingredients

- 1 medium head cabbage
- 1 can (28 ounces) sauerkraut, divided
- 1/2 pound ground beef
- 1/2 pound ground pork
- 1/2 cup long grain rice, cooked
- 1 teaspoon salt
- 1/2 teaspoon pepper
- 1 egg
- 2 bacon strips, diced
- 1 cup chopped onion
- 2 garlic cloves, minced
- 1 tablespoon Hungarian paprika
- 1/4 teaspoon cayenne pepper
- 1 can (14-1/2 ounces) diced tomatoes, undrained
- 1 tablespoon caraway seeds
- 2 cups water
- 2 tablespoons all-purpose flour
- 1 cup sour cream

Direction

- Remove the core a head of cabbage. Put the head of cabbage in a big saucepan; pour in water to cover. Heat to a boil, then boil till outer leaves loosen from the head. Take cabbage out and remove the softened leaves. Bring back to boiling water so as to soften other leaves. Repeat until there is no leaf left. Remove the tough center stalk of every leaf. Put 12 big leaves aside for rolls; keep the balance to use as recipe instructions.
- Use a spoon to transfer 1/2 of the sauerkraut to a Dutch oven; put aside. Combine egg, pepper, salt, rice, pork, and beef in a bowl. Cook bacon in a saucepan until crisp. Remove to paper towels to drain. Sauté garlic and onion in drippings until tender. To meat mixture, add half of the onion mixture and bacon; combine nicely.
- Transfer about 3 tablespoons onto each cabbage leaf. Roll up, tucking in sides. Arrange rolls over sauerkraut in the Dutch oven with seam side down. Coarsely chop any unused cabbage leaves; arrange atop rolls. Add remaining sauerkraut, water, caraway seeds, tomatoes, cayenne, and paprika to the remaining onion mixture. Cook through, then spread over rolls.
- Cover and bake for 1 3/4 hours at 325 degrees. Slowly mix flour into sour cream in a small bowl. Mix in 1 or 2 tablespoons of hot cooking liquid; combine well. With a spoon, spread over cabbage rolls. Without cover, bake until sauce is thickened, about 15-20 minutes more.

Nutrition Information

- Calories: 451 calories
- Cholesterol: 117mg cholesterol
- Protein: 24g protein.
- Total Fat: 23g fat (11g saturated fat)
- Sodium: 1558mg sodium
- Fiber: 9g fiber)
- Total Carbohydrate: 37g carbohydrate (10g sugars

162. Idaho Tacos

Serving: 4 servings. | Prep: 20mins | Ready in:

Ingredients

- 1 pound ground beef
- 1 envelope taco seasoning
- 4 hot baked potatoes
- 1/2 cup shredded cheddar cheese
- 1 cup chopped green onions
- Salsa, optional

Direction

- In a large skillet over medium heat, cook beef until no longer pink; drain. Add taco

seasoning; prepare following the instructions on packaging.
- Cut an X in the top of each potato using a sharp knife; fluff pulp with a fork. Have cheese, onions and taco meat to top. If wished, serve with salsa.

Nutrition Information

- Calories: 601 calories
- Sodium: 990mg sodium
- Fiber: 7g fiber)
- Total Carbohydrate: 76g carbohydrate (6g sugars
- Cholesterol: 90mg cholesterol
- Protein: 34g protein.
- Total Fat: 18g fat (9g saturated fat)

163. Indian Fry Bread Tacos

Serving: 2 servings. | Prep: 20mins | Ready in:

Ingredients

- 3/4 cup all-purpose flour
- 1/2 teaspoon baking powder
- 1/4 teaspoon salt
- 1/3 cup hot water
- 1/2 pound lean ground beef (90% lean)
- 2 tablespoons taco seasoning
- 1/3 cup water
- Oil for frying
- 2 tablespoons chopped lettuce
- 2 tablespoons chopped tomato
- 2 tablespoons salsa
- 2 tablespoons sour cream

Direction

- Mix salt, baking powder and flour in a small bowl. Mix in hot water and create a soft dough. Cover the dough and leave to sit for 1 hour.

- Over medium heat, cook the beef in small skillet until no pink color remains. Drain beef. Mix in water and taco seasoning. Simmer for 10 minutes while uncovered. Keep the contents warm.
- Separate the dough in half. Roll every portion to form a 4-inch circle onto a lightly floured surface.
- Heat one inch of oil in an electric skillet to 350°. Then fry the bread circles for about 3 to 4 minutes per side in the hot oil or until turned golden. Place on paper towels to drain. Add tomato, lettuce, and meat mixture on top of each. Serve together with sour cream and salsa.

Nutrition Information

- Calories: 407 calories
- Total Carbohydrate: 45g carbohydrate (2g sugars
- Cholesterol: 66mg cholesterol
- Protein: 27g protein.
- Total Fat: 11g fat (5g saturated fat)
- Sodium: 1361mg sodium
- Fiber: 1g fiber)

164. Iowa Ham Balls Main Dish

Serving: 8 servings. | Prep: 15mins | Ready in:

Ingredients

- 2 pound ground ham
- 2 pounds ground beef
- 2 cups graham cracker crumbs
- 2 large eggs
- 1-1/2 cups milk
- SAUCE:
- 2 cans (10-3/4 ounces each) tomato soup, undiluted
- 3/4 cup white vinegar
- 2-1/4 cups brown sugar

- 2 teaspoons ground mustard

Direction

- Mix milk, eggs, and crumbs in a large bowl. Break beef and ham into crumbles over mixture. Form meat mixture, 1/2 cup each time, into balls individually and arrange in a 13x9-inch baking dish.
- Blend the sauce ingredients and transfer over balls. Bake, without covering, at 350° in 1 hour, or until a thermometer shows 160°.

Nutrition Information

- Calories: 897 calories
- Fiber: 1g fiber)
- Total Carbohydrate: 84g carbohydrate (70g sugars
- Cholesterol: 198mg cholesterol
- Protein: 49g protein.
- Total Fat: 40g fat (15g saturated fat)
- Sodium: 1924mg sodium

165. Italian Beef

Serving: 14 servings. | Prep: 5mins | Ready in:

Ingredients

- 1 beef top round roast (4 pounds)
- 2 cups water
- 2 tablespoons Italian seasoning
- 1 teaspoon each salt, dried oregano, dried basil, garlic powder, dried parsley flakes and pepper
- 1 bay leaf
- 14 French rolls (5 inches long)

Direction

- Halve the roast; put in a 5-quart slow cooker. Mix together seasonings and water; spread over the roast. Put the lid on and cook on low until the meat has completely softened, about 10-12 hours. Remove the bay leaf. Take the meat out and use a fork to shred. Remove the fat from the cooking juices; put the meat back into the slow cooker. Enjoy on rolls.

Nutrition Information

- Calories: 386 calories
- Cholesterol: 80mg cholesterol
- Protein: 34g protein. Diabetic Exchanges: 3 lean meat
- Total Fat: 11g fat (5g saturated fat)
- Sodium: 557mg sodium
- Fiber: 2g fiber)
- Total Carbohydrate: 36g carbohydrate (0 sugars

166. Italian Beef Tortellini Stew

Serving: 6 servings (2-1/4 quarts). | Prep: 25mins | Ready in:

Ingredients

- 1/3 cup all-purpose flour
- 1 teaspoon pepper, divided
- 1 pound beef stew meat, cut into 1-inch cubes
- 3 tablespoons olive oil, divided
- 2 medium zucchini, cut into 1/2-inch pieces
- 1 large onion, chopped
- 2 celery ribs, sliced
- 3 small carrots, sliced
- 3 garlic cloves, minced
- 1-1/2 teaspoons each dried oregano, basil and marjoram
- 1/2 cup dry red wine or reduced-sodium beef broth
- 1 can (28 ounces) crushed tomatoes
- 3 cups reduced-sodium beef broth
- 1 teaspoon sugar
- 1 package (9 ounces) refrigerated cheese tortellini
- 1 package (6 ounces) fresh baby spinach

Direction

- Mix 1/2 teaspoon of pepper and flour together in a big resealable plastic bag. Add beef, several pieces each time, and shake to cover.
- Brown beef with 2 tablespoons of oil in a Dutch oven; strain. Take out and put aside. Sauté carrots, celery, onion, and zucchini in the leftover oil in the same pan until soft. Add marjoram, basil, oregano, and garlic; cook for another 1 minute.
- Pour in the wine, you stir to get the browned bits loosened from the pan. Put the beef back to the pan; add the leftover peppers, sugar, broth, and tomatoes. Boil it. Lower the heat, simmer with a cover until the beef is soft, about 1-1/2 hours. Add spinach and tortellini. Boil again. Cook without a cover until the tortellini are soft, about 7- 9 minutes.

Nutrition Information

- Calories: 416 calories
- Total Fat: 16g fat (5g saturated fat)
- Sodium: 642mg sodium
- Fiber: 7g fiber)
- Total Carbohydrate: 43g carbohydrate (6g sugars
- Cholesterol: 68mg cholesterol
- Protein: 26g protein. Diabetic Exchanges: 3 starch

167. Italian Beef With Mushrooms

Serving: 2 servings. | Prep: 10mins | Ready in:

Ingredients

- 1-1/2 cups sliced fresh mushrooms
- 2 tablespoons butter
- 1/3 cup thinly sliced green onions
- 1 garlic clove, minced
- 1/2 cup spaghetti sauce
- 2 tablespoons water
- 2 tablespoons dry red wine or beef broth
- 1/4 teaspoon dried basil
- 1/4 teaspoon dried thyme
- 1/8 teaspoon salt
- Dash pepper
- 1 cup cubed cooked roast beef
- Hot cooked noodles or mashed potatoes

Direction

- Sauté mushrooms with butter for 3 minutes in a saucepan. Put garlic and green onions; sauté for 2 more minutes. Mix in the pepper, salt, thyme, basil, wine or broth, water and spaghetti sauce. Heat to a boil. Turn heat down; simmer for 35 minutes while covered. Mix in beef. Simmer 10 more minutes while covered, until meat is heated through. Serve on top of noodles.

Nutrition Information

- Calories: 327 calories
- Total Carbohydrate: 10g carbohydrate (5g sugars
- Cholesterol: 96mg cholesterol
- Protein: 29g protein.
- Total Fat: 17g fat (9g saturated fat)
- Sodium: 576mg sodium
- Fiber: 2g fiber)

168. Italian Mushroom Meat Loaf

Serving: 8 servings. | Prep: 30mins | Ready in:

Ingredients

- 1 large egg, lightly beaten
- 1/4 pound fresh mushrooms, chopped
- 1/2 cup old-fashioned oats
- 1/2 cup chopped red onion
- 1/4 cup ground flaxseed

- 1/2 teaspoon pepper
- 1 package (19-1/2 ounces) Italian turkey sausage links, casings removed, crumbled
- 1 pound lean ground beef (90% lean)
- 1 cup marinara or spaghetti sauce

Direction

- Mix pepper, flax, onion, oats, mushrooms and egg in a big bowl. Crumble turkey and beef over the mixture and combine well.
- Form into a 10x4-inch loaf. Put in a greased 13x9-inch baking dish. Bake without a cover at 350° for 50 minutes; drain. Use marinara sauce to top the loaf. Bake until no longer pink and a thermometer indicates 165 degrees, about 10-15 minutes more.

Nutrition Information

- Calories: 261 calories
- Total Carbohydrate: 10g carbohydrate (3g sugars
- Cholesterol: 103mg cholesterol
- Protein: 25g protein. Diabetic Exchanges: 3 lean meat
- Total Fat: 14g fat (3g saturated fat)
- Sodium: 509mg sodium
- Fiber: 2g fiber)

169. Italian Noodles

Serving: 4-6 servings. | Prep: 10mins | Ready in:

Ingredients

- 4 cups uncooked egg noodles
- 1/2 pound ground beef
- 1/4 pound miniature smoked sausage links
- 2 cups frozen corn, thawed
- 1 jar (26 ounces) spaghetti sauce
- 1 cup (8 ounces) 4% cottage cheese
- 1/4 teaspoon garlic powder
- 1/2 cup shredded part-skim mozzarella cheese

Direction

- Following package directions to cook noodles. In the meantime, cook sausage and beef together in a big skillet on moderate heat until beef is not pink anymore, then drain. Put in garlic powder, cottage cheese, spaghetti sauce and corn, then heat through. Drain noodles and put into the beef mixture, stir. Use cheese to sprinkle over top, then cook, covered, until cheese has melted, about 5 minutes.

Nutrition Information

- Calories: 439 calories
- Total Carbohydrate: 43g carbohydrate (11g sugars
- Cholesterol: 79mg cholesterol
- Protein: 24g protein.
- Total Fat: 19g fat (7g saturated fat)
- Sodium: 993mg sodium
- Fiber: 4g fiber)

170. Italian Pot Roast

Serving: 8 servings. | Prep: 20mins | Ready in:

Ingredients

- 1 boneless beef chuck roast (3 to 4 pounds)
- 1 can (28 ounces) diced tomatoes, drained
- 3/4 cup chopped onion
- 3/4 cup Burgundy wine or beef broth
- 1-1/2 teaspoons salt
- 1 teaspoon dried basil
- 1/2 teaspoon dried oregano
- 1 garlic clove, minced
- 1/4 teaspoon pepper
- 1/4 cup cornstarch
- 1/2 cup cold water

Direction

- Halve the roast. Add into 5-quart slow cooker. Put in pepper, garlic, oregano, basil, salt, wine,

onion and tomatoes. Cook with cover over low heat till the meat softens, or for 5-6 hours.
- Transfer meat to serving platter; keep it warm. Skim fat off the cooking juices; move into small-sized saucepan. Mix the water and cornstarch till smooth. Slowly whisk into the pan. Boil; cook and whisk till thicken or for 2 minutes. Serve along with the meat.

Nutrition Information

- Calories: 345 calories
- Total Fat: 16g fat (6g saturated fat)
- Sodium: 641mg sodium
- Fiber: 2g fiber)
- Total Carbohydrate: 10g carbohydrate (4g sugars
- Cholesterol: 111mg cholesterol
- Protein: 34g protein.

171. Italian Turkey Burgers

Serving: 4 servings. | Prep: 10mins | Ready in:

Ingredients

- 1/4 cup canned crushed tomatoes
- 2 tablespoons grated Parmesan cheese
- 1/2 teaspoon garlic powder
- 1/2 teaspoon dried oregano
- 1/4 teaspoon salt
- 1/4 teaspoon pepper
- 1 pound ground turkey
- 8 slices Italian bread, toasted
- 1/2 cup meatless spaghetti sauce, warmed

Direction

- Mix the first six ingredients in a large mixing bowl. Break turkey into small pieces and stir into the mixture. Separate the mixture into four balls and pat into oval shaped patties 3/4-in. thick. Place a small amount of cooking oil on paper towel and use long-handled tongs to lightly grease the grill rack with paper towel. Place patties on grill over medium heat uncovered, or broil for 6-8 minutes placing the patties 4 in. from the heat. Both methods require 6-8 minutes per side or until juices are clear and temperature is 165 degrees. Put one patty on a slice of bread, spread with warm spaghetti sauce, and top with another slice of bread.

Nutrition Information

- Calories: 306 calories
- Sodium: 680mg sodium
- Fiber: 2g fiber)
- Total Carbohydrate: 24g carbohydrate (0 sugars
- Cholesterol: 92mg cholesterol
- Protein: 25g protein. Diabetic Exchanges: 3 lean meat
- Total Fat: 12g fat (3g saturated fat)

172. Italian Style Beef Liver

Serving: 4 servings. | Prep: 10mins | Ready in:

Ingredients

- 1/3 cup all-purpose flour
- 1/4 teaspoon salt
- 1 pound beef liver, cut into bite-size pieces
- 4 teaspoons canola oil, divided
- 1 cup thinly sliced onion
- 1/2 cup chopped celery
- 2 cans (14-1/2 ounces each) diced tomatoes, undrained
- 1 bay leaf
- 2 tablespoons chopped fresh parsley
- 1 tablespoon minced fresh basil or 1 teaspoon dried basil
- 1 teaspoon salt
- 1/4 teaspoon pepper
- Hot cooked spaghetti
- Grated Parmesan cheese

Direction

- Combine salt and flour; toss with the liver. Heat 2 teaspoons oil in a skillet, and cook liver until no longer pink. Take out and put aside.
- Sauté onion and celery in the same skillet with remaining oil until tender. Stir in pepper, salt, basil, parsley, bay leaf and tomatoes. Simmer with cover, stirring occasionally, about 20 minutes. Put in liver; heat through. Get rid of bay leaf.
- Add over spaghetti and sprinkle cheese over to serve.

Nutrition Information

- Calories:
- Total Fat:
- Sodium:
- Fiber:
- Total Carbohydrate:
- Cholesterol:
- Protein:

173.   Jack N Jill Burgers

Serving: 6 servings. | Prep: 10mins | Ready in:

Ingredients

- 1 medium onion
- 1/2 cup finely crushed seasoned salad croutons
- 1/4 cup dill pickle relish
- 2 tablespoons ketchup
- 1-1/2 pounds ground beef
- 6 slices Monterey Jack cheese
- 6 hamburger buns, split
- 6 lettuce leaves
- 6 slices tomato

Direction

- Mix the first 4 ingredients together in a large mixing bowl. Crush beef into small pieces over the mixture; stir to combine. Form beef mixture into 6 patties, about 1/2-inch thick; arrange patties on an ungreased broiler pan.
- Broil about 4 inches away from the heat source until no longer pink, for 7 to 9 minutes per side. Place a cheese slice on top of each patty. Broil until cheese is melted, for 1 to 2 minutes more. Serve cooked patties on buns with lettuce and slices of tomato.

Nutrition Information

- Calories:
- Fiber:
- Total Carbohydrate:
- Cholesterol:
- Protein:
- Total Fat:
- Sodium:

174.   Lakes Burgoo

Serving: 8 servings (3 quarts). | Prep: 20mins | Ready in:

Ingredients

- 1-1/2 pounds ground beef
- 2 cups diced potatoes
- 1 large onion, chopped
- 3/4 cup chopped green pepper
- 1 can (14-1/2 ounces) diced tomatoes, undrained
- 1 can (14-1/2 ounces) peas, drained
- 1 can (14-1/2 ounces) cut green beans, drained
- 1 can (14-1/2 ounces) whole kernel corn, drained
- 1 bottle (18 ounces) barbecue sauce
- 2 cups water
- 1 can (14-1/2 ounces) tomato puree
- 1/2 cup ketchup
- 1/2 teaspoon salt
- 1/2 teaspoon pepper

Direction

- Cook beef in a big frying pan over medium heat until not pink anymore; strain. Move to a Dutch oven. Add the rest of the ingredients. Boil it. Lower the heat; simmer until the potatoes are soft, about 1 to 1-1/4 hours.

Nutrition Information

- Calories:
- Protein:
- Total Fat:
- Sodium:
- Fiber:
- Total Carbohydrate:
- Cholesterol:

175. Lasagna With White Sauce

Serving: 10-12 servings. | Prep: 40mins | Ready in:

Ingredients

- 1 pound ground beef
- 1 large onion, chopped
- 1 can (14-1/2 ounces) diced tomatoes, undrained
- 2 tablespoons tomato paste
- 1 teaspoon beef bouillon granules
- 1-1/2 teaspoons Italian seasoning
- 1 teaspoon salt
- 1/2 teaspoon pepper
- 1/4 teaspoon cayenne pepper
- WHITE SAUCE:
- 2 tablespoons butter
- 3 tablespoons all-purpose flour
- 1 teaspoon salt
- 1/4 teaspoon pepper
- 2 cups 2% milk
- 1-1/4 cups shredded mozzarella cheese, divided
- 10 to 12 uncooked lasagna noodles

Direction

- Put onion and beef in a Dutch oven and cook over medium heat until the meat is not pink; then drain excess oil. Mix in the bouillon, seasonings, tomatoes and tomato paste. Cover the Dutch oven and cook for about 20 minutes over medium-low heat while occasionally stirring.
- While the meat sauce is cooking, melt butter in a big pan then mix in the salt, pepper and flour until fully combined. Slowly put in the milk. Let it boil and cook for 1 minute or until sauce is thick in consistency. Remove the pan from heat then add 1/2 of cheese and mix; put aside.
- In an ungreased 13x9-inch pan, put in 1/2 of meat sauce on bottom. Layer on 1/2 of the lasagna noodles and the remaining meat sauce. Put the remaining lasagna noodles on top. Put the white sauce evenly on top of the noodles. Finish with the remaining cheese on top.
- Put the covered baking dish in the preheated oven at 400°F and bake for 40 minutes or until bubbling and the noodles are soft.

Nutrition Information

- Calories: 232 calories
- Protein: 14g protein.
- Total Fat: 10g fat (5g saturated fat)
- Sodium: 639mg sodium
- Fiber: 1g fiber)
- Total Carbohydrate: 22g carbohydrate (5g sugars
- Cholesterol: 38mg cholesterol

176. Layer Cake Meat Loaf

Serving: 8-10 servings. | Prep: 30mins | Ready in:

Ingredients

- 2 eggs, lightly beaten
- 1 can (5-1/2 ounces) spicy hot V8 juice

- 1 cup chopped green pepper
- 2/3 cup chopped onion
- 1/2 cup seasoned bread crumbs
- 1/2 cup quick-cooking oats
- 1 teaspoon chili powder
- 1/2 teaspoon salt
- 1/2 teaspoon pepper
- 2 pounds ground beef
- MASHED POTATOES:
- 4-2/3 cups water
- 1 cup plus 2 tablespoons milk
- 7 tablespoons butter, cubed
- 1-3/4 teaspoons salt
- 4-2/3 cups mashed potato flakes
- Ketchup and mustard

Direction

- Mix the first 9 ingredients together in a large mixing bowl. Crush beef into crumbles over mixture and stir to combine. Press mixture into 2 ungreased 9x9-inch baking pans.
- Bake for 15 to 20 minutes at 350° until center is no longer pink and a thermometer reaches 160°. Drain. Allow to sit for 10 minutes.
- In the meantime, bring milk, water, salt, and butter in a large saucepan to a boil. Mix in potato flakes. Take off the heat.
- Turn one meatloaf upside down onto a serving platter; and put the other upside down onto a cutting board. Spread 1 1/2 cups mashed potatoes over top of the loaf in the serving platter. Gently lay the second loaf atop potatoes.
- Distribute 3 1/2 cups mashed potatoes over sides and top. Spoon the remainder of mashed potatoes into a pastry bag with open star tip #195. Pipe a shell border around the top and bottom edges. Put mustard and ketchup into individual resealable plastic bags; snip a small hole in a corner of each bag. Pipe onto mashed potato border.

Nutrition Information

- Calories: 439 calories
- Sodium: 851mg sodium
- Fiber: 3g fiber)
- Total Carbohydrate: 36g carbohydrate (3g sugars
- Cholesterol: 126mg cholesterol
- Protein: 25g protein.
- Total Fat: 22g fat (10g saturated fat)

177. Layered Potato Beef Casserole

Serving: 6 servings. | Prep: 25mins | Ready in:

Ingredients

- 3 tablespoons butter, divided
- 2 tablespoons all-purpose flour
- 3/4 teaspoon dried rosemary, crushed
- 1/4 teaspoon pepper
- 1/8 teaspoon salt
- 2 cups 2% milk
- 2 cups shredded sharp cheddar cheese
- 4 cups leftover beef stew
- 4 medium Yukon potatoes, thinly sliced
- 1/3 cup crushed butter-flavored crackers (about 8 crackers)
- 1 tablespoon dried parsley flakes
- 1/4 teaspoon garlic powder

Direction

- In a large pot, melt 2 tablespoons of butter. Mix in salt, rosemary, pepper, and flour until combined. Slowly add the milk. Heat to a boil. Stirring constantly, cook until thick, 2 minutes. Take it off the heat and mix in cheese until it melts. Put 2 cups of stew in a 2-1/2 qt. greased dish. Layer half the potatoes and then sauce mixture. Layer the rest of the stew, potatoes, and sauce. Cover; bake in a 400-degree oven until potatoes are tender, 45-50 minutes. Melt remaining butter in microwave. Stir in garlic powder, crackers, and parsley. Sprinkle on top of dish. Do not cover; bake until topping turns golden brown and bubbling, 5-10 minutes. Let it cool for 10 minutes before enjoying.

Nutrition Information

- Calories: 541 calories
- Sodium: 872mg sodium
- Fiber: 5g fiber)
- Total Carbohydrate: 48g carbohydrate (8g sugars
- Cholesterol: 88mg cholesterol
- Protein: 26g protein.
- Total Fat: 28g fat (14g saturated fat)

178. Life Preserver Meat Loaves

Serving: 6 servings. | Prep: 20mins | Ready in:

Ingredients

- 1 large egg
- 1 can (5-1/2 ounces) spicy hot V8 juice
- 1/4 cup milk
- 1 cup seasoned bread crumbs
- 1-1/2 teaspoons seasoned salt
- 1 teaspoon chili powder
- 1-1/2 pounds lean ground beef (90% lean)
- Ketchup and mustard

Direction

- Mix the first 6 ingredients in a big bowl. Crumble beef over the mixture and blend well. Roll into 6 balls, then lightly flatten. Use the end of a wooden spoon handle to create a hole in the middle of each ball.
- Put the ball in a 15x10x1" baking pan that greased. Bake without a cover for 25-30 minutes at 350 degrees or until no pink remains and a thermometer reaches 160 degrees. Garnish with mustard and ketchup.

Nutrition Information

- Calories: 274 calories
- Sodium: 1056mg sodium
- Fiber: 1g fiber)
- Total Carbohydrate: 15g carbohydrate (0 sugars
- Cholesterol: 41mg cholesterol
- Protein: 27g protein. Diabetic Exchanges: 3 lean meat
- Total Fat: 11g fat (4g saturated fat)

179. Lighter Lasagna Corn Carne

Serving: 12 servings. | Prep: 30mins | Ready in:

Ingredients

- 1 pound lean ground beef (90% lean)
- 1 jar (16 ounces) salsa
- 1 can (16 ounces) kidney beans, rinsed and drained
- 1 can (14-3/4 ounces) cream-style corn
- 1 large onion, chopped
- 1 medium green pepper, chopped
- 1 celery rib, chopped
- 3 garlic cloves, minced
- 1 tablespoon minced fresh basil or 1 teaspoon dried basil
- 1 teaspoon salt
- 1 teaspoon chili powder
- 12 lasagna noodles, cooked, rinsed and drained
- 2 cups shredded part-skim mozzarella cheese
- 1/2 cup grated Parmesan cheese

Direction

- Cook beef until not pink on medium heat. Drain excess fat. Mix in the salsa, vegetables, beans, garlic and seasonings. Let it boil. Put heat to low and cover. Gently boil 15 minutes.
- Place 1/4 meat sauce in a greased 13 in. x 9 in. baking pan. Put four pieces of pasta on top

and repeat the layering one time. Top with 1/2 of remaining sauce. Drizzle on 1/2 of cheeses. Top with left, pasta noodles, sauce, and the cheeses.
- Cover and let it bake for 30 minutes at 350 degrees. Remove the cover. Bake for 15 to 20 minutes until cooked completely. Let sit 15 minutes before slicing.

Nutrition Information

- Calories: 292 calories
- Cholesterol: 37mg cholesterol
- Protein: 20g protein. Diabetic Exchanges: 2-1/2 starch
- Total Fat: 8g fat (4g saturated fat)
- Sodium: 674mg sodium
- Fiber: 4g fiber
- Total Carbohydrate: 36g carbohydrate (5g sugars

180. Lots A Veggies Stew

Serving: 10 servings. | Prep: 10mins | Ready in:

Ingredients

- 1 pound ground beef
- 1 medium onion, diced
- 2 garlic cloves, minced
- 1 can (16 ounces) baked beans, undrained
- 1 can (16 ounces) kidney beans, rinsed and drained
- 1 can (16 ounces) butter beans, rinsed and drained
- 1 can (14-1/2 ounces) beef broth
- 1 can (11 ounces) whole kernel corn, undrained
- 1 can (10-1/2 ounces) condensed vegetable soup, undiluted
- 1 can (6 ounces) tomato paste
- 1 medium green pepper, diced
- 1 cup sliced carrots
- 1 cup sliced celery
- 2 tablespoons chili powder
- 1 teaspoon dried oregano
- 1 teaspoon dried thyme
- 1 teaspoon salt, optional
- 1/2 teaspoon dried marjoram
- 1/2 teaspoon pepper

Direction

- Cook beef and onion until meat is not pink anymore in a large skillet over medium heat. Add garlic; cook for another 1 minute. Drain. Transfer to a slow cooker (5 qt). Put in the remaining ingredients and stir. Cover and cook on low for 5-6 hours until vegetables are tender.

Nutrition Information

- Calories: 272 calories
- Total Fat: 6g fat (2g saturated fat)
- Sodium: 1088mg sodium
- Fiber: 9g fiber)
- Total Carbohydrate: 40g carbohydrate (0 sugars
- Cholesterol: 21mg cholesterol
- Protein: 20g protein. Diabetic Exchanges: 2 starch

181. Louisiana Round Steak

Serving: 6 servings. | Prep: 20mins | Ready in:

Ingredients

- 2 pounds sweet potatoes, peeled and cut into 1-inch pieces
- 1 large onion, chopped
- 1 medium green pepper, sliced
- 2 beef top round steaks (3/4 inch thick and 1 pound each)
- 1 teaspoon salt, divided
- 2 tablespoons olive oil
- 1 garlic clove, minced

- 3 tablespoons all-purpose flour
- 1 can (28 ounces) diced tomatoes, undrained
- 1/2 cup beef broth
- 1 teaspoon sugar
- 1/2 teaspoon dried thyme
- 1/2 teaspoon pepper
- 1/4 teaspoon hot pepper sauce

Direction

- In 6-qt. slow cooker, put green pepper, onion and sweet potatoes. Cut every steak to 3 serving-sized pieces; sprinkle 1/2 tsp. salt. Brown steaks in batches in oil on both sides in a big skillet on medium heat. Put steaks on veggies; keep drippings in the pan.
- Put garlic in drippings; mix and cook for 1 minute. Mix in flour till blended; mix in leftover salt and leftover ingredients. Boil, constantly mixing; mix and cook till thick for 4-5 minutes. Put on meat; cover. Cook till beef is tender for 7-9 hours on low.

Nutrition Information

- Calories: 576 calories
- Total Fat: 14g fat (4g saturated fat)
- Sodium: 1031mg sodium
- Fiber: 5g fiber)
- Total Carbohydrate: 37g carbohydrate (16g sugars
- Cholesterol: 170mg cholesterol
- Protein: 71g protein.

182. Macaroni Scramble

Serving: 3 servings. | Prep: 10mins | Ready in:

Ingredients

- 1 cup uncooked cellentani (spiral pasta) or elbow macaroni
- 1/2 pound lean ground beef (90% lean)
- 1 small onion, chopped
- 1 celery rib, chopped
- 1 small green pepper, chopped
- 1 garlic clove, minced
- 1 can (10-3/4 ounces) reduced-sodium condensed tomato soup, undiluted
- 1 tablespoon minced fresh parsley or 1 teaspoon dried parsley flakes
- 1 teaspoon dried oregano
- 1/4 teaspoon salt
- 1/4 teaspoon pepper
- 1/2 cup shredded reduced-fat cheddar cheese

Direction

- Following the package instructions, cook the pasta. At the same time, cook green pepper, celery, onion, and beef in a large skillet on medium heat until the meat is not pink anymore. Put in garlic; cook for 1 more minute. Let drain.
- Drain the pasta; put into the beef mixture. Stir in pepper, salt, oregano, parsley, and soup. Boil. Turn down the heat; simmer without a cover until cooked thoroughly, 4-5 minutes. Dust with the cheese.

Nutrition Information

- Calories: 351 calories
- Sodium: 758mg sodium
- Fiber: 3g fiber)
- Total Carbohydrate: 38g carbohydrate (13g sugars
- Cholesterol: 50mg cholesterol
- Protein: 24g protein. Diabetic Exchanges: 3 medium-fat meat
- Total Fat: 11g fat (5g saturated fat)

183. Makeover Li'l Cheddar Meat Loaves

Serving: 8 servings. | Prep: 15mins | Ready in:

Ingredients

- 2 large egg whites, beaten
- 3/4 cup fat-free milk
- 1 cup shredded reduced-fat cheddar cheese
- 3/4 cup quick-cooking oats
- 1 medium onion, chopped
- 1 medium carrot, shredded
- 1/2 teaspoon salt
- 3/4 pound lean ground beef (90% lean)
- 2/3 cup ketchup
- 2 tablespoons brown sugar
- 1-1/2 teaspoons prepared mustard

Direction

- Whisk the milk and egg whites in a big bowl. Stir in salt, carrot, onion, oats and cheese, then crumble the beef on top of the mixture and stir well.
- Form it into 8 loaves, then put it in a cooking spray coated 13x9-inch baking dish. Mix together the mustard, brown sugar and ketchup in a small bowl, then scoop on top of the loaves.
- Let it bake for 25 to 30 minutes at 350 degrees without a cover or until the thermometer registers 160 degrees and no pink color remains.

Nutrition Information

- Calories: 187 calories
- Sodium: 550mg sodium
- Fiber: 1g fiber)
- Total Carbohydrate: 18g carbohydrate (11g sugars
- Cholesterol: 36mg cholesterol
- Protein: 15g protein. Diabetic Exchanges: 2 lean meat
- Total Fat: 7g fat (3g saturated fat)

184. Mardi Gras Beef

Serving: 4 servings. | Prep: 20mins | Ready in:

Ingredients

- 1 medium onion, chopped
- 1 small green pepper, cut into strips
- 1 teaspoon dried thyme
- 2 teaspoons garlic powder, divided
- 2 tablespoons canola oil
- 1 to 1-1/2 pounds beef top sirloin steak (1 inch thick)
- 1 can (14-1/2 ounces) stewed tomatoes, juice drained and reserved
- 2 teaspoons cornstarch
- Salt and pepper to taste

Direction

- In a big oiled pan, cook and stir onion, half teaspoon garlic powder, thyme, and green pepper until tender-crisp. Season steak with leftover garlic powder.
- Grill steak or broil 5 inches from heat for 3-4 mins per side (for medium-rare steak) or until it reaches the preferred doneness.
- Add tomatoes in the pan. Mix together cornstarch and reserved tomato juice; pour slurry in the vegetable mixture. Cook for 2 minutes until thick, stirring regularly. Sprinkle pepper and salt to taste. Slice the steak thinly and serve with veggies.

Nutrition Information

- Calories: 263 calories
- Fiber: 2g fiber)
- Total Carbohydrate: 15g carbohydrate (8g sugars
- Cholesterol: 63mg cholesterol
- Protein: 23g protein.
- Total Fat: 13g fat (3g saturated fat)
- Sodium: 234mg sodium

185. Marinated Iowa Beef

Serving: 6-8 servings. | Prep: 15mins | Ready in:

Ingredients

- 1 boneless beef chuck roast (3 pounds)
- 1/3 cup tarragon wine vinegar
- 1/4 cup olive oil
- 1 envelope zesty Italian salad dressing mix
- 1/2 teaspoon meat tenderizer, optional

Direction

- Using meat fork, prick the meat liberally; flip the meat and prick once more. Mix meat tenderizer (if wished), salad dressing mix, oil and vinegar in a big resealable plastic bag. Put the roast; Enclose bag and coat by flipping. Chill for 8 hours or up to overnight, flipping frequently.
- Grill for 6 to 9 minutes per side on moderate heat or till meat achieves preferred doneness.

Nutrition Information

- Calories: 303 calories
- Sodium: 505mg sodium
- Fiber: 0 fiber)
- Total Carbohydrate: 3g carbohydrate (0 sugars
- Cholesterol: 36mg cholesterol
- Protein: 37g protein. Diabetic Exchanges: 5 lean meat.
- Total Fat: 15g fat (0 saturated fat)

186. Marinated Ostrich Steak

Serving: 4 servings. | Prep: 15mins | Ready in:

Ingredients

- 3/4 cup vegetable oil
- 1/3 cup soy sauce
- 1/4 cup cider or white wine vinegar
- 3 tablespoons lemon juice
- 2 tablespoons Worcestershire sauce
- 1 tablespoon ground mustard
- 1 teaspoon salt
- 1 teaspoon pepper
- 1 teaspoon dried parsley flakes
- 1/2 teaspoon garlic powder
- 4 ostrich or beef tenderloin steaks (4 ounces each)

Direction

- Initially combine the first 10 ingredients in either a shallow glass container or a resealable plastic bag. Drop the meat into the marinade, flip over a couple of times to ensure that the entire meat is well coated. Cover the container or seal the bag and store in the fridge overnight. Occasionally flip the meat all throughout. Remove the meat from the marinade, drain and throw away the excess liquid mixture. For 5 minutes, either grill or broil your meat over medium heat. Flip the meat and cook the other side for 6 to 8 minutes or depending on the person's preference for doneness (well-done, 170 degrees; medium 160 degrees; or medium-rare, 145 degrees). Make sure to cover the meat all throughout the cooking process.

Nutrition Information

- Calories:
- Total Carbohydrate:
- Cholesterol:
- Protein:
- Total Fat:
- Sodium:
- Fiber:

187. Matthew's Best Ever Meat Loaf

Serving: 8 servings. | Prep: 30mins | Ready in:

Ingredients

- 3 slices white bread, torn into small pieces
- 1/2 cup beef stock

- 2 large portobello mushrooms (about 6 ounces), cut into chunks
- 1 medium onion, cut into wedges
- 1 medium carrot, cut into chunks
- 1 celery rib, cut into chunks
- 3 garlic cloves, halved
- 1 tablespoon olive oil
- 2 tablespoons tomato paste
- 2 large eggs, lightly beaten
- 1-1/4 pounds ground beef
- 3/4 pound ground pork
- 1 tablespoon Worcestershire sauce
- 1 tablespoon reduced-sodium soy sauce
- 1-1/4 teaspoons salt
- 3/4 teaspoon pepper
- GLAZE:
- 1/2 cup ketchup
- 2 tablespoons tomato paste
- 2 tablespoons brown sugar
- 1 teaspoon ground mustard

Direction

- Set oven to 350°and start preheating. Mix stock and bread; let it rest until liquid is absorbed.
- At the same time, pulse garlic, celery, carrot, onion, and mushrooms in a food processor until they are finely chopped. Heat oil in a big skillet on medium heat. Put in the mushroom mixture; cook while stirring for 5 to 6 minutes until soft and the liquid burns off. Stir in tomato paste; cook for 1 minute more. Let it cool slightly.
- Put in the next 7 ingredients and cooked vegetables to the bread mixture; mix thoroughly. Put a 12x7-inch piece of foil on a rack in a foil-lined rimmed baking pan. Pour the meat mixture to the foil and form into a 10x6-inch loaf.
- Bake for 1 hour. Combine together glaze ingredients; drizzle over loaf. Bake for about 15-25 minutes more until a thermometer indicates 160 degrees. Let it rest for 10 minutes before you slice.
- Freeze option: Form meat loaf on a plastic wrap-lined baking sheet; wrap and freeze until firm. Take out of pan and carefully wrap in foil; put back to freezer. To use, unwrap meat loaf and bake as instructed, increasing initial baking time to 2 hours. Combine together glaze ingredients; drizzle over loaf. Bake for 15-25 minutes more until a thermometer inserted in the center reads 160°. Let it rest for 10 minutes before you slice.

Nutrition Information

- Calories: 341 calories
- Protein: 25g protein.
- Total Fat: 18g fat (6g saturated fat)
- Sodium: 832mg sodium
- Fiber: 2g fiber)
- Total Carbohydrate: 19g carbohydrate (11g sugars
- Cholesterol: 119mg cholesterol

188. Meat 'n' Potato Kabobs

Serving: 4 servings. | Prep: 20mins | Ready in:

Ingredients

- 1 pound beef top sirloin steak, cut into 1-inch cubes
- 1-1/2 teaspoons steak seasoning, divided
- 1 garlic clove, minced
- 1 cup cola
- 3 small red potatoes (about 8 ounces), cubed
- 1 tablespoon water
- 1 cup cherry tomatoes
- 1 medium sweet orange pepper, cut into 1-inch pieces
- 1 teaspoon canola oil
- 1 cup pineapple chunks

Direction

- Season beef with 1 teaspoon steak seasoning and garlic. Pour cola in a large bowl and toss in the beef. Cover the potatoes in water in a microwaveable bowl. Set the microwave on high, cover the bowl, and cook for 4-5 minutes or just until tender. Drain the potatoes and return them to the bowl. Add in oil, tomatoes, pepper, and remaining steak seasoning. Toss to coat the potatoes, gently, so that the potatoes are not damaged. Drain the beef of its marinade, discarding the liquid. Alternate the beef, pineapple, and vegetables on eight metal or pre-soaked wooden skewers. Cook in a covered grill over medium heat, or broil 4 in. from heat, until peppers are crisp on the outside and tender on the inside, and the beef is cooked to liking, about 6-8 minutes with occasional turning.

Nutrition Information

- Calories: 279 calories
- Total Carbohydrate: 30g carbohydrate (19g sugars
- Cholesterol: 46mg cholesterol
- Protein: 26g protein. Diabetic Exchanges: 3 lean meat
- Total Fat: 6g fat (2g saturated fat)
- Sodium: 321mg sodium
- Fiber: 3g fiber)

189. Meat Loaf From The Slow Cooker

Serving: 8 servings. | Prep: 25mins | Ready in:

Ingredients

- 1/2 cup tomato sauce
- 2 large eggs, lightly beaten
- 1/4 cup ketchup
- 1 teaspoon Worcestershire sauce
- 1 small onion, chopped
- 1/3 cup crushed saltines (about 10 crackers)
- 3/4 teaspoon minced garlic
- 1/4 teaspoon seasoned salt
- 1/8 teaspoon seasoned pepper
- 1-1/2 pounds lean ground beef (90% lean)
- 1/2 pound reduced-fat bulk pork sausage
- SAUCE:
- 1/2 cup ketchup
- 3 tablespoons brown sugar
- 3/4 teaspoon ground mustard
- 1/4 teaspoon ground nutmeg

Direction

- Create three 25x3-in. pieces of heavy-duty foil by cutting; crisscross to make them shape like spokes of a wheel. Put the strips up the sides and on the bottom of a 4-qt. or 5-qt. slow cooker. Grease the strips using cooking spray.
- Mix together the first nine ingredients in a large bowl. Put crumbled sausage and beef into the mixture and stir well (the mixture should be moist). Form it into a loaf. Put the meat loaf in the middle of the strips.
- Combine sauce ingredients in a small bowl. Pour the sauce over meat loaf using a spoon. Put on a cover and cook for 3-4 hours on low until a thermometer reaches 160° and the meat is no longer pink. Remove the meat loaf to a platter with foil strips as handles.

Nutrition Information

- Calories: 284 calories
- Protein: 24g protein. Diabetic Exchanges: 3 lean meat
- Total Fat: 14g fat (5g saturated fat)
- Sodium: 681mg sodium
- Fiber: 1g fiber)
- Total Carbohydrate: 16g carbohydrate (12g sugars
- Cholesterol: 119mg cholesterol

190. Meat Loaf Patty

Serving: 2 servings. | Prep: 5mins | Ready in:

Ingredients

- 1/3 cup seasoned bread crumbs
- 3 tablespoons milk
- 1 teaspoon Worcestershire sauce
- 1 teaspoon finely chopped onion
- 1/4 teaspoon salt
- 1/2 pound lean ground beef
- Ketchup

Direction

- Mix the first 5 ingredients together in a big bowl. Crumble over the mixture with beef and combine well. Form into a big patty.
- Put in a shallow microwavable dish, then microwave on high setting without a cover until a thermometer reaches 160 degrees, about 2 to 3 minutes. Allow to stand about 3 minutes and serve together with ketchup.

Nutrition Information

- Calories: 262 calories
- Total Carbohydrate: 15g carbohydrate (2g sugars
- Cholesterol: 72mg cholesterol
- Protein: 25g protein.
- Total Fat: 11g fat (4g saturated fat)
- Sodium: 670mg sodium
- Fiber: 1g fiber)

191. Meat Loaf Potato Surprise

Serving: 8 servings. | Prep: 20mins | Ready in:

Ingredients

- 1 cup soft bread crumbs
- 1/2 cup beef broth
- 1 egg, lightly beaten
- 4 teaspoons dried minced onion
- 1 teaspoon salt
- 1/4 teaspoon Italian seasoning
- 1/4 teaspoon pepper
- 1-1/2 pounds ground beef
- 4 cups frozen shredded hash brown potatoes, thawed
- 1/3 cup grated Parmesan cheese
- 1/4 cup minced fresh parsley
- 1 teaspoon onion salt
- SAUCE:
- 1 can (8 ounces) tomato sauce
- 1/4 cup beef broth
- 2 teaspoons prepared mustard
- Additional Parmesan cheese, optional

Direction

- Mix together the seasonings, egg, broth and crumbs in a large bowl; allow to sit for 2 minutes. Top the mixture with a sprinkle of beef and mix thoroughly.
- Shape meat mixture into a 10-in. square on a piece of waxed paper. Mix together onion salt, parsley, cheese and hash browns and pour over the meat using a spoon.
- Roll up in the jelly-roll style, discarding waxed paper while rolling. Seal ends and edges by pinching; place in a shallow baking pan without grease, putting the seam side down.
- Bake for 40 minutes at 375°. Mix the first three sauce ingredients; pour over the loaf using a spoon. Put back into the oven for 10 more minutes. Top with a sprinkle of Parmesan if wanted.

Nutrition Information

- Calories: 249 calories
- Sodium: 889mg sodium
- Fiber: 1g fiber)
- Total Carbohydrate: 12g carbohydrate (2g sugars
- Cholesterol: 86mg cholesterol
- Protein: 21g protein.
- Total Fat: 12g fat (5g saturated fat)

192. Meat Loaf For 120

Serving: 120 servings. | Prep: 20mins | Ready in:

Ingredients

- 40 pounds ground beef
- 16 large eggs, lightly beaten
- 8 cups old-fashioned oats
- 5 cups tomato juice
- 3 large onions, chopped
- 1/3 cup salt
- 2 tablespoons pepper
- SAUCE:
- 3 cups water
- 1-1/2 cup ketchup
- 6 tablespoons vinegar
- 2 tablespoons prepared mustard
- 2 tablespoons brown sugar

Direction

- Mix pepper, onions, eggs, tomato juice, salt, beef, and oats. Form mixture into 16 loaves. Put them in 9x5-in. loaf pans. Mix the sauce ingredients; on each loaf put 3 tablespoons. Bake in a 350-degree oven until not pink, 1 1/2-2 hours. Baste once with the rest of the sauce.

Nutrition Information

- Calories: 333 calories
- Fiber: 1g fiber)
- Total Carbohydrate: 6g carbohydrate (1g sugars
- Cholesterol: 129mg cholesterol
- Protein: 32g protein.
- Total Fat: 20g fat (8g saturated fat)
- Sodium: 470mg sodium

193. Meat Loaf For A Mob

Serving: 4 meat loaves. | Prep: 20mins | Ready in:

Ingredients

- 8 eggs, lightly beaten
- 1 can (46 ounces) V8 juice
- 2 large onions, finely chopped
- 4 celery ribs, finely chopped
- 4-1/4 cups seasoned bread crumbs
- 2 envelopes onion soup mix
- 2 teaspoons pepper
- 8 pounds ground beef
- 3/4 cup ketchup
- 1/3 cup packed brown sugar
- 1/4 cup prepared mustard

Direction

- Set oven at 350° to preheat. Mix the pepper, soup mix, bread crumbs, celery, onions, V8 juice and eggs in a huge bowl. Break the beef into crumbs and blend well into the mixture. Form into 4 loaves, lay each on a 13x9-inch baking dish coated with cooking spray. Bake while uncovered for 45 minutes.
- In the meantime, mix the mustard, brown sugar and ketchup together. Add on top of loaves and spread out. Bake until a thermometer reaches 160° and they are not pink any longer, about 15 minutes.

Nutrition Information

- Calories: 332 calories
- Total Carbohydrate: 18g carbohydrate (6g sugars
- Cholesterol: 128mg cholesterol
- Protein: 27g protein.
- Total Fat: 16g fat (6g saturated fat)
- Sodium: 656mg sodium
- Fiber: 1g fiber)

194. Meat Lover's Pizza Casserole

Serving: 6 servings. | Prep: 10mins | Ready in:

Ingredients

- 1 pound ground beef
- 1 medium onion, chopped
- 1 can (15 ounces) pizza sauce
- 8 ounces elbow macaroni, cooked and drained
- 2 cups shredded part-skim mozzarella cheese
- 1 package (3-1/2 ounces) sliced pepperoni, quartered
- 1/2 teaspoon salt

Direction

- In a big skillet, cook the onion and beef on medium heat till the meat is not pink anymore; drain off. Whisk in the rest of the ingredients.
- Move into a greased 2-quart baking dish. Bake, with no cover, at 350 degrees till heated completely or for 40 to 45 minutes.

Nutrition Information

- Calories: 379 calories
- Protein: 29g protein.
- Total Fat: 20g fat (10g saturated fat)
- Sodium: 926mg sodium
- Fiber: 2g fiber)
- Total Carbohydrate: 19g carbohydrate (5g sugars
- Cholesterol: 73mg cholesterol

195. Meatball Pie

Serving: 6 servings. | Prep: 50mins | Ready in:

Ingredients

- 1 pound ground beef
- 3/4 cup soft bread crumbs
- 1/4 cup chopped onion
- 2 tablespoons minced fresh parsley
- 1 teaspoon salt
- 1/2 teaspoon dried marjoram
- 1/8 teaspoon pepper
- 1/4 cup milk
- 1 large egg, lightly beaten
- 1 can (14-1/2 ounces) stewed tomatoes
- 1 tablespoon cornstarch
- 2 teaspoons beef bouillon granules
- 1 cup frozen peas
- 1 cup sliced carrots, cooked
- CRUST:
- 2-2/3 cups all-purpose flour
- 1/2 teaspoon salt
- 1 cup shortening
- 7 to 8 tablespoons ice water
- Half-and-half cream

Direction

- Mix the first 9 ingredients together in a big bowl (the mixture should be tender). Separate into 4 portions, forming each portion into 12 small meatballs. Working in batches, in a big skillet, brown the meatballs; strain and put aside.
- Strain the tomatoes, saving the liquid. Mix the liquid with cornstarch, adding to the skillet. Add bouillon and tomatoes; boil it over medium heat, whisking continually. Mix in carrots and peas. Take away from heat and put aside.
- Start preheating the oven to 400°. To prepare the crust, mix salt with flour in a big bowl. Cut in shortening until the mixture looks like coarse crumbs. Add water, 1 tablespoon each time; use a fork to gently stir. Remove onto a surface lightly scattered with flour. Lightly knead to make a dough. (The mixture will be crumbly in the beginning, but it will come together and make a dough when you knead it). Split the dough into 2 portions.
- Between 2 pieces of waxed paper lightly scattered with flour, roll each portion of the dough to a 1/8-inch thick circle. Discard the top piece of the waxed paper from 1 pastry circle, flipping onto a 9-inch deep-dish pie plate. Discard the leftover waxed paper. Snip the pastry to even with the rim. Put in the meatballs, spooning over the top with the tomato mixture.

- Discard the top piece of the waxed paper from the leftover pastry circle, flipping onto the pie. Discard the leftover waxed paper. Snip, seal, and flute the edge. Cut vents in the top, brushing cream over.
- Bake for 45-50 minutes until the crust turns golden brown. Use a foil to loosely cover the edges during the final 10 minutes if necessary to avoid over-browning. Allow to sit before slicing, about 10 minutes.

Nutrition Information

- Calories: 735 calories
- Fiber: 4g fiber)
- Total Carbohydrate: 58g carbohydrate (8g sugars
- Cholesterol: 87mg cholesterol
- Protein: 25g protein.
- Total Fat: 43g fat (12g saturated fat)
- Sodium: 1094mg sodium

196. Meatball Submarine Casserole

Serving: 4 servings. | Prep: 15mins | Ready in:

Ingredients

- 1 package (12 ounces) frozen fully cooked Italian meatballs
- 4 slices sourdough bread
- 1-1/2 teaspoons olive oil
- 1 garlic clove, halved
- 1-1/2 cups pasta sauce with mushrooms
- 1/2 cup shredded part-skim mozzarella cheese, divided
- 1/2 cup grated Parmesan cheese, divided

Direction

- Start heating the broiler. Set microwave on high and cook meatballs, covered, for 4-6 minutes or until heated. In the meantime, put bread on a cookie sheet that is not greased. Use a brush to put oil on one side of bread. Place pan 4-6 in. from heat and broil 1-2 minutes or until golden brown. Rub garlic on the cut side of the bread; throw out the garlic. Break bread into small pieces. Place bread pieces in an 11x7-in. greased dish. Reduce oven to 350 degrees. Add 1/4 cup Parmesan, pasta sauce, and 1/4 cup mozzarella to the meatballs. Mix to combine. Pour meatball mixture over the bread and sprinkle the rest of the cheeses on top. Do not cover; bake 15-18 minutes until cheeses melt.

Nutrition Information

- Calories: 417 calories
- Total Fat: 28g fat (13g saturated fat)
- Sodium: 1243mg sodium
- Fiber: 3g fiber)
- Total Carbohydrate: 22g carbohydrate (8g sugars
- Cholesterol: 59mg cholesterol
- Protein: 23g protein.

197. Meaty Macaroni

Serving: 6 servings. | Prep: 10mins | Ready in:

Ingredients

- 1 pound ground beef
- 1 medium onion, chopped
- 1/2 cup chopped green pepper
- 1 jar (14 ounces) spaghetti sauce
- 1-1/2 cups uncooked elbow macaroni
- 1 cup water
- Salt and pepper to taste
- 1 cup shredded part-skim mozzarella cheese

Direction

- Crumble the beef over a 2-quart microwave-safe dish. Put in green pepper and onion. Put

on a cover and microwave on high heat setting, stirring once, until the meat is not pink anymore, 3-5 minutes; drain. Stir in pepper, salt, water, macaroni, and spaghetti sauce.
- Microwave, covered, on high heat setting, stirring once for 9 minutes. Dust with cheese. Before serving, allow to stand for 5 minutes.

Nutrition Information

- Calories: 338 calories
- Total Carbohydrate: 24g carbohydrate (7g sugars
- Cholesterol: 66mg cholesterol
- Protein: 23g protein.
- Total Fat: 16g fat (7g saturated fat)
- Sodium: 462mg sodium
- Fiber: 2g fiber)

198. Mexican Beef Cobbler

Serving: 6 servings. | Prep: 20mins | Ready in:

Ingredients

- 1-1/2 pounds ground beef
- 1 envelope taco seasoning
- 1 jar (16 ounces) salsa
- 1 can (8-3/4 ounces) whole kernel corn, drained
- 2 cups shredded sharp cheddar cheese
- 1-1/2 cups biscuit/baking mix
- 1/2 cup 2% milk
- 1/8 teaspoon freshly ground pepper

Direction

- Cook beef on medium heat in a big skillet till not pink anymore or for 8 to 10 minutes, crumble; drain. Mix in corn, salsa and taco seasoning; heat through. Move to an 11x7-in. baking dish; drizzle along with cheese.

- Whisk milk and biscuit mix in a small-sized bowl just till blended; drop by tablespoonfuls on top of cheese. Drizzle along with pepper.
- Bake, while uncovered, at 350 degrees for 35 to 45 minutes or till becoming bubbly and topping turns golden brown.

Nutrition Information

- Calories:
- Total Carbohydrate:
- Cholesterol:
- Protein:
- Total Fat:
- Sodium:
- Fiber:

199. Mexican Lasagna

Serving: 12 | Prep: 30mins | Ready in:

Ingredients

- 1 pound extra-lean ground beef
- 1 (16 ounce) can refried beans
- 2 teaspoons dried oregano
- 1 teaspoon ground cumin
- 3/4 teaspoon garlic powder
- 12 dry lasagna noodles
- 2 1/2 cups water
- 2 1/2 cups salsa
- 2 cups sour cream
- 3/4 cup chopped green onions
- 1 (2 ounce) can sliced black olives
- 1 cup shredded Pepper Jack cheese

Direction

- Put a skillet on medium-high heat and cook ground beef until browned evenly. Drain grease. Mix refried beans, cooked beef, oregano, cumin, and garlic powder in a bowl.
- Put 4 uncooked pasta in the bottom of a 13 in x 9 in baking pan. Pour 1/2 of beef mixture on

top of the pasta. Layer with 4 more uncooked pasta, the remaining 1/2 of beef mixture, and the remaining pasta. Mix salsa and water in a bowl and pour on top.
- Use foil to tightly cover and bake in oven at 175°C (350°F). Cook for 1 1/2 hours until pasta is soft.
- Mix green onions, sour cream, and olives in a bowl. Scoop over lasagna and put shredded cheese on top. Put it back in oven and bake for 5-10 min. until cheese melts.

Nutrition Information

- Calories: 559 calories;
- Total Fat: 19.1
- Sodium: 604
- Total Carbohydrate: 72.3
- Cholesterol: 60
- Protein: 25.6

200. Mexicana Skillet Stew

Serving: 4 servings. | Prep: 5mins | Ready in:

Ingredients

- 1 pound lean ground beef (90% lean)
- 2 large potatoes, peeled and cut into 1/2-inch cubes
- 1 large onion, chopped
- 1 large green pepper, chopped
- 1 can (4 ounces) mushroom stems and pieces, undrained
- 3/4 cup picante sauce
- Garlic salt and pepper to taste

Direction

- Cook beef, mushrooms, green pepper, onion, and potatoes over medium heat in a large skillet until meat is no longer pink; drain. Lower heat; simmer, covered, stirring from time to time until potatoes are tender, or for 20 minutes.
- Add pepper, garlic salt, and picante sauce. Cook until thoroughly heated or for 5 more minutes.

Nutrition Information

- Calories: 344 calories
- Sodium: 527mg sodium
- Fiber: 4g fiber)
- Total Carbohydrate: 35g carbohydrate (0 sugars
- Cholesterol: 35mg cholesterol
- Protein: 27g protein. Diabetic Exchanges: 3-1/2 meat
- Total Fat: 11g fat (4g saturated fat)

201. Microwave Meatball Stew

Serving: 4-6 servings. | Prep: 15mins | Ready in:

Ingredients

- 1 egg, lightly beaten
- 1/2 cup dry bread crumbs
- 1/2 cup finely chopped onion
- 2 tablespoons onion soup mix
- 1 pound ground beef
- 1 can (15 ounces) whole potatoes, drained and quartered
- 1-1/4 cups frozen sliced carrots
- 1-1/4 cups frozen peas
- 1 can (10-3/4 ounces) condensed cream of mushroom soup, undiluted
- 1 can (10-1/2 ounces) condensed beef broth, undiluted
- 1/2 teaspoon dried savory
- 1/4 teaspoon dried thyme
- 2 tablespoons cornstarch
- 2 tablespoons water
- 1/4 teaspoon browning sauce, optional

Direction

- Combine soup mix, onion, crumbs, and egg in a large bowl. Break beef apart and sprinkle over the mixture; stir well. Form the mixture into 1 1/2-inch balls.
- Transfer the balls to a microwaveable baking dish. Microwave, covered for 3 to 4 minutes on high power. Turn meatballs over and cook in microwave for 3 to 4 more minutes; drain.
- Combine the next 7 ingredients in a large bowl; ladle over meatballs. Cook, covered at 50% power until meat is no longer pink, or for 8 to 10 minutes. Combine water, cornstarch, and browning sauce (if using) until no lumps remain; slowly mix into the stew. Microwave, covered for 1 to 2 minutes on high power, stirring from time to time, or until bubbly and thickened.

Nutrition Information

- Calories: 333 calories
- Protein: 22g protein.
- Total Fat: 14g fat (5g saturated fat)
- Sodium: 1274mg sodium
- Fiber: 5g fiber)
- Total Carbohydrate: 29g carbohydrate (5g sugars
- Cholesterol: 88mg cholesterol

202. Microwave Swiss Steak

Serving: 6 servings. | Prep: 10mins | Ready in:

Ingredients

- 1-1/2 pounds beef top round steak (1/4 inch thick)
- 3 tablespoons onion soup mix
- 1 can (4 ounces) mushroom stems and pieces, drained
- 1 can (14-1/2 ounces) diced tomatoes
- 2 tablespoons cornstarch
- 1/4 to 1/2 teaspoon pepper
- Dash cayenne pepper, optional

Direction

- Take steak and cut into serving-size pieces; use a mallet to pound, tenderizing it. In a shallow ungreased microwave-safe pan put the steak. Sprinkle on mushrooms and soup mix. Keeping the liquid, drain the tomatoes. Set the tomatoes aside. Mix tomato liquid and cornstarch in a bowl until smooth. Mix in tomatoes, pepper, and cayenne if desired. Pour mixture over steak. Cover; with microwave on high cook until it starts boiling, 4-6 minutes. Leave covered; microwave on 50% power until steak is tender, 14-19 minutes.

Nutrition Information

- Calories: 201 calories
- Protein: 28g protein. Diabetic Exchanges: 3 lean meat
- Total Fat: 4g fat (0 saturated fat)
- Sodium: 308mg sodium
- Fiber: 2g fiber)
- Total Carbohydrate: 10g carbohydrate (0 sugars
- Cholesterol: 70mg cholesterol

203. Midwest Meatball Casserole

Serving: 6 servings. | Prep: 40mins | Ready in:

Ingredients

- 2 cans (8 ounces each) tomato sauce, divided
- 1 large egg
- 1/4 cup dry bread crumbs
- 1/4 cup chopped onion
- 1 teaspoon salt
- 1 pound lean ground beef (90% lean)
- 1 package (10 ounces) frozen mixed vegetables
- 1/2 teaspoon dried thyme
- 1/8 teaspoon pepper

- 1 package (16 ounces) frozen shredded hash brown potatoes, thawed
- 1 tablespoon butter, melted
- 3 slices process American cheese, cut into 1/2-inch strips

Direction

- Combine egg, 2 tbsp. of tomato sauce, bread crumbs, salt and onion in a large bowl. Crumble beef over mixture and mix well. Form into balls of 1-inch.
- On a greased rack in a shallow baking pan, place meatballs and bake at 375° for approximately 15 to 20 minutes until meatballs are not pink anymore; drain.
- In the meantime, in a large skillet, combine the rest tomato sauce with seasonings and vegetables. Simmer while covered for around 10 to 15 minutes until heated through; mix in meatballs and leave aside.
- In a greased baking dish of 11x7-inch, place potatoes. Brush with butter and bake at 375° for nearly 15 to 20 minutes until lightly browned. Take away from the oven; put meatball mixture on top. Place cheese strips in a lattice pattern on top. Uncovered while baking for an addition of 20 to 25 minutes until cheese is melted and heated through.

Nutrition Information

- Calories: 310 calories
- Protein: 23g protein.
- Total Fat: 12g fat (6g saturated fat)
- Sodium: 884mg sodium
- Fiber: 4g fiber)
- Total Carbohydrate: 27g carbohydrate (4g sugars
- Cholesterol: 97mg cholesterol

204. Mini Cheese Meat Loaves

Serving: 6 servings. | Prep: 20mins | Ready in:

Ingredients

- 1 large egg, beaten
- 1 cup soft bread cubes
- 1/4 cup whole milk
- 1-1/2 teaspoons onion salt
- 1 teaspoon dried parsley flakes
- Dash pepper
- 1-1/2 pounds lean ground beef (90% lean)
- 6 sticks (2-1/2 inches x 1/2 inch each) cheddar or mozzarella cheese
- SAUCE:
- 2 cans (15 ounces each) tomato sauce
- 1/2 cup chopped onion
- 1 tablespoon dried parsley flakes
- 1/2 teaspoon dried oregano
- 1/4 teaspoon garlic salt

Direction

- Stir together the first 6 ingredients in a bowl. Add in beef. Split into 6 parts. Form each part around a cheese stick and shape into a loaf. Put aside.
- Mix all the sauce ingredients in a big skillet. Put in loaves and spoon the sauce onto each piece. Cover and boil. Lower heat to simmer for 20 minutes, until the meat thermometer reaches 160 degrees.

Nutrition Information

- Calories: 342 calories
- Total Fat: 19g fat (10g saturated fat)
- Sodium: 1152mg sodium
- Fiber: 1g fiber)
- Total Carbohydrate: 9g carbohydrate (3g sugars
- Cholesterol: 122mg cholesterol
- Protein: 32g protein.

205. Minute Steaks Parmesan

Serving: 4 servings. | Prep: 10mins | Ready in:

Ingredients

- 1 large egg white, lightly beaten
- 2 teaspoons water
- Dash pepper
- 1/2 cup finely crushed saltine crackers
- 1/2 cup grated Parmesan cheese
- 4 beef cube steaks (4 ounces each)
- 2 tablespoons butter
- 1 can (8 ounces) pizza sauce

Direction

- Mix together pepper, water and egg white in a shallow bowl, then set aside. Mix together cheese and cracker crumbs on a plate, then dip each cube of steak into the egg mixture. Coat dipped steak cubes with cracker and cheese mixture.
- Melt butter in a big skillet and brown both sides of steaks. Put in pizza sauce and simmer for 3 to 5 minutes. Decorate with the leftover crumb mixture and serve promptly.

Nutrition Information

- Calories: 185 calories
- Total Carbohydrate: 10g carbohydrate (3g sugars
- Cholesterol: 39mg cholesterol
- Protein: 13g protein.
- Total Fat: 10g fat (6g saturated fat)
- Sodium: 521mg sodium
- Fiber: 1g fiber)

206. Moist Hungarian Goulash

Serving: 2 servings. | Prep: 15mins | Ready in:

Ingredients

- 2 tablespoons all-purpose flour
- 1/8 teaspoon salt
- 1/8 teaspoon pepper
- 3/4 pound beef top round steak, cut into 1-inch cubes
- 1/2 cup coarsely chopped onion
- 1 teaspoon butter
- 1 teaspoon canola oil
- 1/2 cup reduced-sodium beef broth
- 1 tablespoon tomato paste
- 1 garlic clove, minced
- 1 teaspoon paprika
- 1/8 teaspoon dried marjoram
- 1/8 teaspoon caraway seeds
- 1/8 teaspoon lemon juice
- Hot cooked noodles, optional

Direction

- Combine pepper, salt, and flour in a big plastic resealable bag. Add in the beef cubes, shaking to coat.
- Cook onion and beef with oil and butter in a large skillet until the onion becomes tender. Stir in lemon juice, caraway seeds, marjoram, paprika, garlic, tomato paste, and broth, then allow to boil. Lower the heat then simmer while covered for 1 - 1 1/2 hours or until the meat is really tender.
- If desired, you can serve the soup over noodles.

Nutrition Information

- Calories: 310 calories
- Total Carbohydrate: 13g carbohydrate (4g sugars
- Cholesterol: 102mg cholesterol
- Protein: 41g protein. Diabetic Exchanges: 5 lean meat
- Total Fat: 10g fat (3g saturated fat)
- Sodium: 333mg sodium
- Fiber: 2g fiber)

207. Mom's Beef Stew

Serving: 10 servings. | Prep: 40mins | Ready in:

Ingredients

- 2 pounds meaty beef soup bones (beef shanks or short ribs)
- 6 cups water
- 5 medium potatoes, peeled and cubed
- 5 medium carrots, chopped
- 1 medium onion, chopped
- 1/2 cup medium pearl barley
- 1 can (28 ounces) plum tomatoes, undrained
- 1 to 1-1/2 teaspoons salt
- 1/2 teaspoon pepper
- 2 garlic cloves, minced, optional
- 1 bay leaf, optional
- 3 tablespoons cornstarch
- 1/2 cup cold water

Direction

- In a soup kettle or a Dutch oven, combine water and soup bones. Bring to a boil slowly. Lower the heat and simmer, covered, for 2 hours.
- Allow beef bones to cool until safe to handle. Remove meat from bones; throw away the bones and add meat back to the broth. Add bay leaf (optional), garlic, pepper, salt, tomatoes, barley, onion, carrots and potatoes. Simmer, covered for 50 to 60 minutes or until barley and vegetables are softened.
- Throwaway bay leaf. Mix together cold water and cornstarch until smooth; stir into stew. Bring to a boil and cook, stirring, for 2 minutes or until mixture is thickened.

Nutrition Information

- Calories: 256 calories
- Protein: 15g protein.
- Total Fat: 5g fat (2g saturated fat)
- Sodium: 420mg sodium
- Fiber: 5g fiber)
- Total Carbohydrate: 37g carbohydrate (7g sugars
- Cholesterol: 28mg cholesterol

208. Mushroom Pizza Burgers

Serving: 6 servings. | Prep: 15mins | Ready in:

Ingredients

- 1/2 cup sliced fresh mushrooms
- 1/4 cup chopped onion
- 1 garlic clove, minced
- 1/2 teaspoon dried oregano
- 1 cup crushed tomatoes, undrained
- BURGERS:
- 1-1/2 cups finely chopped fresh mushrooms
- 1/3 cup minced fresh basil
- 1 egg white, lightly beaten
- 2 tablespoons grated Parmesan cheese
- 2 tablespoons dry bread crumbs
- 1/2 teaspoon salt
- 1/8 teaspoon pepper
- 1 pound lean ground beef (90% lean)
- 6 slices part-skim mozzarella cheese (3 ounces)
- 6 hamburger buns, split and toasted

Direction

- Sauté the onion and mushrooms for 3 minutes in a small frying pan that is coated with cooking spray. Add oregano and garlic and let it cook for another 1 minute. Mix in tomatoes and let it cook for 5 minutes on medium-low heat without cover, stirring from time to time. Put aside and keep it warm.
- Mix together the pepper, salt, breadcrumbs, Parmesan cheese, egg white, basil and mushrooms in a big bowl. Crumble the beef on top of the mixture and stir well. Form it into 6 patties.
- Grill the patties on a grill rack that's lightly oiled on medium-hot heat with cover, or let it broil for 4-5 minutes per side, placed 4-inches from the heat source or until the meat juices

run clear and a thermometer registers 160 degrees. Put tomato sauce and cheese on top of the patties, then serve it on buns.

Nutrition Information

- Calories: 333 calories
- Protein: 25g protein. Diabetic Exchanges: 3 lean meat
- Total Fat: 12g fat (5g saturated fat)
- Sodium: 757mg sodium
- Fiber: 3g fiber)
- Total Carbohydrate: 28g carbohydrate (0 sugars
- Cholesterol: 36mg cholesterol

209. Mushroom Pot Roast

Serving: 8-10 servings. | Prep: 15mins | Ready in:

Ingredients

- 1 boneless beef chuck roast (3 to 4 pounds)
- 1 teaspoon garlic powder
- 1/2 teaspoon pepper
- 2 tablespoons olive oil
- 4 cups water
- 1 large onion, chopped
- 1 celery rib, sliced
- 4 garlic cloves, peeled and sliced
- 4 teaspoons beef bouillon granules
- 2 bay leaves
- 1/2 pound sliced fresh mushrooms

Direction

- Season beef with pepper and garlic powder. Cook beef in oil over medium-high heat in a Dutch oven until all sides are browned. Add bay leaves, bouillon, garlic, celery, onion, and water; bring to a boil. Lower heat; simmer, covered for 60 minutes.
- Add mushroom into the pan. Simmer, covered until meat is tender, for 30 more minutes. Pick out bay leaves. Thicken pan juices if desired; serve beef with sauce.

Nutrition Information

- Calories: 272 calories
- Sodium: 376mg sodium
- Fiber: 1g fiber)
- Total Carbohydrate: 3g carbohydrate (1g sugars
- Cholesterol: 89mg cholesterol
- Protein: 28g protein.
- Total Fat: 16g fat (5g saturated fat)

210. Mushroom Ribeyes

Serving: 2 servings. | Prep: 20mins | Ready in:

Ingredients

- 2 beef ribeye steaks (8 ounces each)
- 1/4 teaspoon seasoned salt
- 1/8 teaspoon pepper
- 2 teaspoons canola oil
- 1 small onion, thinly sliced
- 1 cup sliced fresh mushrooms
- 1 envelope brown gravy mix
- 1/3 cup sour cream

Direction

- Sprinkle pepper and seasoned salt over steaks. Brown both sides of steaks with oil in a big skillet, then turn to an 11"x7" baking dish.
- Sauté mushrooms and onion together in the same skillet until softened, then scoop over steaks. Following package directions to prepare gravy and stir in sour cream, then pour over steaks.
- Cover and bake at 350 degrees until meat reaches wanted doneness (for medium-rare, a thermometer should read 145 degrees; medium, 160 degrees and well-done, 170 degrees), about 10 to 15 minutes.

Nutrition Information

- Calories: 448 calories
- Protein: 26g protein.
- Total Fat: 31g fat (13g saturated fat)
- Sodium: 1341mg sodium
- Fiber: 1g fiber)
- Total Carbohydrate: 14g carbohydrate (7g sugars
- Cholesterol: 94mg cholesterol

211. Mushroom Steak

Serving: 6 servings. | Prep: 20mins | Ready in:

Ingredients

- 1/3 cup all-purpose flour
- 1/2 teaspoon salt
- 1/2 teaspoon pepper, divided
- 1 beef top round steak (2 pounds), cut into 1-1/2-inch strips
- 2 cups sliced fresh mushrooms
- 1 small onion, cut into thin wedges
- 1 can (10-3/4 ounces) condensed golden mushroom soup, undiluted
- 1/4 cup sherry or beef broth
- 1/2 teaspoon dried oregano
- 1/4 teaspoon dried thyme
- Hot cooked egg noodles

Direction

- Mix 1/4 teaspoon pepper, flour, and salt together in a big resealable plastic bag. Add in beef, several pieces each time, and shake to coat.
- Combine the mushrooms, onion, and beef in a 3-qt slow cooker. Mix the leftover pepper, thyme, oregano, sherry, and soup together; pour over the top. Put the lid on and cook on low until the beef is soft, about 7-9 hours. Enjoy with noodles.

Nutrition Information

- Calories: 265 calories
- Sodium: 612mg sodium
- Fiber: 1g fiber)
- Total Carbohydrate: 12g carbohydrate (1g sugars
- Cholesterol: 87mg cholesterol
- Protein: 36g protein. Diabetic Exchanges: 5 lean meat
- Total Fat: 6g fat (2g saturated fat)

212. Mustard Crusted Prime Rib With Madeira Glaze

Serving: 8 servings. | Prep: 20mins | Ready in:

Ingredients

- 1 bone-in beef rib roast (about 5 pounds)
- 1/2 cup stone-ground mustard
- 6 small garlic cloves, minced
- 1 tablespoon brown sugar
- 1/2 teaspoon salt
- 1/2 teaspoon coarsely ground pink peppercorns, optional
- VEGETABLES:
- 2 pounds medium Yukon Gold potatoes, cut into eighths (about 2-inch chunks)
- 4 medium carrots, halved lengthwise and cut into 2-inch pieces
- 1 medium red onion, cut into eighths (but with root end intact)
- 1 medium fennel bulb, cut into eighths
- 3 tablespoons olive oil
- 1 tablespoon balsamic vinegar
- 1 teaspoon brown sugar
- 3/4 teaspoon salt
- 1/2 teaspoon pepper
- MADEIRA GLAZE:
- 1 cup balsamic vinegar
- 1/2 cup Madeira wine

- 1 teaspoon brown sugar
- Cracked pink peppercorns and fennel fronds, optional

Direction

- Allow the roast to stand at room temperature for about 1 hour. Preheat oven to 450°. Stir salt, brown sugar, garlic, mustard and, if wanted, peppercorns; evenly brush over sides and top of the roast, but not on the bones (the mixture might look loose, but will stick). Set on a rack in a shallow roasting pan with the bone side facing down. Position the pan on the center of oven rack; instantly lower heat to 350°. Let roast for 1 hour.
- Toss fennel, onion, carrots and potatoes with the next 5 ingredients. In a 15x10x1-inch baking pan on the lowest rack of oven, place vegetables in a single layer. Roast vegetables and meat, mix vegetables halfway through baking for around 1 and a half hours, till meat reaches the wanted doneness (a thermometer should show 135° for medium-rare, 140° for medium and 145° for medium-well). Use a foil to loosely cover the roast during the last 30 minutes to avoid overbrowning. Allow to stand for 15 minutes before carving.
- Meanwhile, for glaze, stir the brown sugar, Madeira wine and balsamic vinegar together in a small saucepan. Let it boil over medium-high heat; cook for around 15 minutes till lessened to a half cup. Allow the glaze to come to room temperature. Serve roast along with glaze and vegetables and, if wanted, fennel fronds and pink peppercorns.

Nutrition Information

- Calories: 575 calories
- Protein: 42g protein.
- Total Fat: 25g fat (8g saturated fat)
- Sodium: 828mg sodium
- Fiber: 5g fiber)
- Total Carbohydrate: 44g carbohydrate (18g sugars
- Cholesterol: 0 cholesterol

213. Nacho Cheese Beef Bake

Serving: 4 servings. | Prep: 25mins | Ready in:

Ingredients

- 2 cups uncooked egg noodles
- 1 pound ground beef
- 1 can (14-1/2 ounces) diced tomatoes, undrained
- 1 can (10-3/4 ounces) condensed nacho cheese soup, undiluted
- 1 jar (5-3/4 ounces) sliced pimiento-stuffed olives, drained
- 1 can (4 ounces) chopped green chilies
- 1-1/2 cups shredded cheddar cheese
- 2 cups crushed tortilla chips
- 1/3 cup prepared ranch salad dressing
- Shredded lettuce, sour cream and/or salsa, optional

Direction

- Following the package instructions, cook the noodles; drain. At the same time, cook the beef in a large saucepan over medium heat until it is not pink anymore; then drain the beef. Stir in chilies, olives, soup, and tomatoes. Boil. Turn down the heat; simmer without covering for 10 minutes. Add noodles and stir.
- Place into an 11x7-inch baking dish coated with cooking spray. Dust with cheese. Bake at 350 degrees until heated through, 15-20 minutes. Put tortilla chips on top; sprinkle with the salad dressing. If desired, serve alongside sour cream, lettuce, or/and salsa.

Nutrition Information

- Calories: 827 calories
- Cholesterol: 158mg cholesterol
- Protein: 42g protein.
- Total Fat: 55g fat (24g saturated fat)

- Sodium: 2131mg sodium
- Fiber: 4g fiber)
- Total Carbohydrate: 41g carbohydrate (6g sugars

214. Nebraska Beef Rolls

Serving: 8 servings. | Prep: 20mins | Ready in:

Ingredients

- 2 large eggs, beaten
- 1/4 cup ketchup
- 2 tablespoons Worcestershire sauce
- 1 cup shredded cheddar cheese
- 1/4 cup finely chopped onion
- 2 tablespoons grated Parmesan cheese
- 1 teaspoon salt
- 1/4 teaspoon pepper
- 2 pounds ground beef
- 12 bacon strips

Direction

- Blend the first 8 ingredients together in a bowl. Put in beef and stir well. Form the mixture into two 6" rolls. On a big waxed paper sheet, lay 6 bacon strips side by side. Transfer one roll onto the bacon. Wrap bacon around the loaf while rolling up, then use toothpicks to secure. Do the same thing to the other loaf. Put into a 13x9" ungreased baking pan. Bake for 45-50 minutes at 375 degrees or until the meat thermometer reaches 160 degrees and no longer pink on the inside. Remove toothpicks.

Nutrition Information

- Calories: 498 calories
- Total Carbohydrate: 4g carbohydrate (1g sugars
- Cholesterol: 167mg cholesterol
- Protein: 31g protein.
- Total Fat: 39g fat (16g saturated fat)

- Sodium: 852mg sodium
- Fiber: 0 fiber)

215. New Year's Eve Tenderloin Steaks

Serving: 2 servings. | Prep: 30mins | Ready in:

Ingredients

- 2 beef tenderloin steaks (1 inch thick and 5 ounces each)
- 1/4 teaspoon pepper
- 1 tablespoon canola oil
- 3 shallots, finely chopped
- 2 tablespoons Cognac
- 1/4 teaspoon whole peppercorns, crushed
- 1/2 cup dry red wine or beef broth
- 1/4 cup beef broth
- 2 ounces fresh goat cheese, crumbled

Direction

- Sprinkle pepper over steaks. Cook steaks with oil in a big skillet over moderate heat until the meat reaches wanted doneness (for medium-rare, a thermometer should read 145 degrees; medium, 160 degrees; well-done, 170 degrees), about 4 to 6 minutes per side. Remove to a baking sheet and keep warm.
- Lower heat to low, put in peppercorns, Cognac and shallots while stirring to loosen browned bits from pan. Stir in broth and wine, bring to a boil over moderate heat and cook until liquid is reduced to 1/2 cup.
- Put cheese on top of steaks, broil 6 inches from the heat until cheese is softened, about 2 to 3 minutes. Serve steaks and sauce mixture together.

Nutrition Information

- Calories: 444 calories
- Sodium: 234mg sodium

- Fiber: 0 fiber)
- Total Carbohydrate: 14g carbohydrate (3g sugars
- Cholesterol: 81mg cholesterol
- Protein: 35g protein.
- Total Fat: 19g fat (6g saturated fat)

- Total Fat: 10g fat (4g saturated fat)
- Sodium: 1152mg sodium
- Fiber: 5g fiber)
- Total Carbohydrate: 39g carbohydrate (18g sugars
- Cholesterol: 36mg cholesterol

216. Okie Beans

Serving: 16-20 servings. | Prep: 10mins | Ready in:

Ingredients

- 1-1/2 pounds ground beef
- 1 medium onion, chopped
- 1 pound Johnsonville® Fully Cooked Smoked Sausage Rope, cut into 1/2-inch slices
- 1 cup cubed fully cooked ham
- 1 cup packed brown sugar
- 2 tablespoons prepared mustard
- 2 tablespoons vinegar
- 1 bottle (32 ounces) ketchup
- 1 can (16 ounces) kidney beans, undrained
- 1 can (16 ounces) great northern beans, undrained
- 1 can (15 ounces) pinto beans, undrained
- 1 can (16 ounces) butter beans, undrained

Direction

- Add onion and ground beef to a Dutch oven or a big frying pan, cook until the onion gets tender and beef turns brown; drain. Add the ham and sausage.
- Mix the ketchup, vinegar, mustard and brown sugar together and mix into the beef mixture. Mix in all beans. Simmer while uncovered until the sauce gets thick, about 2 to 2 1/2 hours, stirring periodically.

Nutrition Information

- Calories: 299 calories
- Protein: 16g protein.

217. Old Fashioned Beef Brisket

Serving: 12 servings. | Prep: 20mins | Ready in:

Ingredients

- 1 fresh beef brisket (4 pounds)
- 2 tablespoons canola oil
- 2 large sweet onions, sliced
- 2 cups ketchup
- 2 cups water
- 1/2 cup dry red wine or beef broth

Direction

- Brown the meat on all sides in oil in a Dutch oven and then drain. Add onions on top. Mix wine, water and ketchup. Spread atop onions and meat.
- Cover and then bake for 3 to 3-1/2 hours at 350° or until the meat becomes tender. Allow to sit for five minutes. Slice brisket thinly across the grain. If desired, thicken the sauce and then serve along with beef.

Nutrition Information

- Calories: 277 calories
- Total Carbohydrate: 15g carbohydrate (13g sugars
- Cholesterol: 64mg cholesterol
- Protein: 31g protein. Diabetic Exchanges: 4 lean meat
- Total Fat: 9g fat (3g saturated fat)
- Sodium: 562mg sodium
- Fiber: 0 fiber)

218. Old World Corned Beef And Vegetables

Serving: 8 servings. | Prep: 25mins | Ready in:

Ingredients

- 2-1/2 pounds red potatoes, quartered
- 2 cups fresh baby carrots
- 1 package (10 ounces) frozen pearl onions
- 1 corned beef brisket with spice packet (3 to 3-1/2 pounds)
- 1/2 cup water
- 1 tablespoon marinade for chicken
- 1/8 teaspoon pepper
- 3 tablespoons cornstarch
- 1/4 cup cold water

Direction

- Mix onions, carrots and potatoes in 5-qt. slow cooker. Add beef; throw corned beef spice packet/keep for another time. Mix pepper, marinade for chicken and water; put on meat. Cover; cook till veggies and meat are tender for 8-10 hours on low.
- Put veggies and meat on serving platter; keep them warm. From cooking juices, skim fat; put in small saucepan. Boil. Mix cold water and cornstarch till smooth; mix into pan slowly. Boil; mix and cook till thick for 1-2 minutes. Serve with veggies and meat.

Nutrition Information

- Calories: 446 calories
- Total Fat: 23g fat (8g saturated fat)
- Sodium: 1419mg sodium
- Fiber: 3g fiber)
- Total Carbohydrate: 34g carbohydrate (5g sugars
- Cholesterol: 117mg cholesterol
- Protein: 25g protein.

219. One Pot Saucy Beef Rotini

Serving: 4 servings. | Prep: 10mins | Ready in:

Ingredients

- 3/4 pound lean ground beef (90% lean)
- 2 cups sliced fresh mushrooms
- 1 medium onion, chopped
- 3 garlic cloves, minced
- 3/4 teaspoon Italian seasoning
- 2 cups tomato basil pasta sauce
- 1/4 teaspoon salt
- 2-1/2 cups water
- 3 cups uncooked whole wheat rotini (about 8 ounces)
- 1/4 cup grated Parmesan cheese

Direction

- Cook the first 5 ingredients together in a 6-quart stock pot on medium high heat until beef is not pink anymore, or about 6 to 8 minutes. Break up cooked beef into crumbles and drain.
- Put in pasta sauce, water and salt, then bring the mixture to a boil. Stir in rotini and bring mixture back to a boil. Lower the heat and simmer with a cover until pasta is al dente while stirring sometimes, or about 8 to 10 minutes. Serve together with cheese.

Nutrition Information

- Calories: 414 calories
- Cholesterol: 57mg cholesterol
- Protein: 28g protein.
- Total Fat: 11g fat (4g saturated fat)
- Sodium: 806mg sodium
- Fiber: 8g fiber)
- Total Carbohydrate: 49g carbohydrate (12g sugars

220. Orange Flank Steak

Serving: 4 servings. | Prep: 10mins | Ready in:

Ingredients

- 1/4 cup orange juice
- 1/4 cup canola oil
- 2 tablespoons ketchup
- 4-1/2 teaspoons soy sauce
- 2 garlic cloves, minced
- 1 teaspoon grated orange zest
- 1/8 teaspoon hot pepper sauce
- 1 beef flank steak (1 pound)
- 1 medium orange, sliced

Direction

- Mix all the initial 7 ingredients together in a big bowl. Put in the beef and turn to coat evenly with the mixture. Cover the bowl and keep in the fridge for 8 hours or throughout the night.
- Put the steak in a broiler and let it broil 4-6 inches away from heat or put the steak on a grill over medium-hot heat then cover and let it grill for 4 to 6 minutes on every side until the preferred meat doneness is achieved (a thermometer inserted on the meat should indicate 145°F for medium-well, 140°F for medium and 135°F for medium-rare). Let it sit for 10 minutes.
- While the meat is grilling, let the sliced oranges grill or broil for 2 minutes. Cut the steak into thin slices perpendicular to the grain then serve. Top it with grilled sliced oranges.

Nutrition Information

- Calories: 322 calories
- Sodium: 509mg sodium
- Fiber: 0 fiber
- Total Carbohydrate: 6g carbohydrate (5g sugars
- Cholesterol: 54mg cholesterol
- Protein: 23g protein.
- Total Fat: 22g fat (5g saturated fat)

221. Oven Stew And Biscuits

Serving: 6-8 servings. | Prep: 20mins | Ready in:

Ingredients

- 1/3 cup all-purpose flour
- 1 teaspoon salt
- 1/2 teaspoon pepper
- 2 pounds beef top sirloin, cut into 1-inch cubes
- 1/4 cup canola oil
- 1 can (14-1/2 ounces) stewed tomatoes
- 1 jar (4-1/2 ounces) sliced mushrooms, drained
- 1 large onion, thinly sliced
- 3 tablespoons soy sauce
- 3 tablespoons molasses
- 1 medium green pepper, cut into 1-inch pieces
- 1 tube (12 ounces) refrigerated buttermilk biscuits
- 1 teaspoon butter, melted
- Sesame seeds

Direction

- Combine pepper, salt, and flour in a large resealable plastic bag. Working in batches, add beef into the bag and shake until evenly coated. Cook beef in batches in oil over medium heat until browned in a large skillet. Add all of the cooked beef back into the pan; mix in molasses, soy sauce, onion, mushrooms, and tomatoes.
- Pour the mixture into an oiled 13x9-inch baking dish. Bake, covered for 20 minutes at 375°. Mix in green pepper. Bake, covered for 10 more minutes.
- Remove cover; lay biscuits on top. Brush butter over biscuits; scatter with sesame seeds.

Bake until biscuits turn golden brown, or about 15 to 18 minutes longer.
- \

Nutrition Information

- Calories: 387 calories
- Sodium: 1222mg sodium
- Fiber: 2g fiber)
- Total Carbohydrate: 37g carbohydrate (8g sugars
- Cholesterol: 47mg cholesterol
- Protein: 30g protein.
- Total Fat: 13g fat (3g saturated fat)

222. Papa Burger

Serving: 4 servings. | Prep: 20mins | Ready in:

Ingredients

- 1 pound ground beef or ground buffalo
- 1/3 cup finely chopped onion
- 1 slice whole wheat or white bread, broken into small pieces
- 2 tablespoons red wine vinegar
- 1 tablespoon liquid smoke
- 2 teaspoons Worcestershire sauce
- 1 teaspoon hamburger or steak seasoning
- 1/4 to 1/2 teaspoon garlic salt
- 1/4 to 1/2 teaspoon pepper
- 1/4 cup all-purpose flour
- 4 onion hamburger buns, split
- 4 Bibb or Boston lettuce leaves
- 1/3 cup prepared Thousand Island salad dressing
- 4 slices red onion
- 1 large heirloom tomato, sliced

Direction

- Mix the first 9 ingredients together lightly; form into 4, 3/4-inch thick patties. Press and lightly coat each side of the patties in flour.
- On medium heat, cook burgers for 4-5mins on each side in a big non-stick pan until an inserted thermometer registers 160 degrees F. In a layer, arrange lettuce and burgers on bun bottoms. Add salad dressing then top with tomato and onion slices; place the bun tops.

Nutrition Information

- Calories: 464 calories
- Cholesterol: 77mg cholesterol
- Protein: 26g protein.
- Total Fat: 22g fat (6g saturated fat)
- Sodium: 713mg sodium
- Fiber: 3g fiber)
- Total Carbohydrate: 37g carbohydrate (8g sugars

223. Pepper Jack Smothered Cheeseburgers

Serving: 4 servings. | Prep: 30mins | Ready in:

Ingredients

- 1/2 cup honey mustard salad dressing
- 1 tablespoon lime juice
- 1 tablespoon minced chipotle pepper in adobo sauce
- BURGERS:
- 1 egg white, beaten
- 1/4 cup crushed tortilla chips
- 3 tablespoons minced seeded jalapeno peppers
- 1/2 teaspoon salt
- 1 pound ground chicken
- TOPPINGS:
- 2 poblano peppers, julienned
- 2 Anaheim peppers, julienned
- 1 medium sweet red pepper, julienned
- 1 small onion, halved and sliced
- 2 tablespoons canola oil
- 3 tablespoons minced fresh cilantro
- 1/4 teaspoon salt

- 4 slices pepper Jack cheese
- 4 hamburger buns, split

Direction

- To make glaze, combine chipotle pepper, lime juice, and salad dressing in a blender; put the lid on, and puree until blended. Put to one side.
- Mix salt, jalapenos, tortilla chips, and egg white together in a large bowl. Crumble chicken over the mixture and mix well. Form mixture into 4 patties. Arrange in an oiled 15x10x1-inch baking pan. Bake for 9 to 11 minutes on each side at 375° until juices run clear and a thermometer reaches 165°, basting with glaze occasionally.
- In the meantime, sauté onion and peppers in oil in a large skillet until tender but crisp. Turn off the heat; mix in salt and cilantro.
- Top burgers with pepper mixture and cheese. Broil 4 inches away from the heat until cheese is melted, for 2 to 3 minutes. Serve on buns.

Nutrition Information

- Calories: 581 calories
- Protein: 30g protein.
- Total Fat: 36g fat (9g saturated fat)
- Sodium: 1113mg sodium
- Fiber: 4g fiber)
- Total Carbohydrate: 38g carbohydrate (11g sugars
- Cholesterol: 98mg cholesterol

- 1/2 to 1 teaspoon salt
- 1/2 teaspoon pepper
- 1-1/2 pounds lean ground beef (90% lean)
- 1 cup (4 ounces) pepper jack cheese, divided
- 1 cup salsa, optional

Direction

- Combine pepper, salt, onion, bread crumbs, and egg in a large mixing bowl. Crumble beef over mixture and stir to combine. Pat 1/2 of the beef mixture onto the bottom and halfway up the sides of an oiled 8x4-inch loaf pan. Scatter 3/4 cup cheese over meat to within 1/2 inch of the sides. Press the remainder of beef mixture over cheese.
- Bake without covering for 50 to 55 minutes at 350° until center is no longer pink and thermometer registers 160°. Scatter top with the remainder of cheese. Bake until cheese is melted, for 5 more minutes. Allow to rest for 10 minutes before cutting. If desired, serve meatloaf with salsa.

Nutrition Information

- Calories: 331 calories
- Fiber: 1g fiber)
- Total Carbohydrate: 15g carbohydrate (1g sugars
- Cholesterol: 111mg cholesterol
- Protein: 30g protein.
- Total Fat: 16g fat (7g saturated fat)
- Sodium: 681mg sodium

224. Pepper Jack Meat Loaf

Serving: 6 servings. | Prep: 20mins | Ready in:

Ingredients

- 1 egg, lightly beaten
- 1 cup seasoned bread crumbs
- 1/4 cup chopped onion

225. Peppered Meatballs

Serving: 1-1/2 dozen. | Prep: 35mins | Ready in:

Ingredients

- 1/2 cup sour cream
- 2 teaspoons grated Parmesan or Romano cheese

- 2 to 3 teaspoons pepper
- 1 teaspoon salt
- 1 teaspoon dry bread crumbs
- 1/2 teaspoon garlic powder
- 1-1/2 pounds ground beef
- SAUCE:
- 1 can (10-3/4 ounces) condensed cream of mushroom soup, undiluted
- 1 cup (8 ounces) sour cream
- 2 teaspoons dill weed
- 1/2 teaspoon sugar
- 1/2 teaspoon pepper
- 1/4 teaspoon garlic powder

Direction

- Combine cheese and sour cream in a large bowl. Add garlic powder, bread crumbs, salt, and pepper. Crumble the meat over the mixture and mix well. Roll into 1-in. balls.
- In a shallow baking pan, place the meatballs on a greased rack. Bake at 350° until no more pink, for 20-25 minutes; drain.
- Transfer the meatballs to a 1-1/2-qt. slow cooker. Mix the sauce ingredients, then pour over the meatballs. Cook on high, covered, until heated through, for 2-3 hours.

Nutrition Information

- Calories: 259 calories
- Fiber: 0 fiber)
- Total Carbohydrate: 5g carbohydrate (2g sugars
- Cholesterol: 77mg cholesterol
- Protein: 17g protein.
- Total Fat: 18g fat (9g saturated fat)
- Sodium: 565mg sodium

226. Peppered Ribeye Roast

Serving: 24-30 servings. | Prep: 15mins | Ready in:

Ingredients

- 1/3 to 1/2 cup coarsely ground pepper
- 1 teaspoon ground cardamom
- 2 beef ribeye roasts (5 to 6 pounds each)
- 2 cups soy sauce
- 1-1/2 cups cider vinegar
- 2 tablespoons tomato paste
- 2 teaspoons garlic powder
- 2 teaspoons paprika

Direction

- Mix the cardamom and pepper; rub it all over roasts. Combine paprika, garlic powder, tomato paste, vinegar and soy sauce in a big bowl. Divide the mixture into 2 halves and separately pour into two big resealable plastic bags; put each roast in each bag. Seal the bags and turn to coat; store in the fridge overnight.
- Drain and remove marinade. Transfer each roast to a roasting pan. Bake at 350° without a cover for 2 hours or until the meat is done as desired (a food thermometer should read 145° for medium-rare, 160° for medium, and 170° for well-done).

Nutrition Information

- Calories:
- Total Carbohydrate:
- Cholesterol:
- Protein:
- Total Fat:
- Sodium:
- Fiber:

227. Peppered Steaks With Salsa

Serving: 4 servings. | Prep: 25mins | Ready in:

Ingredients

- 1/2 cup red wine vinegar
- 2 tablespoons lime juice

- 2 tablespoons olive oil
- 2 teaspoons chili powder
- 1 garlic clove, minced
- 1 to 2 teaspoons crushed red pepper flakes
- 1 teaspoon salt
- 1/2 teaspoon pepper
- 4 beef eye round steaks (6 ounces each)
- SALSA:
- 1 large tomato, seeded and chopped
- 1 medium ripe avocado, chopped
- 2 green onions, thinly sliced
- 1 tablespoon lime juice
- 1 tablespoon minced fresh cilantro
- 1 garlic clove, minced
- 1/4 to 1/2 teaspoon salt
- 1/4 teaspoon pepper

Direction

- Mix the initial 8 ingredients together in a bowl. Transfer half cup of the mixture in a bog ziplock bag; put in steak. Seal and flip the bag to coat beef with marinade. Let it chill in the refrigerator for eight hours to overnight. Cover the leftover marinade for basting and refrigerate.
- Mix the salsa ingredients together; cover and refrigerate.
- Drain steaks and get rid of the marinade. On medium heat, grill steaks for 7-8 mins per side while covered until it reaches the preferred doneness (an inserted thermometer in the steak should register 170° Fahrenheit for well-done, 160 degrees F for medium done, and 145° Fahrenheit for medium rare). Use the reserved marinade to baste. Serve steak with salsa.

Nutrition Information

- Calories:
- Fiber:
- Total Carbohydrate:
- Cholesterol:
- Protein:
- Total Fat:

- Sodium:

228. Peppy Potato Casserole

Serving: 4 servings. | Prep: 15mins | Ready in:

Ingredients

- 2 cans (8 ounces each) tomato sauce
- 1-1/2 cups water
- 1-1/2 teaspoons Italian seasoning
- 1 package (4.9 ounces) scalloped potatoes
- 1/2 pound ground beef
- 24 pepperoni slices
- 4 ounces sliced provolone cheese
- 1/2 cup shredded part-skim mozzarella cheese
- 1 tablespoon grated Parmesan cheese

Direction

- Mix Italian seasoning, water, and tomato sauce together in a big saucepan; boil it. Add contents of sauce mix and potatoes. Remove into a non-oiled 2-quart baking dish.
- In the meantime, cook beef in a big frying pan over medium heat until no pink remains; strain. Add to the potatoes, put pepperoni on top.
- Bake without a cover for 20 minutes at 400°. Put cheeses on top. Bake until the potatoes are soft, about another 15-20 minutes.

Nutrition Information

- Calories: 455 calories
- Sodium: 1392mg sodium
- Fiber: 4g fiber)
- Total Carbohydrate: 30g carbohydrate (3g sugars
- Cholesterol: 81mg cholesterol
- Protein: 28g protein.
- Total Fat: 25g fat (12g saturated fat)

229. Philly Cheesesteak Rolls

Serving: 4 servings. | Prep: 30mins | Ready in:

Ingredients

- 1/2 pound sliced fresh mushrooms
- 1 medium onion, halved and sliced
- 1 small green pepper, cut into thin strips
- 1 beef top round steak (1 pound)
- 4 wedges The Laughing Cow light Swiss cheese
- 1/4 teaspoon pepper
- 3 cups hot mashed potatoes (made with fat-free milk)

Direction

- Set oven to 450° to preheat. Put a big nonstick skillet greased with cooking spray over medium-high heat. Put in green pepper, onion and mushrooms; cook and mix for 8-10 minutes until tender. Take out of pan; let rest to cool a little.
- Chop steak into 4 slices; pound with a meat mallet to 1/4 inch thickness. Scatter cheese on top. Dust with pepper; top with mushroom mixture. From the shorter side, roll it up; secure with toothpicks. Put in a 15x10x1 inch baking dish that has been foil-lined.
- Bake 12 to 17 minutes until meat comes to the doneness as desired (medium 160°; medium-rare 145°). Let sit 5 minutes prior to serving. Serve together with mashed potatoes.

Nutrition Information

- Calories: 364 calories
- Sodium: 822mg sodium
- Fiber: 4g fiber)
- Total Carbohydrate: 34g carbohydrate (5g sugars
- Cholesterol: 68mg cholesterol
- Protein: 33g protein. Diabetic Exchanges: 4 lean meat
- Total Fat: 10g fat (3g saturated fat)

230. Philly Steak Potatoes

Serving: 4 servings. | Prep: 10mins | Ready in:

Ingredients

- 4 large baking potatoes
- 1-1/2 cups frozen pepper strips
- 1 cup chopped onion
- 1/4 cup butter, cubed
- 1 pound sliced deli roast beef, cut into thin strips
- 1 cup shredded Colby cheese
- 1/4 cup mayonnaise
- 3/4 teaspoon prepared horseradish

Direction

- Scrub and pierce the potatoes; put onto a microwavable plate. Microwave, with no cover, over high setting till soften or for 15 to 17 minutes, flipping one time.
- At the same time, in the big skillet, cook the onion and peppers in butter on medium heat till soften. Whisk in the roast beef; heat completely.
- Cut one "X" in each potato's tops; fluff the pulp using fork. Scoop the meat mixture in the potatoes; scatter cheese over.
- Mix the horseradish and mayonnaise; scoop on the tops.

Nutrition Information

- Calories: 747 calories
- Protein: 37g protein.
- Total Fat: 35g fat (16g saturated fat)
- Sodium: 987mg sodium
- Fiber: 7g fiber)
- Total Carbohydrate: 73g carbohydrate (9g sugars
- Cholesterol: 123mg cholesterol

231. Picante Cranberry Meatballs

Serving: 8 servings. | Prep: 20mins | Ready in:

Ingredients

- 2 eggs, lightly beaten
- 1/3 cup ketchup
- 1/3 cup minced fresh parsley
- 2 tablespoons soy sauce
- 2 tablespoons dried minced onion
- 1/2 teaspoon garlic powder
- 1/4 teaspoon pepper
- 1 cup crushed saltines (about 30 crackers)
- 2 pounds lean ground beef (90% lean)
- SAUCE:
- 1 can (14 ounces) jellied cranberry sauce
- 1 cup chili sauce
- 1/4 cup picante sauce
- 2 tablespoons brown sugar
- 1 tablespoon lemon juice
- Hot cooked noodles, optional

Direction

- Blend pepper, garlic powder, onion, soy sauce, parsley, ketchup, and eggs in the large bowl. Put in cracker crumbs. Crumble the beef and place over the mixture, combine properly. Form into 1 1/2-inch balls.
- Brown the meatballs in a skillet on medium heat. Place into a 13x9-inch baking dish coated with cooking spray.
- Blend the lemon juice, brown sugar, Picante sauce, chili sauce, and cranberry sauce in a large saucepan. Stir and cook until the mixture is cooked thoroughly and the cranberry sauce melts. Add to the meatballs.
- Put a cover on and bake at 350 degrees until the meat is not pink anymore, 30-35 minutes. If desired, serve alongside noodles.

Nutrition Information

- Calories: 363 calories
- Protein: 25g protein.
- Total Fat: 10g fat (4g saturated fat)
- Sodium: 1043mg sodium
- Fiber: 1g fiber)
- Total Carbohydrate: 42g carbohydrate (26g sugars
- Cholesterol: 109mg cholesterol

232. Pineapple Beef Stir Fry

Serving: Makes 4 servings. | Prep: 15mins | Ready in:

Ingredients

- 1 can (8 oz.) pineapple chunks in juice, undrained
- 1 Tbsp. oil
- 1 beef flank steak (1 lb.), cut across the grain into thin strips
- 1/2 cup chopped green onions
- 1 clove garlic, minced
- 2 Tbsp. water
- 1 Tbsp. cornstarch
- 1/4 cup A.1. Original Sauce

Direction

- Drain the pineapple and reserve its liquid; put aside. Put oil into the large skillet and heat it over medium-high. Stir in steak and cook for 5 minutes until cooked through. Add the garlic, onions, and pineapple. Cook for 2 minutes while stirring the mixture. Adjust the heat to low.
- Mix the cornstarch, reserved pineapple liquid, and water until well-combined. Add this mixture into the steak mixture. Cook for 1 minute, stirring constantly until thickened. Remove it from the heat.
- Mix in steak sauce and serve it over rice.

Nutrition Information

- Calories: 250
- Total Fat: 11 g
- Sodium: 340 mg
- Cholesterol: 65 mg
- Saturated Fat: 3.5 g
- Fiber: 0.8055 g
- Sugar: 9 g
- Total Carbohydrate: 14 g
- Protein: 22 g

233. Pineapple Red Pepper Beef Stir Fry

Serving: 4 servings. | Prep: 10mins | Ready in:

Ingredients

- 1/2 cup soy sauce
- 2 garlic cloves, minced
- 1 teaspoon ground ginger
- 1 pound beef top sirloin steak, cut into 1/4-inch thin strips
- 1 tablespoon canola oil
- 2 celery ribs, thinly sliced
- 1 cup cubed sweet red pepper
- 1 cup sliced green onions
- 1 cup sliced fresh mushrooms
- 1 can (20 ounces) pineapple chunks
- 1 can (8 ounces) sliced water chestnuts, drained
- 2 to 3 tablespoons cornstarch
- 1/2 cup water
- Hot cooked rice

Direction

- Mix ginger, garlic and soy sauce in a big resealable plastic bag. Add beef; flip to coat. Stand for 15 minutes.
- Stir-fry beef mixture for 2 minutes in oil in a big skillet. Add red pepper and celery; stir-fry it for 2 minutes. Add mushrooms and onions; cook for 2 minutes.
- Drain pineapple; keep juice. Mix water chestnuts and pineapple into skillet. Mix reserved pineapple juice, water and cornstarch till smooth in a small bowl; mix into veggies and beef slowly. Boil; mix and cook till thick for 1-2 minutes. Serve with rice.

Nutrition Information

- Calories: 351 calories
- Total Fat: 9g fat (3g saturated fat)
- Sodium: 1916mg sodium
- Fiber: 5g fiber)
- Total Carbohydrate: 39g carbohydrate (21g sugars
- Cholesterol: 63mg cholesterol
- Protein: 28g protein.

234. Pineapple Sirloin Kabobs

Serving: 4 servings. | Prep: 20mins | Ready in:

Ingredients

- 1 can (8 ounces) unsweetened pineapple chunks
- 1/2 cup water
- 1/2 cup soy sauce
- 1 teaspoon garlic powder
- 1/2 teaspoon salt
- 1/4 teaspoon ground ginger
- 1/4 teaspoon paprika
- 1 pound beef top sirloin steak, cut into 1-inch pieces
- 16 medium fresh mushrooms
- 1 large onion, cut into chunks
- 1 medium green pepper, cut into 1-inch pieces
- 1/2 cup butter, melted

Direction

- Reserve the juice from the pineapples and refrigerate the fruit. Pour the pineapple juice in a large re-sealable plastic bag along with the soy sauce, water, salt, garlic powder, paprika, and ginger. Add the steak, zip the top, and turn to coat the steak with marinade. Keep refrigerated for at least half hour. Drain the steak, discarding its marinade. Alternately thread the steak, onions, mushrooms, pineapples, and green peppers. Place on the medium-hot grill, cover, and cook for 4-5 minutes on each side, or until meat is cooked to liking. You may also broil 4-6 in. from the heat. Turn and baste frequently with butter.

Nutrition Information

- Calories:
- Cholesterol:
- Protein:
- Total Fat:
- Sodium:
- Fiber:
- Total Carbohydrate:

235. Pinwheel Pizza Loaf

Serving: 12 servings. | Prep: 15mins | Ready in:

Ingredients

- 2 large eggs
- Salt and pepper to taste
- 3 pounds lean ground beef (90% lean)
- 6 thin slices deli ham
- 2 cups shredded part-skim mozzarella cheese
- 1 jar (14 ounces) pizza sauce

Direction

- In a big bowl, whip pepper, salt and eggs. Break up the beef on top of eggs and stir them well. On a heavy-duty foil piece, pat the beef mixture into a rectangle 12x10-inchin size. Use cheese and ham to cover to within half an inch of the edges. Roll up like jelly-roll, beginning with the short side and peeling away the foil when rolling. Seal the seam and ends.
- Position loaf with the seam-side facing downward in the greased 13x9-inch baking dish. Add the pizza sauce on top. Bake, with no cover, at 350 degrees till the meat is not pink anymore and a thermometer reaches 160 degrees or for 1.25 hours. Allow it to rest for 10 minutes prior to slicing.

Nutrition Information

- Calories:
- Total Carbohydrate:
- Cholesterol:
- Protein:
- Total Fat:
- Sodium:
- Fiber:

236. Pizza Burgers

Serving: 6 servings. | Prep: 10mins | Ready in:

Ingredients

- 1 can (6 ounces) tomato paste
- 1/2 teaspoon salt
- 1/2 teaspoon dried oregano
- 1/4 teaspoon garlic salt
- 1/4 teaspoon pepper
- 1/4 teaspoon aniseed
- 1-1/2 pounds lean ground beef (90% lean)
- 1/2 cup shredded part-skim mozzarella cheese
- 6 hamburger buns, split
- 6 lettuce leaves
- 6 tomato slices

Direction

- Mix together the initial 6 ingredients in a big bowl. Crumble the beef on top of the mixture and stir well, then form it into 6 patties. Put it on a cooking spray coated broiler pan.
- Let it broil for 5 to 6 minutes per side, placed 6 inches from the heat source or until the juices

run clear. Sprinkle cheese on top and let it broil for 1 minute more or until the cheese melts. Serve with tomato and lettuce on buns.

Nutrition Information

- Calories: 346 calories
- Protein: 28g protein. Diabetic Exchanges: 3 lean meat
- Total Fat: 13g fat (5g saturated fat)
- Sodium: 628mg sodium
- Fiber: 3g fiber)
- Total Carbohydrate: 28g carbohydrate (8g sugars
- Cholesterol: 75mg cholesterol

237. Pizza Hot Dish

Serving: 12-16 servings. | Prep: 10mins | Ready in:

Ingredients

- 2 large eggs
- 1/2 cup whole milk
- 1 package (7 ounces) elbow macaroni, cooked and drained
- 1 pound ground beef
- 1 medium onion, chopped
- 1 can (10-3/4 ounces) condensed tomato soup, undiluted
- 1 teaspoon salt
- 1/2 teaspoon dried basil
- 1/2 teaspoon dried oregano
- 1/4 teaspoon pepper
- 2 cups shredded cheddar cheese

Direction

- Whisk eggs in a big bowl. Stir in macaroni and milk. Transfer into a 13x9-inch baking dish that is greased; reserve.
- Cook onion and beef in a big skillet over medium heat until meat is not pink; strain. Mix in the seasonings and soup.

- Scoop over the macaroni. Top with cheese. Place in the oven and bake for 20-25 minutes, uncovered, at 350°F or until heated through.

Nutrition Information

- Calories: 153 calories
- Sodium: 370mg sodium
- Fiber: 1g fiber)
- Total Carbohydrate: 8g carbohydrate (3g sugars
- Cholesterol: 61mg cholesterol
- Protein: 11g protein.
- Total Fat: 8g fat (5g saturated fat)

238. Pizza Lasagna

Serving: 12 | Prep: 20mins | Ready in:

Ingredients

- 1 (8 ounce) package lasagna noodles
- 6 Cajun-style sausage links, casings removed
- 2 (24 ounce) jars marinara sauce
- 1 (7 ounce) package sliced pepperoni
- 1 (8 ounce) package sliced fresh mushrooms
- 1 onion, sliced
- 1 large green bell pepper, chopped
- 2 (2.25 ounce) cans sliced black olives
- 2 (8 ounce) packages shredded pizza cheese blend

Direction

- Preheat oven to 175° C (350°F). Put light salt in water using a large pot and let it boil. Cook lasagna pasta in the boiling water, stir from time to time until tender yet firm to the bite for 8 minutes Drain.
- Put a large skillet to medium-high heat. Cook sausage in the hot skillet, break into bite size pieces until brown; about 5 -7 min.
- Pour layer of sauce in the bottom of a 9x13 inch baking dish. Place lasagna pasta side by

side. Pour more sauce. Ladle more sauce on top. Add pepperoni on the noodles and put sausage on top of pepperoni. Make a layer of mushrooms, onion, green bell pepper, black olives, and cheese blend on top. Continue to layer until all ingredients are used.
- Bake in the preheated oven until heated completely and bubbling about 35 min.

Nutrition Information

- Calories: 409 calories;
- Cholesterol: 50
- Protein: 17.9
- Total Fat: 23.1
- Sodium: 1153
- Total Carbohydrate: 33.2

239. Pizza With Hash Brown Crust

Serving: 8 servings. | Prep: 10mins | Ready in:

Ingredients

- 1 package (30 ounces) frozen shredded hash brown potatoes, thawed
- 1 can (10-3/4 ounces) condensed cheddar cheese soup, undiluted
- 1 pound ground beef
- 3 celery ribs, chopped
- 1 medium onion, chopped
- 1 can (8 ounces) tomato sauce
- 1 jar (6 ounces) sliced mushrooms, drained
- 1-1/4 teaspoons chili powder
- 3/4 teaspoon seasoned salt
- 1/2 teaspoon garlic powder
- 1/4 teaspoon pepper
- 2 cups shredded Colby-Monterey Jack cheese

Direction

- Mix the soup and hash browns in a large bowl. Transfer to a greased 15x10x1-inch baking pan and spread. Bake for 30 minutes at 400 degrees.
- In the meantime, cook the onion, celery, and beef in a large skillet over medium heat until vegetables are tender and meat is not pink; drain.
- Add pepper, garlic powder, seasoned salt, chili powder, mushrooms, and tomato sauce.
- Pour over the crust and spread. Scatter with cheese. Bake for 10 more minutes or until the cheese melts.

Nutrition Information

- Calories: 348 calories
- Fiber: 3g fiber)
- Total Carbohydrate: 28g carbohydrate (3g sugars
- Cholesterol: 67mg cholesterol
- Protein: 23g protein.
- Total Fat: 18g fat (10g saturated fat)
- Sodium: 884mg sodium

240. Plantation Supper

Serving: 8 servings. | Prep: 10mins | Ready in:

Ingredients

- 1-1/2 pounds ground beef
- 1 medium onion, chopped
- 1 can (15-1/4 ounces) whole kernel corn, drained
- 1 can (10-3/4 ounces) condensed cream of mushroom soup, undiluted
- 1 package (8 ounces) cream cheese, cubed
- 1 cup milk
- 1 teaspoon beef bouillon granules
- 1/4 teaspoon pepper
- 4-1/2 cups uncooked wide egg noodles

Direction

- In a big skillet on medium heat, cook onion and beef until the latter is not pink. Drain then add pepper, bouillon, milk, cream cheese, soup and corn. Cook until the cheese melts, stirring all throughout. Follow the instructions on the package to cook the noodles. Strain and rinse the noodles then add it into the skillet. Heat thoroughly.

Nutrition Information

- Calories: 444 calories
- Protein: 25g protein.
- Total Fat: 25g fat (12g saturated fat)
- Sodium: 657mg sodium
- Fiber: 2g fiber)
- Total Carbohydrate: 28g carbohydrate (6g sugars
- Cholesterol: 114mg cholesterol

241. Portobello Beef Burgundy

Serving: 6 servings. | Prep: 30mins | Ready in:

Ingredients

- 1/4 cup all-purpose flour
- 1/2 teaspoon salt
- 1/2 teaspoon seasoned salt
- 1-1/2 teaspoons minced fresh thyme or 1/2 teaspoon dried thyme
- 3/4 teaspoon minced fresh marjoram or 1/4 teaspoon dried thyme
- 1/2 teaspoon pepper
- 2 pounds beef sirloin tip steak, cubed
- 2 bacon strips, diced
- 3 tablespoons canola oil
- 1 garlic clove, minced
- 1 cup Burgundy wine or beef broth
- 1 teaspoon beef bouillon granules
- 1 pound sliced baby portobello mushrooms
- Hot cooked noodles, optional

Direction

- Combine the first 6 ingredients in a large resealable plastic bag. Add a few pieces of beef at a time until finish, and shake to coat.
- Cook bacon in a large skillet over medium heat until it's crispy. Transfer to paper towels to drain using a slotted spoon. Cook beef in batches in hot oil until browned in the same skillet, adding garlic to the last batch; cook for 1 to 2 minutes longer. Drain well.
- Transfer to a 4-quart slow cooker. Pour in wine into the skillet, stirring to loosen browned bits from the pan. Add bouillon; bring to a boil. Mix into slow cooker. Mix in bacon. Cook, covered on low setting until meat is tender, or for 7 to 9 hours.
- Mix in mushrooms. Cook, covered on high setting until sauce thickens slightly and mushrooms are tender, or for 30 to 45 minutes longer. Enjoy with noodles if desired.

Nutrition Information

- Calories: 321 calories
- Fiber: 1g fiber)
- Total Carbohydrate: 8g carbohydrate (2g sugars
- Cholesterol: 100mg cholesterol
- Protein: 34g protein.
- Total Fat: 15g fat (3g saturated fat)
- Sodium: 552mg sodium

242. Portobello Pizza Burgers

Serving: 4 servings. | Prep: 10mins | Ready in:

Ingredients

- 4 large portobello mushrooms (4 to 4-1/2 inches)
- 4 teaspoons plus 1 tablespoon olive oil, divided
- 1-1/2 cups finely chopped plum tomatoes
- 3/4 cup shredded part-skim mozzarella cheese
- 1-1/2 teaspoons Italian seasoning

- 4 hamburger buns, split

Direction

- Start heating broiler. Take the mushrooms and cut off and through away stems. Use a spoon to carefully take off the gills by scraping. Take 4 teaspoons of oil and brush mushroom caps. In a 15x10x1-in. ungreased pan, place mushrooms with stem side facing down. Put pan 4 in. from heat and broil for 5 minutes. In separate bowl, mix remaining oil, tomatoes, Italian seasoning, and cheese. Take the mushrooms out of the broiler and place tomato mixture in caps. Place back in broiler and broil until cheese is melty and mushrooms are tender, 4-6 minutes. Tastes great on buns.

Nutrition Information

- Calories: 284 calories
- Sodium: 314mg sodium
- Fiber: 3g fiber)
- Total Carbohydrate: 29g carbohydrate (7g sugars
- Cholesterol: 12mg cholesterol
- Protein: 12g protein. Diabetic Exchanges: 2 starch
- Total Fat: 13g fat (4g saturated fat)

243. Potato Beef Lasagna

Serving: 8 servings. | Prep: 20mins | Ready in:

Ingredients

- 1 pound lean ground beef
- 1/2 pound Johnsonville® Ground Mild Italian sausage
- 1 can (19 ounces) ready-to-serve tomato-basil soup
- 1 can (14-1/2 ounces) Italian diced tomatoes, undrained
- 1 package (20 ounces) refrigerated sliced potatoes
- 1 medium onion, thinly sliced
- 1 cup shredded part-skim mozzarella cheese
- 1-1/2 cups shredded Gruyere or Swiss cheese
- 3 tablespoons minced fresh parsley

Direction

- Let sausage and beef cook on medium fire in a big skillet. When beef is cooked with no pink color; drain the excess water. Add tomatoes and soup, stir. Put aside.
- Halve potatoes and onions and place into a 13x9 inches greased baking dish. Make the other half into layers. Use meat mixture and mozzarella cheese as topping.
- Place cover and let it bake for an hour at 350°. Remover the cover and top with Gruyere cheese. Let it bake for 10 to 15 minutes more. When cheese melts and potatoes become tender, wait for 10 minutes then serve. Top with parsley.

Nutrition Information

- Calories: 372 calories
- Total Fat: 17g fat (8g saturated fat)
- Sodium: 765mg sodium
- Fiber: 2g fiber)
- Total Carbohydrate: 26g carbohydrate (7g sugars
- Cholesterol: 71mg cholesterol
- Protein: 27g protein.

244. Pressure Cooker Beef Brisket In Beer

Serving: 6 servings. | Prep: 15mins | Ready in:

Ingredients

- 1 fresh beef brisket (2-1/2 to 3 pounds)
- 2 teaspoons liquid smoke, optional
- 1 teaspoon celery salt
- 1/2 teaspoon pepper

- 1/4 teaspoon salt
- 1 large onion, sliced
- 1 can (12 ounces) beer or nonalcoholic beer
- 2 teaspoons Worcestershire sauce
- 2 tablespoons cornstarch
- 1/4 cup cold water

Direction

- Slice brisket in half; rub liquid smoke (optional), together with pepper and salt, celery salt over brisket. Put brisket in a 6 quarts electric pressure cooker, fat side up. Top with onion Mix Worcestershire sauce and beer; put on top of meat. Close the lid; check if the vent is closed. Choose manual setting; turn pressure to high, set timer for 70 minutes. When completed cooking, let the pressure release naturally for 10 minutes, then quick release any leftover pressure following manufacturer's directions. Reseal cooker if meat isn't fork-tender and cook for 10 to 15 mins more.
- Take out brisket, put foil on brisket to cover and keep warm. Strain cooking juices, then pour juices into pressure cooker again. Choose sauté setting and turn on high heat; heat the liquid to a boil. Stir water and cornstarch in a small bowl until smooth; mix into juices slowly. Cook and mix for about 2 minutes until the sauce is thickened. Serve beef together with the sauce.

Nutrition Information

- Calories:
- Sodium:
- Fiber:
- Total Carbohydrate:
- Cholesterol:
- Protein:
- Total Fat:

245. Presto Beef Stew

Serving: 2 servings. | Prep: 10mins | Ready in:

Ingredients

- 2 individually frozen biscuits
- 2 tablespoons butter
- 2 cups sliced fresh mushrooms
- 1 package (17 ounces) refrigerated beef roast au jus
- 1/4 teaspoon pepper
- 2 tablespoons cornstarch
- 1 cup cold water

Direction

- Bake biscuits following the package's instructions.
- In the meantime, melt butter over medium heat in a big saucepan. Add mushrooms, stir and cook until soft. Use two forks to shred beef; add to the pan. Add pepper. Mix water and cornstarch together until smooth; mix into the stew. Boil it, stir and cook until thickened, or for about 1-2 minutes.
- Distribute the stew among 2 bowls; put a biscuit on top each.

Nutrition Information

- Calories: 710 calories
- Total Carbohydrate: 38g carbohydrate (10g sugars
- Cholesterol: 176mg cholesterol
- Protein: 54g protein.
- Total Fat: 40g fat (18g saturated fat)
- Sodium: 1595mg sodium
- Fiber: 2g fiber)

246. Prime Rib Of Beef

Serving: 8-10 servings. | Prep: 15mins | Ready in:

Ingredients

- 1/3 cup each chopped onion, carrot and celery
- 2 teaspoons salt
- 1/2 teaspoon pepper
- 1/2 teaspoon garlic powder
- 1 bone-in beef rib roast (6 to 8 pounds)
- 1 can (14-1/2 ounces) beef broth

Direction

- In a greased roasting pan, mix celery, carrot and onion. Mix garlic powder, pepper and salt; massage over the roast. Put on top of vegetables, fat side up. Bake at 350°, uncovered, for 2-1/2 to 3-1/2 hours or until meat comes to the doneness as desired (well-done, 170°; medium, 160°; medium-rare, 145°). Let it sit for 10 to 15 minutes before carving. Skim fat from pan drippings; pour in beef broth, mixing to remove browned chunks. Strain, throw veggies away. Serve au jus together with the roast.

Nutrition Information

- Calories:
- Protein:
- Total Fat:
- Sodium:
- Fiber:
- Total Carbohydrate:
- Cholesterol:

247. Prime Rib With Horseradish Cream

Serving: 12 servings (1-1/2 cups cream). | Prep: 30mins | Ready in:

Ingredients

- 1 bone-in beef rib roast (6 to 8 pounds)
- 3 garlic cloves, sliced
- 1 teaspoon pepper
- HORSERADISH CREAM:
- 1 cup heavy whipping cream
- 2 tablespoons prepared horseradish
- 2 teaspoons red wine vinegar
- 1 teaspoon ground mustard
- 1/4 teaspoon sugar
- 1/8 teaspoon salt
- Dash pepper

Direction

- In a shallow roasting pan, set roast, fat side-up. Make slits into roast; put in garlic slices. Scatter with pepper. Bake with no cover at 450° for about 15 minutes. Lessen heat to 325°; bake for 2-3/4 to 3-1/4 more hours, or till meat attains the desired doneness (a thermometer should read 145° for medium-rare, 160° for medium, and 170° for well-done).
- Meanwhile, in a small pot, beat cream to form soft peaks. Fold in the pepper, salt, sugar, mustard, vinegar and horseradish. Refrigerate with cover for 1 hour.
- Transfer roast to a serving platter. Keep warm and let rest for 15 minutes. Serve along with cream.

Nutrition Information

- Calories:
- Sodium:
- Fiber:
- Total Carbohydrate:
- Cholesterol:
- Protein:
- Total Fat:

248. Quick Chili Mac

Serving: 6 servings. | Prep: 5mins | Ready in:

Ingredients

- 1 cup uncooked elbow macaroni

- 1 pound ground beef
- 1 small green pepper, chopped
- 1 small onion, chopped
- 2 cans (15 ounces each) chili with beans
- 1 can (11 ounces) whole kernel corn, drained
- 1 cup shredded cheddar cheese

Direction

- Following the instructions on package, cook macaroni; drain off. At the same time, in the big skillet, cook and break up the beef with the onion and pepper on medium heat for 5 to 7 minutes or till not pink anymore; drain off.
- Whisk in the macaroni, corn and chili; thoroughly heat. Drizzle with the cheese.

Nutrition Information

- Calories: 422 calories
- Total Carbohydrate: 27g carbohydrate (6g sugars
- Cholesterol: 89mg cholesterol
- Protein: 30g protein.
- Total Fat: 21g fat (9g saturated fat)
- Sodium: 898mg sodium
- Fiber: 4g fiber)

249. Quick Corned Beef Hash

Serving: 6 servings. | Prep: 10mins | Ready in:

Ingredients

- 3 tablespoons butter, divided
- 4 cups refrigerated diced potatoes with onion
- 1-1/2 cups leftover cooked corned beef, diced
- 1 medium green pepper, diced
- 1 cup sliced fresh mushrooms
- 1 teaspoon salt
- 6 eggs
- 1/2 teaspoon pepper

Direction

- In a big skillet, melt 2 tbsp. of the butter; whisk in salt, mushrooms, green pepper, beef and potatoes. Cook on medium heat, with a cover, till the veggies soften or for 10 to 12 minutes, whisk once in a while.
- At the same time, in a small-sized bowl, stir the pepper and egg. In a separate skillet, heat the rest of butter on medium heat. Put in egg mixture; cook and whisk till eggs set totally. Whisk into the potato mixture.

Nutrition Information

- Calories: 261 calories
- Total Carbohydrate: 15g carbohydrate (1g sugars
- Cholesterol: 255mg cholesterol
- Protein: 13g protein.
- Total Fat: 16g fat (7g saturated fat)
- Sodium: 1051mg sodium
- Fiber: 2g fiber)

250. Quick Spaghetti Skillet

Serving: 4 servings. | Prep: 10mins | Ready in:

Ingredients

- 1/2 pound lean ground beef (90% lean)
- 1/4 pound Johnsonville® Ground Mild Italian sausage
- 2 cans (8 ounces each) no-salt-added tomato sauce
- 1 can (14-1/2 ounces) stewed tomatoes
- 1 cup water
- 1 can (4 ounces) mushroom stems and pieces, drained
- 2 celery ribs, sliced
- 4 ounces uncooked spaghetti, broken in half
- 1/4 teaspoon dried oregano
- Salt and pepper to taste

Direction

- In the big skillet, cook the sausage and beef on medium heat till not pink anymore; drain off. Put in rest ingredients. Boil. Lower the heat; put cover on and let simmer till the spaghetti softens or for 14 to 16 minutes.

Nutrition Information

- Calories: 314 calories
- Total Fat: 8g fat (3g saturated fat)
- Sodium: 514mg sodium
- Fiber: 3g fiber)
- Total Carbohydrate: 38g carbohydrate (13g sugars
- Cholesterol: 39mg cholesterol
- Protein: 19g protein. Diabetic Exchanges: 2 starch

251. Quick Tater Tot Bake

Serving: 2-3 servings. | Prep: 15mins | Ready in:

Ingredients

- 3/4 to 1 pound ground beef or turkey
- 1 small onion, chopped
- Salt and pepper to taste
- 1 package (16 ounces) frozen Tater Tot potatoes
- 1 can (10-3/4 ounces) condensed cream of mushroom soup, undiluted
- 2/3 cup 2% milk or water
- 1 cup shredded cheddar cheese

Direction

- Start preheating the oven to 350°. Cook onion and beef in a big skillet over medium heat until the meat is not pink anymore; strain. Use pepper and salt to season.
- Remove into a 2-quart baking dish coated with cooking spray. Put potatoes on top. Mix together milk and soup; add on top of the potatoes. Sprinkle cheese over. Bake without a cover until thoroughly heated, about 30-40 minutes.

Nutrition Information

- Calories: 740 calories
- Sodium: 1634mg sodium
- Fiber: 5g fiber)
- Total Carbohydrate: 52g carbohydrate (6g sugars
- Cholesterol: 127mg cholesterol
- Protein: 38g protein.
- Total Fat: 46g fat (19g saturated fat)

252. Quicker Mushroom Beef Stew

Serving: 8 servings. | Prep: 15mins | Ready in:

Ingredients

- 1 pound sliced baby portobello mushrooms
- 1 pound fresh baby carrots, sliced
- 1 large onion, chopped
- 3 tablespoons butter
- 3 garlic cloves, minced
- 1 teaspoon dried rosemary, crushed
- 3 tablespoons all-purpose flour
- 1 teaspoon pepper
- 4 cups water
- 4 teaspoons beef base
- 2 packages (17 ounces each) refrigerated beef tips with gravy
- Hot cooked egg noodles
- Crumbled blue cheese

Direction

- In a Dutch oven, sauté onion, carrots, and mushrooms until soft. Add rosemary and garlic, cook for another 1 minute. Mix in pepper and flour until combined, slowly add water. Mix in the beef base.

- Boil it, stir and cook until thickened, or for about 2 minutes. Add beef tips with gravy, heat thoroughly. Enjoy with cheese and noodles.

Nutrition Information

- Calories: 237 calories
- Protein: 20g protein.
- Total Fat: 11g fat (5g saturated fat)
- Sodium: 1077mg sodium
- Fiber: 3g fiber)
- Total Carbohydrate: 16g carbohydrate (8g sugars
- Cholesterol: 59mg cholesterol

253. Reuben Hot Dish

Serving: 10 | Prep: 20mins | Ready in:

Ingredients

- 2 (10.75 ounce) cans condensed cream of mushroom soup
- 1 1/2 cups milk
- 1/4 cup finely chopped onion
- 12 ounces deli sliced corned beef, chopped
- 3 tablespoons prepared mustard
- 2 (16 ounce) cans sauerkraut, drained and rinsed
- 1 (8 ounce) package uncooked egg noodles
- 2 cups shredded Swiss cheese
- 2 tablespoons butter, melted
- 3/4 cup cubed rye bread

Direction

- Preheat the oven to 120 degrees C (250 degrees F). Spread a single layer of bread cubes on a baking sheet and then toast until dry. Crush and set aside. Raise the temperature of oven to 175 degrees C (350 degrees F).
- Combine the corned beef, soup, mustard, onion, and milk in a medium bowl. Reserve.
- Evenly arrange sauerkraut at the bottom of a 9x13 inch baking dish that is lightly greased. Pour the uncooked noodles atop sauerkraut. Scoop the soup mixture atop the noodles and drizzle with cheese. Combine melted butter and rye bread crumbs in a small bowl and then drizzle the mixture atop cheese.
- Cover and then bake for 50 minutes. Uncover and then bake for 10 more minutes.

Nutrition Information

- Calories: 363 calories;
- Cholesterol: 67
- Protein: 19.6
- Total Fat: 17
- Sodium: 1682
- Total Carbohydrate: 33.9

254. Reuben Noodle Casserole

Serving: 5 servings. | Prep: 20mins | Ready in:

Ingredients

- 5 cups uncooked egg noodles
- 2 cans (14 ounces each) sauerkraut, rinsed and well drained
- 2 cans (10-3/4 ounces each) condensed cream of chicken soup, undiluted
- 3/4 cup whole milk
- 1/2 cup chopped onion
- 3 tablespoons prepared mustard
- 3/4 pound sliced deli corned beef, chopped
- 2 cups shredded Swiss cheese
- 2 slices day-old light rye bread
- 2 tablespoons butter, melted

Direction

- Prepare noodles following package directions. In the meantime, mix the mustard, onion, milk, soup and sauerkraut in a large bowl.

- Drain noodles; mix into sauerkraut mixture. Pour into a greased 13x9 inch baking pan. Scatter corned beef and cheese over top.
- In a food processor, put bread; cover and blend until it forms coarse crumbs. Stir crumbs and butter; scatter on top of the casserole.
- Bake at 350° while uncovered until bubbly, about 40-45 minutes.

Nutrition Information

- Calories: 621 calories
- Sodium: 3130mg sodium
- Fiber: 7g fiber)
- Total Carbohydrate: 53g carbohydrate (8g sugars
- Cholesterol: 141mg cholesterol
- Protein: 35g protein.
- Total Fat: 30g fat (15g saturated fat)

255. Rice Mix Meatballs

Serving: 8-10 servings. | Prep: 15mins | Ready in:

Ingredients

- 1 package (6.8 ounces) beef-flavored rice mix
- 1 egg, lightly beaten
- 1 pound ground beef
- 2-1/2 cups boiling water
- 2 tablespoons cornstarch
- 3 tablespoons cold water

Direction

- Put the rice seasoning packet aside. Mix egg and rice in a big bowl. Crumble beef over bowl and stir well. Make into 1-in. balls. Brown meatballs on all sides in a big frying pan on medium heat. In the meantime, mix the seasoning packer with boiling water in a small bowl. Mix into frying pan. Cover; simmer until rice is tender, 30 minutes. Mix cold water and cornstarch until smooth; add to frying pan.

Heat to a boil. Stirring constantly, cook until thick, 2 minutes.

Nutrition Information

- Calories:
- Fiber:
- Total Carbohydrate:
- Cholesterol:
- Protein:
- Total Fat:
- Sodium:

256. Roasted Garlic Herb Prime Rib

Serving: 12 servings. | Prep: 60mins | Ready in:

Ingredients

- 1 whole garlic bulb
- 1/4 teaspoon plus 2 tablespoons olive oil, divided
- 3 green onions, finely chopped
- 1 tablespoon dried rosemary, crushed
- 1 teaspoon dried thyme
- 1 teaspoon dill weed
- 1 teaspoon onion powder
- 1/2 teaspoon salt
- 1/4 teaspoon pepper
- 1/2 cup dry red wine or beef broth
- 1 bone-in beef rib roast (6 to 8 pounds)
- 2 cups beef broth
- SAUCE:
- 1 cup (8 ounces) sour cream
- 1 tablespoon prepared horseradish
- 1-1/2 teaspoons dill weed

Direction

- Preheat oven to 425°. Remove papery exterior skin from garlic (do not peel or distinct cloves). Chop top off of garlic bulb. Brush with 1/4 teaspoon oil. Enclose garlic bulb in heavy

duty foil. Bake for 30 to 35 minutes, until softened. Cool for 10 to 15 minutes.
- Preheat oven to 450°. In a small bowl, squeeze softened garlic; mix in pepper, salt, onion powder, herbs and onions. Put in reserved oil and wine. In a shallow roasting pan, position roast fat side up. Score slits into roast; spoon garlic blend into slits. Rub reserved garlic blend over roast. Put beef broth in the bottom of pan.
- Bake for 15 minutes, uncovered. Lower heat to 325°; bake for another 2 1/4 to 2 3/4 hours, until the desired doneness of meat is reached (a thermometer should read 145° for medium-rare; 160° for medium; 170° for well-done).
- In the meantime, mix sauce ingredients in a small bowl. Cover then chill until served. Place roast on a serving platter and keep warm; let stand for 15 minutes before cutting. Serve with sauce.

Nutrition Information

- Calories:
- Protein:
- Total Fat:
- Sodium:
- Fiber:
- Total Carbohydrate:
- Cholesterol:

257. Roasted Tenderloin And Red Potatoes

Serving: 4 servings. | Prep: 25mins | Ready in:

Ingredients

- 1 beef tenderloin roast (1-1/2 pounds)
- 2 garlic cloves, thinly sliced
- 1 tablespoon minced fresh thyme or 1 teaspoon dried thyme
- 1-1/2 teaspoons coarsely ground pepper, divided
- 3 tablespoons olive oil
- 8 small red potatoes, cut into chunks
- 1/2 cup reduced-sodium beef broth

Direction

- Make small slashes in tenderloin; put in every slit one garlic slice. Mix a teaspoon of pepper and thyme; massage on beef. Let beef brown in oil in skillet on every side. Put in one a shallow, small roasting pan.
- Scatter leftover pepper on potatoes; put in into skillet. Cook and mix till browned slightly. Transfer to roasting pan.
- Little by little pour broth into skillet, mixing to detach browned bits. Put on potatoes and meat.
- Bake for 25 to 40 minutes at 375°, with no cover, or till meat attains preferred doneness, thermometer must register 145° to get a medium-rare; 160° for medium; 170° for well-done, and potatoes become soft.

Nutrition Information

- Calories: 0g saturated fat (0 sugars
- Total Fat: 0 fiber).

258. Round Steak 'N' Dumplings

Serving: 8 servings. | Prep: 45mins | Ready in:

Ingredients

- 1/3 cup all-purpose flour
- 1 teaspoon paprika
- 2 pounds boneless beef round steak, cut into 1/2-inch cubes
- 2 cups frozen pearl onions, thawed
- 1/4 cup canola oil
- 2-1/2 cups water
- 1/2 teaspoon salt
- 1/4 teaspoon pepper

- 1 can (10-3/4 ounces) condensed cream of mushroom soup, undiluted
- 2 jars (4-1/2 ounces each) whole mushrooms, drained
- DUMPLINGS:
- 2 cups all-purpose flour
- 4 teaspoons baking powder
- 1 teaspoon dried minced onion
- 1 teaspoon celery seed
- 1 teaspoon poultry seasoning
- 1/2 teaspoon salt
- 1/2 teaspoon rubbed sage
- 1 cup milk
- 1/4 cup canola oil
- 1-1/2 cups soft bread crumbs
- 1/4 cup butter, melted

Direction

- In a large resealable plastic bag, combine the paprika and flour; add beef in batches then shaking to cover. In a Dutch oven over medium heat, cook onion and beef in oil until meat is no longer pink. Add the pepper, salt and water; let come to boil. Decrease heat; simmer with cover for 35-45 minutes. Add in mushrooms and soup.
- For dumplings, combine the first seven ingredients in a large bowl. Pour in milk and oil and mix just to moisten. Combine bread crumbs and butter in a shallow dish. Drop dumpling batter into crumb mixture by heaping tablespoonful; turn to coat.
- In a greased baking dish of 2 and a half quart, transfer hot beef mixture. Put dumplings on top. Bake with no cover at 425° for nearly 25 to 30 minutes until golden brown and bubbly and a toothpick pinned in dumplings comes out clean.

Nutrition Information

- Calories:
- Protein:
- Total Fat:
- Sodium:
- Fiber:
- Total Carbohydrate:
- Cholesterol:

259. Santa Fe Stew

Serving: 8 | Prep: 10mins | Ready in:

Ingredients

- 2 pounds ground beef
- 1 onion, chopped
- 2 (1 ounce) packets taco seasoning mix
- 2 (1 ounce) packets ranch dressing mix
- 2 (16 ounce) cans shoepeg corn
- 2 (10 ounce) cans diced tomatoes with green chile peppers (such as RO*TEL®)
- 1 (15 ounce) can red kidney beans
- 1 (15 ounce) can black beans
- 1 (15 ounce) can pinto beans
- 1 (14.5 ounce) can chicken broth
- 1 (14.5 ounce) can diced tomatoes

Direction

- Heat a large skillet on medium-high. Cook beef and stir onion until the color turns brown and beef is crumbly, about 5 to 7 minutes; remove excess oil.
- Sprinkle in taco seasoning mix and the ranch dressing mix into the cooked beef; add diced tomatoes with green chile peppers, pinto beans, black beans, red kidney beans, diced tomatoes, shoepeg corn, and chicken broth. Bring to a simmer. Stir occasionally and cook until tomatoes are tender, about 30 to 60 minutes.

Nutrition Information

- Calories: 525 calories;
- Total Fat: 15.3
- Sodium: 2402
- Total Carbohydrate: 61.5

- Cholesterol: 72
- Protein: 31.3

260. Saucy Skillet Lasagna

Serving: 8 servings. | Prep: 5mins | Ready in:

Ingredients

- 1 pound ground beef
- 1 can (14-1/2 ounces) diced tomatoes, undrained
- 2 large eggs, lightly beaten
- 1-1/2 cups ricotta cheese
- 4 cups marinara sauce
- 1 package (9 ounces) no-cook lasagna noodles
- 1 cup shredded part-skim mozzarella cheese, optional

Direction

- Using a large skillet, cook beef in medium heat for 6 to 8 minutes until no longer pink, smash into smaller crumbles; let it drain. Place in a large bowl and add in tomatoes. In a small bowl, mix ricotta cheese and eggs. Put 1 cup of the meat mixture back in a skillet, spread out evenly. Place in a layer 1 cup ricotta mixture, half of the pasta (cut to fit), 1 1/2 cups marinara sauce. Repeat the layers and put the remaining marinara sauce on top.
- Let it boil and lower down the heat, let it simmer with cover for 15-17 min. Until pasta are soft. Take out from the heat. Can be sprinkled with mozzarella cheese if desired. Let it set for 2 min. until cheese melts.

Nutrition Information

- Calories: 430 calories
- Protein: 27g protein.
- Total Fat: 18g fat (8g saturated fat)
- Sodium: 750mg sodium
- Fiber: 4g fiber)

- Total Carbohydrate: 41g carbohydrate (11g sugars
- Cholesterol: 108mg cholesterol

261. Saucy Swiss Steak

Serving: 4-6 servings. | Prep: 25mins | Ready in:

Ingredients

- 1-1/2 pounds boneless beef round steak (1/2 inch thick)
- 2 tablespoons all-purpose flour
- 1/2 teaspoon salt
- 1/4 teaspoon pepper
- 2 tablespoons canola oil
- 2 medium carrots, chopped
- 1 medium onion, chopped
- 1 cup chopped green pepper
- 3/4 cup chopped celery
- 1 teaspoon cornstarch
- 1/2 cup cold water
- 1 can (10-3/4 ounces) condensed tomato soup, undiluted
- 1 teaspoon prepared horseradish

Direction

- Cut steak to serving-sized pieces. Mix pepper, salt and flour; sprinkle on both steak sides. Brown steaks in oil on both sides in a pressure cooker; drain. Add celery, green pepper, onion and carrots.
- Mix water and cornstarch till smooth in a bowl; add horseradish and soup. Put on veggies.
- Securely close cover; put pressure regulator on the vent pipe. On high heat, put cooker on fully pressure; lower heat to medium. Cook for 12 minutes; the pressure regulator should maintain release of steam/slow steady rocking motion; as needed, adjust heat. Take off heat; follow manufacturer's instructions to cool immediately till pressure is fully reduced.

Nutrition Information

- Calories: 253 calories
- Total Carbohydrate: 16g carbohydrate (8g sugars
- Cholesterol: 64mg cholesterol
- Protein: 28g protein.
- Total Fat: 8g fat (2g saturated fat)
- Sodium: 552mg sodium
- Fiber: 3g fiber)

262. Sauerbraten

Serving: 8 | Prep: | Ready in:

Ingredients

- Marinade
- 2 cups dry red wine, such as pinot noir
- 1 cup red-wine vinegar
- 2 cups water
- 1 medium onion, finely chopped
- 2 tablespoons pickling spice
- 2 teaspoons whole black peppercorns
- 4 sprigs fresh thyme
- Roast
- 1 4-pound boneless beef roast, such as rump roast or chuck roast, trimmed
- 1 teaspoon ground ginger
- ½ teaspoon ground allspice
- 1 teaspoon salt
- ¾ teaspoon ground pepper
- 1½ tablespoons extra-virgin olive oil
- 1 medium onion, chopped
- 2 parsnips, peeled and chopped
- 2 stalks celery, chopped
- 1 cup low-sodium beef broth
- ⅓ cup ground gingersnap cookies
- Fresh thyme sprigs for garnish

Direction

- In a 5-6-qt. non-reactive, ovenproof pot, mix together thyme, peppercorns, pickling spice, onion, water, vinegar and wine 5 days prior to serving; boil. Switch to low heat to low and bring to a simmer in 10 minutes. Turn off the heat and rest for half an hour. Refrigerate for another half an hour until it achieves room temperature.
- Bring roast into cooled marinade. Leave in the fridge, covered, for 3 days; flip over once a day.
- Take roast out of the marinade and pat until fully dried using paper towels 2 days prior to serving. Strain, reserving marinade (without solids). Stir allspice and ginger into the marinade; put aside. Rinse and dry the pot.
- Set oven to 325 degrees F and start preheating.
- Add pepper and salt to the roast. Bring oil into the pot and heat on medium-high. Put in the roast and brown all sides for about 10 minutes; lower the heat if the pot begins to get very darkened. Bring roast to a plate.
- Switch to medium heat; put celery, parsnips and onion in the pot, then cook and stir for 4-6 minutes until begin to brown. Arrange vegetables to the sides of the pot and set roast in the middle. Add in marinade reserved earlier, along with broth, and simmer. Using a tight-fitting lid to cover the pot.
- Bring pot to oven and bake for half an hour. The liquid should be simmering, not boiling intensely; in case it is boiling, lower heat to 300°. Keep baking for another 2-2.5 hours until the top is fork-tender; invert once halfway through. Cool, uncovered, for about 60 minutes at room temperature. Refrigerate until cold before covering one more time. Leave in the fridge for 1 day.
- Start preheating oven to 350 degrees 60 minutes prior to serving.
- Cut the roast in thin slices. Add vegetables and liquid to a blender. Blend, in batches if needed, until smoothened. Return the sauce to the pot; mix in gingersnaps until no crumbs remain. Settle sliced roast into the sauce; simmer on medium heat. Cover and put into the oven; bake for about 40 minutes until hot. Place meat on a platter and pour on sauce. Add thyme to decorate.

Nutrition Information

- Calories: 450 calories;
- Protein: 49
- Saturated Fat: 4
- Total Carbohydrate: 16
- Sodium: 457
- Fiber: 2
- Cholesterol: 129
- Sugar: 5
- Total Fat: 14

263. Sauerbraten Patties

Serving: 6-8 servings. | Prep: 20mins | Ready in:

Ingredients

- 2 eggs
- 1 cup water, divided
- 1 cup seasoned bread crumbs
- 1/4 cup chopped onion
- 3/4 teaspoon poultry seasoning
- 3/4 teaspoon salt
- 1/4 teaspoon pepper
- 1-1/2 pounds ground beef
- 1 cup beef broth
- 1/4 cup red wine vinegar
- 1 to 2 tablespoons brown sugar
- 10 whole cloves
- 1 bay leaf
- 12 gingersnaps, crumbled

Direction

- In a big bowl, combine the pepper, salt, poultry seasoning, onion, bread crumbs, 3/4 cup water, and eggs. Crumble beef over mixture; stir well. Form into eight patties.
- In a large skillet, brown both sides of patties; let drain. Add the remaining water, gingersnaps, bay leaf, brown sugar, cloves, vinegar and broth. Boil over medium heat. Lower heat; simmer while covered for 1 hour or till meat is no longer pink. Discard bay leaf and cloves.

Nutrition Information

- Calories: 297 calories
- Total Carbohydrate: 21g carbohydrate (6g sugars
- Cholesterol: 110mg cholesterol
- Protein: 21g protein.
- Total Fat: 14g fat (5g saturated fat)
- Sodium: 665mg sodium
- Fiber: 1g fiber)

264. Savory Braised Beef

Serving: 2 servings. | Prep: 10mins | Ready in:

Ingredients

- 1/2 pound boneless beef chuck roast
- 3/4 cup water
- 1 small apple, thinly sliced
- 1 small onion, thinly sliced
- 1/4 teaspoon salt, optional
- 1/4 teaspoon pepper
- 4 small new potatoes, halved
- 2 cabbage wedges (about 2 inches thick)
- 1 can (14-1/2 ounces) stewed tomatoes
- 1-1/2 teaspoons cornstarch
- 1-1/2 teaspoons water

Direction

- Trim meat's fat and cube into 1-inch bits, then brown in a skillet sprayed with cooking spray. Put in pepper, salt, if wanted, onion, apple and water, then cover and simmer about 1 1/4 hours.
- Put in cabbage and potatoes, then cover and simmer until vegetables are softened, about 35 minutes. Stir in tomatoes, then cover and simmer about 10 minutes. Mix water and cornstarch then stir into skillet. Bring the

mixture to a boil, then cook and stir about 2 minutes.

Nutrition Information

- Calories: 401 calories
- Total Fat: 13g fat (0 saturated fat)
- Sodium: 560mg sodium
- Fiber: 0 fiber)
- Total Carbohydrate: 46g carbohydrate (0 sugars
- Cholesterol: 101mg cholesterol
- Protein: 38g protein. Diabetic Exchanges: 2 starch

265. Savory Grilled T Bones

Serving: 6 servings. | Prep: 15mins | Ready in:

Ingredients

- 1/4 cup chopped onion
- 1/4 cup olive oil
- 2 tablespoons lemon juice
- 2 tablespoons soy sauce
- 1 tablespoon sugar
- 1 tablespoon cider vinegar
- 1 tablespoon honey
- 2 teaspoons minced garlic
- 2 teaspoons Worcestershire sauce
- 1 teaspoon salt
- 1/2 teaspoon pepper
- 6 beef T-bone steaks (16 ounces each)

Direction

- Mix all the first 11 ingredients together in a big ziplock plastic bag and put in the steaks. Seal the ziplock bag and turn to coat the steaks with the marinade; keep in the fridge for 2-4 hours.
- Drain the marinated steaks and throw away the marinade mixture. Put the marinated steaks on a grill over medium heat then cover and let it grill for 6-10 minutes on both sides until the preferred meat doneness is achieved (a thermometer inserted in the meat should indicate 160°F for medium, 170°F for well-done and 145°F for medium-rare).

Nutrition Information

- Calories:
- Sodium:
- Fiber:
- Total Carbohydrate:
- Cholesterol:
- Protein:
- Total Fat:

266. Savory Meatballs

Serving: 8 servings. | Prep: 25mins | Ready in:

Ingredients

- 2 large eggs, lightly beaten
- 1 medium onion, chopped
- 2 teaspoons ground mustard
- 1 teaspoon salt
- 1/2 teaspoon pepper
- 1/2 teaspoon poultry seasoning
- 1/3 cup cornmeal
- 3/4 cup whole milk
- 2 pounds ground beef
- 3 tablespoons vegetable oil
- 2 cans (10-3/4 ounces each) condensed cream of mushroom soup, undiluted
- 1-1/2 cups water

Direction

- In a large bowl, mix the first eight ingredients. Crumble beef over the mixture; mix thoroughly. Form into 2-inch balls. Place a large skillet on medium-high heat; brown meatballs in batches in oil.

- Arrange on a 2-qt baking dish. Mix water and soup; pour over the meatballs. Bake without a cover at 350° till a thermometer reads 160° when inserted in the meatballs, 45-50 minutes.

Nutrition Information

- Calories: 363 calories
- Fiber: 1g fiber)
- Total Carbohydrate: 11g carbohydrate (3g sugars
- Cholesterol: 133mg cholesterol
- Protein: 26g protein.
- Total Fat: 23g fat (8g saturated fat)
- Sodium: 644mg sodium

hour, stirring sporadically. Take the bay leaf out. Serve over spaghetti. You can put oregano on as a garnish.

Nutrition Information

- Calories: 182 calories
- Fiber: 1g fiber)
- Total Carbohydrate: 7g carbohydrate (4g sugars
- Cholesterol: 50mg cholesterol
- Protein: 17g protein.
- Total Fat: 9g fat (4g saturated fat)
- Sodium: 559mg sodium

267. Savory Spaghetti Sauce

Serving: 4-6 servings (about 1 quart). | Prep: 5mins | Ready in:

Ingredients

- 1 pound ground beef
- 1 large onion, chopped
- 2 cans (15 ounces each) tomato sauce
- 1 garlic clove, minced
- 1 bay leaf
- 1 tablespoon minced fresh basil or 1 teaspoon dried basil
- 2 teaspoons minced fresh oregano or 3/4 teaspoon dried oregano
- 2 teaspoon sugar
- 1/2 to 1 teaspoon salt
- 1/2 teaspoon pepper
- Hot cooked spaghetti
- Fresh oregano, optional

Direction

- Cook onion until tender and beef until not pink in a Dutch oven. Drain excess grease. Mix in the next eight ingredients. Heat to a boil. Cover, decrease heat, and gently boil for 1

268. Savory Vegetable Beef Stew

Serving: 12 | Prep: 30mins | Ready in:

Ingredients

- 3 pounds beef stew meat, cut into 1-inch pieces
- 1/3 cup Italian salad dressing
- 2 cups water
- 2 teaspoons beef bouillon granules
- 1 (14.5 ounce) can diced tomatoes, undrained
- 1 (10.5 ounce) can condensed beef broth
- 1 (8 ounce) can tomato sauce
- 1 clove garlic, minced
- 1 bay leaf
- 1 teaspoon salt
- 1 teaspoon dried oregano
- 1/2 teaspoon ground black pepper
- 6 small potatoes, quartered
- 6 carrots, cut into 1-inch pieces
- 1 green bell pepper, cut into 1/2-inch dice
- 1 onion, chopped
- 3 tablespoons all-purpose flour
- 3 tablespoons cold water

Direction

- Heat a Dutch oven or large skillet over medium heat; stir-fry beef stew meat and Italian dressing for about 5 minutes until meat has turned brown evenly. Add pepper, oregano, salt, bay leaf, garlic, tomato sauce, beef broth, diced tomatoes, beef bouillon, and 2 cups of water to the skillet; bring to a boil. Turn heat to medium-low; simmer, covered for about 1 hour and 30 minutes until meat is tender.
- Put onion, bell pepper, carrots, and potatoes into the stew; simmer, covered, for about 45 minutes over medium-low heat until vegetables are tender.
- In a small mixing bowl, combine flour and cold water until no lumps remain. Mix flour mixture into the stew, bring to a boil; cook until stew is thickened, about 2 minutes, stir while cooking. Remove bay leaf before serving.

Nutrition Information

- Calories: 342 calories;
- Protein: 21.8
- Total Fat: 17.5
- Sodium: 680
- Total Carbohydrate: 23.7
- Cholesterol: 63

269. Scotch Braised Beef

Serving: 4 servings. | Prep: 20mins | Ready in:

Ingredients

- 4 bacon strips, diced
- 1 medium carrot, diced
- 1 small turnip, peeled and diced
- 1 small onion, diced
- 2 tablespoons butter
- 1-1/2 pounds beef top round roast
- 2 cans (14-1/2 ounces each) beef broth
- 10 whole peppercorns
- 1 tablespoon minced fresh parsley or 1 teaspoon dried parsley flakes
- 1-1/2 teaspoons minced fresh marjoram or 1/2 teaspoon dried marjoram
- 1/2 teaspoon ground mace
- 1/2 teaspoon ground allspice

Direction

- Sauté onion, turnip, carrot and bacon with butter in a Dutch oven for 3 minutes. Take away vegetables using a slotted spoon; put aside. Put in roast; cook all sides to brown. Put vegetables back to the pan. Add in broth. Put peppercorns on a double thickness of cheesecloth; bring corners together and use string to tie to shape a bag. Put in the pan along with other seasonings. Simmer with a cover for 2 hours, or until meat becomes tender. Take away the roast and discard the spice bag. If desired, thicken the pan drippings to serve along with the roast.

Nutrition Information

- Calories: 417 calories
- Total Carbohydrate: 5g carbohydrate (3g sugars
- Cholesterol: 126mg cholesterol
- Protein: 42g protein.
- Total Fat: 25g fat (10g saturated fat)
- Sodium: 660mg sodium
- Fiber: 1g fiber)

270. Sesame Beef 'n' Veggie Kabobs

Serving: 8 servings. | Prep: 25mins | Ready in:

Ingredients

- 1/2 cup reduced-sodium soy sauce
- 1/4 cup white wine or unsweetened apple juice

- 3 medium green peppers, cut into 1-inch pieces, divided
- 1 medium onion, cut into wedges
- 1 garlic clove, peeled
- 1/2 teaspoon ground ginger
- 1 tablespoon sesame seeds
- 2 pounds beef top sirloin steak, cut into 1-inch pieces
- 32 medium fresh mushrooms
- 32 cherry tomatoes
- 1 tablespoon canola oil

Direction

- Process the following ingredients in a blender until smooth: wine, soy sauce, garlic, onion, ginger, and half cup of green peppers. Add sesame seeds and stir. Refrigerate 1/3 cup of this mixture in a covered container, to use for basting later. Transfer the remaining mixture into a large re-sealable plastic bag with the beef. Zip the bag, turn to coat, and marinate in the refrigerator overnight. Store the remaining peppers in the refrigerator. Drain the beef, discarding its marinade. Skewer the beef, tomatoes, peppers, and mushrooms alternately on 16 metal or water-soaked wooden skewers. Brush the skewers over with a little oil. Lightly coat the grill rack with an oil-moistened paper towel at the end of a pair of long-handled tongs. Cook kabobs in a covered grill over medium heat, or broil 4 in. from the heat, until beef is done to liking, or for 10-15 minutes. Turn skewers occasionally and baste with reserved marinade.

Nutrition Information

- Calories: 216 calories
- Fiber: 3g fiber)
- Total Carbohydrate: 10g carbohydrate (5g sugars
- Cholesterol: 46mg cholesterol
- Protein: 28g protein. Diabetic Exchanges: 3 lean meat
- Total Fat: 7g fat (2g saturated fat)
- Sodium: 364mg sodium

271. Sesame Beef Stir Fry

Serving: 2 servings. | Prep: 15mins | Ready in:

Ingredients

- 2 teaspoons cornstarch
- 1/2 cup reduced-sodium beef broth
- 4 teaspoons reduced-sodium soy sauce
- 1 tablespoon minced fresh gingerroot
- 1 garlic clove, minced
- 1/2 pound beef top sirloin steak, thinly sliced
- 2 teaspoons sesame seeds, toasted, divided
- 2 teaspoons peanut or canola oil, divided
- 2 cups fresh broccoli florets
- 1 small sweet yellow pepper, julienned
- 1 cup hot cooked brown rice

Direction

- Mix the first 5 ingredients in a small bowl until blended; put aside.
- Stir-fry the beef and 1 tsp. of sesame seeds in a wok or large nonstick skillet with 1 tsp. of oil until the beef is not anymore pink. Remove from the heat and keep it warm.
- Add the broccoli into the remaining oil and stir-fry for 2 minutes. Add the pepper and stir-fry for 4-6 more minutes until the vegetables turn crisp-tender.
- Whisk the cornstarch mixture before pouring it into the pan. Let the mixture boil. Cook and stir the mixture for 2 minutes until thick. Add the beef and heat the mixture through. Serve this with rice and remaining sesame seeds sprinkled over it.

Nutrition Information

- Calories: 363 calories
- Cholesterol: 47mg cholesterol
- Protein: 31g protein. Diabetic Exchanges: 3 lean meat

- Total Fat: 12g fat (3g saturated fat)
- Sodium: 606mg sodium
- Fiber: 5g fiber)
- Total Carbohydrate: 33g carbohydrate (4g sugars

- Cholesterol: 70mg cholesterol
- Protein: 28g protein.
- Total Fat: 30g fat (12g saturated fat)
- Sodium: 1264mg sodium

272. Sesame Beef And Mushroom Noodles

Serving: 4 servings. | Prep: 10mins | Ready in:

Ingredients

- 3 packages (3 ounces each) beef ramen noodles
- 1 pound ground beef
- 1 pound fresh mushrooms, thinly sliced
- 2-3/4 cups water
- 1/3 cup coarsely chopped fresh cilantro leaves
- 2 tablespoons sesame oil

Direction

- Break noodles into small pieces and save 1/4 cup.
- Cook beef in a big skillet on medium heat until it is not pink anymore while breaking into crumbles, or for 6 to 8 minutes, then drain. Put in the contents of ramen seasoning packets as well as mushrooms, then cook and stir until mushrooms are softened, or for 3 to 4 minutes more. Put in water and the remaining noodles, then bring to a boil and cook until noodles are softened while stirring from time to time, or for 3 to 4 minutes.
- Take away from the heat and stir in sesame oil as well as cilantro. Put the reserved noodles on top.

Nutrition Information

- Calories: 565 calories
- Fiber: 3g fiber)
- Total Carbohydrate: 46g carbohydrate (5g sugars

273. Short Ribs With Dumplings

Serving: 6-8 servings. | Prep: 40mins | Ready in:

Ingredients

- 3 pounds boneless beef short ribs
- 2 tablespoons canola oil
- 1 medium onion, cut into wedges
- 1 garlic clove, minced
- 1 can (28 ounces) diced tomatoes, undrained
- 1 cup beef broth, divided
- 2 tablespoons soy sauce
- 1 tablespoon sugar
- 1/2 teaspoon salt
- 1/4 teaspoon pepper
- 1/4 teaspoon crushed red pepper flakes
- 1/8 teaspoon ground nutmeg
- 2 to 3 tablespoons cornstarch
- CORNMEAL DUMPLINGS:
- 3/4 cup water
- 1/2 cup cornmeal
- 1/2 teaspoon salt
- 1 egg, beaten
- 1/2 cup all-purpose flour
- 1 teaspoon baking powder
- Dash pepper
- 1 can (7 ounces) whole kernel corn, drained

Direction

- Cut ribs into pieces of 1-inch. In a Dutch oven over medium heat, brown beef in oil on all sides. Add garlic and onion; cook until onion soften, stirring occasionally. Stir in a half cup broth, tomatoes, seasonings and soy sauce; allow to boil. Lower heat; simmer with cover

for 1 and a half to 2 hours or until meat is tender.
- Combine the rest of broth and cornstarch until smooth; then stir into beef mixture. Let come to a boil; cook and stir for around 2 minutes or until thicken.
- For dumplings, in a saucepan, combine the salt, cornmeal and water; and boil. Cook and stir for 1 to 2 minutes until thicken; take away from the heat. Stir a small amount into egg; place all back to the pan, stirring constantly. Combine pepper, baking powder and flour; stir into cornmeal mixture. Mix in corn.
- Drop by rounded tablespoonful into simmering stew. Simmer with cover for approximately 10 to 12 minutes (avoid lifting the lid) or until a toothpick pinned in a dumpling comes out clean.

Nutrition Information

- Calories:
- Sodium:
- Fiber:
- Total Carbohydrate:
- Cholesterol:
- Protein:
- Total Fat:

274. Sicilian Meat Roll

Serving: 8 | Prep: 20mins | Ready in:

Ingredients

- 2 eggs, beaten
- 1/2 cup tomato juice
- 3/4 cup soft bread crumbs
- 2 tablespoons snipped fresh parsley
- 1/2 teaspoon dried oregano, crushed
- 1/4 teaspoon sea salt
- 1/4 teaspoon ground black pepper
- 1 clove garlic, minced
- 2 pounds lean ground beef
- 1 (6 ounce) package thinly sliced ham
- 1 (6 ounce) package sliced mozzarella cheese

Direction

- Combine tomato juice and eggs in a large bowl. Stir in the ground beef, garlic, salt, pepper, oregano, parsley and breadcrumbs. Mix well. Set oven to 350° F (175° C) to preheat.
- Pat and form the meat into a 10x8 inch rectangle on a sheet of waxed paper or foil. Top the meat with ham slices, keeping a small space around edges. Rip the cheese slices, keeping 1 whole slice, and drizzle over the ham.
- Beginning at the short end, roll up the meat carefully, using the waxed paper or foil to lift. Seal the ends and edges of the meat. Put roll in a 9x13 inch baking dish with seam side down.
- Bake for about 75 minutes in a prepared oven. Slice the remaining slice of cheese into 4 triangles. Cover the top of the loaf with overlapped triangles. Bake for 2 minutes more, until cheese is melted.

Nutrition Information

- Calories: 449 calories;
- Total Fat: 30.4
- Sodium: 670
- Total Carbohydrate: 9.7
- Cholesterol: 157
- Protein: 31.8

275. Simple Salisbury Steak

Serving: 6 servings. | Prep: 10mins | Ready in:

Ingredients

- 1 egg
- 1/3 cup dry bread crumbs

- 1 can (10-3/4 ounces) reduced-fat reduced-sodium condensed cream of mushroom soup, undiluted, divided
- 1/4 cup finely chopped onion
- 1 pound lean ground beef (90% lean)
- 1/2 cup fat-free milk
- 1/4 teaspoon browning sauce, optional
- 1/4 teaspoon salt
- 1-1/2 cups sliced fresh mushrooms

Direction

- In the big bowl, mix onion, a quarter cup of the soup, breadcrumbs, and egg. Break up beef on top of mixture and stir them well. Form into 6 patties. In the big nonstick skillet, brown patties on both of the sides; drain off.
- In the small-sized bowl, mix the rest of the soup, salt, browning sauce if you want, and milk; whisk in the mushrooms. Add on top of the patties. Lower the heat; keep covered and let simmer till the thermometer reaches 160 degrees and the meat is not pink anymore or for 15 to 20 minutes.

Nutrition Information

- Calories: 212 calories
- Total Carbohydrate: 11g carbohydrate (0 sugars
- Cholesterol: 67mg cholesterol
- Protein: 20g protein. Diabetic Exchanges: 3 lean meat
- Total Fat: 9g fat (3g saturated fat)
- Sodium: 599mg sodium
- Fiber: 0 fiber)

276. Sloppy Joe Biscuit Cups

Serving: 5 servings. | Prep: 20mins | Ready in:

Ingredients

- 1 pound lean ground beef (90% lean)
- 1/4 cup each finely chopped celery, onion and green pepper
- 1/2 cup barbecue sauce
- 1 tube (12 ounces) refrigerated flaky biscuits (10 count)
- 1/2 cup shredded cheddar cheese

Direction

- Heat oven to 400°. Cook vegetables and beef on medium heat in a big skillet, 5-7 minutes, until beef isn't pink anymore, then crumble beef; drain. Add in barbecue sauce and stir well. Boil. Lower heat and simmer without cover for 2 minutes while stirring sometimes.
- Divide dough into 10 biscuits then flatten to 5-inch circles. Press onto bottom while pulling up to stick around sides of greased muffin cups. Stuff beef mixture into.
- Bake for 9-11 minutes until biscuits have golden brown color. Dredge in cheese and bake for 1-2 minutes more until cheese is melted.

Nutrition Information

- Calories: 463 calories
- Protein: 25g protein.
- Total Fat: 22g fat (8g saturated fat)
- Sodium: 1050mg sodium
- Fiber: 1g fiber)
- Total Carbohydrate: 41g carbohydrate (16g sugars
- Cholesterol: 68mg cholesterol

277. Slow Cooker Beef Tostadas

Serving: 6 servings. | Prep: 20mins | Ready in:

Ingredients

- 1 large onion, chopped
- 1/4 cup lime juice

- 1 jalapeno pepper, seeded and minced
- 1 serrano pepper, seeded and minced
- 1 tablespoon chili powder
- 3 garlic cloves, minced
- 1/2 teaspoon ground cumin
- 1 beef top round steak (about 1-1/2 pounds)
- 1 teaspoon salt
- 1/2 teaspoon pepper
- 1/4 cup chopped fresh cilantro
- 12 corn tortillas (6 inches)
- Cooking spray
- TOPPINGS:
- 1-1/2 cups shredded lettuce
- 1 medium tomato, finely chopped
- 3/4 cup shredded sharp cheddar cheese
- 3/4 cup reduced-fat sour cream, optional

Direction

- In 3-4-qt. slow cooker, put initial 7 ingredients. Halve steak; sprinkle pepper and salt. Put in slow cooker; cook on low for 6-8 hours till meat is tender, covered.
- Remove meat; slightly cool. Use 2 forks to shred meat; put beef in slow cooker. Mix in cilantro then heat through. Spritz cooking spray on both sides of tortillas. Put on baking sheets in 1 layer; broil till crisp for 1-2 minutes per side. Put beef mixture on tortillas; top with sour cream (optional), cheese, tomato and lettuce.

Nutrition Information

- Calories: 372 calories
- Fiber: 5g fiber)
- Total Carbohydrate: 30g carbohydrate (5g sugars
- Cholesterol: 88mg cholesterol
- Protein: 35g protein. Diabetic Exchanges: 4 lean meat
- Total Fat: 13g fat (6g saturated fat)
- Sodium: 602mg sodium

278. Slow Cooker Beef With Red Sauce

Serving: 8 servings. | Prep: 25mins | Ready in:

Ingredients

- 2 tablespoons canola oil
- 2 tablespoons baking cocoa
- 1 tablespoon chili powder
- 2 teaspoons dried oregano
- 1 teaspoon salt
- 1 teaspoon pepper
- 1 teaspoon ground cumin
- 1/2 teaspoon ground cloves
- 1/2 teaspoon ground cinnamon
- 1 beef rump roast or bottom round roast (3 pounds), cut into 1-1/2-in. cubes
- 1 large onion, chopped
- 1 can (28 ounces) whole tomatoes, undrained
- 3 tablespoons cider vinegar
- 1-1/2 cups crushed gingersnap cookies (about 30 cookies)
- 9 garlic cloves, peeled
- 1 tablespoon sugar
- Hot cooked noodles, rice or mashed potatoes

Direction

- Mix the first 9 ingredients together in a small bowl; put aside.
- In a 4-quart slow cooker, put onion and beef; rub the spice mixture over the beef. Pour over the top with tomatoes; sprinkle garlic, gingersnaps, and vinegar over.
- Put the lid on and cook on low until the meat is soft, about 8-10 hours. Mix in sugar. Enjoy with noodles.

Nutrition Information

- Calories: 388 calories
- Total Carbohydrate: 27g carbohydrate (9g sugars
- Cholesterol: 102mg cholesterol
- Protein: 36g protein.

- Total Fat: 14g fat (4g saturated fat)
- Sodium: 685mg sodium
- Fiber: 3g fiber)

279. Slow Cooker Burgundy Beef

Serving: 10 servings. | Prep: 10mins | Ready in:

Ingredients

- 4 pounds beef top sirloin steak, cut into 1-inch cubes
- 3 large onions, sliced
- 1 cup water
- 1 cup burgundy wine or beef broth
- 1 cup ketchup
- 1/4 cup quick-cooking tapioca
- 1/4 cup packed brown sugar
- 1/4 cup Worcestershire sauce
- 4 teaspoons paprika
- 1-1/2 teaspoons salt
- 1 teaspoon minced garlic
- 1 teaspoon ground mustard
- 2 tablespoons cornstarch
- 3 tablespoons cold water
- Hot cooked noodles

Direction

- Mix the first 12 ingredients in a 5-quarter slow cooker. Cook with a cover on low until the meat becomes tender, 8 to 9 hours.
- Mix water and cornstarch until smooth; stir this mixture into pan juices. Cook with a cover on high until the gravy is thickened, approximately 15 minutes. Serve this with noodles.

Nutrition Information

- Calories: 347 calories
- Cholesterol: 74mg cholesterol
- Protein: 40g protein.

- Total Fat: 8g fat (3g saturated fat)
- Sodium: 811mg sodium
- Fiber: 1g fiber)
- Total Carbohydrate: 24g carbohydrate (15g sugars

280. Slow Cooker Chipotle Beef Carnitas

Serving: 16 servings plus 1/4 cup leftover spice mixture. | Prep: 40mins | Ready in:

Ingredients

- 2 tablespoons kosher salt
- 2 tablespoons brown sugar
- 1 tablespoon ground cumin
- 1 tablespoon smoked paprika
- 1 tablespoon chili powder
- 1 teaspoon garlic powder
- 1 teaspoon ground mustard
- 1 teaspoon dried oregano
- 1 teaspoon cayenne pepper
- 1 boneless beef chuck roast (3 pounds)
- 2 large sweet onions, thinly sliced
- 3 poblano peppers, seeded and thinly sliced
- 2 chipotle peppers in adobo sauce, finely chopped
- 3 tablespoons canola oil
- 1 jar (16 ounces) salsa
- 16 flour tortillas (8 inches), warmed
- 3 cups crumbled queso fresco or shredded Monterey Jack cheese
- Optional toppings: cubed avocado, sour cream and minced fresh cilantro

Direction

- Combine the first 9 ingredients. Halve the roast, rub 1/4 cup spice mixture over. Put a cover on and put the leftover mixture in a dry, cool area to store for a maximum of 1 year.
- In a 4-quart slow cooker, put peppers and onions. Heat oil in a big skillet over medium heat. Brown all sides of the roast. Transfer the

drippings and meat to the slow cooker. Put salsa on top. Put the lid on and cook on low for 8-10 hours until the meat is soft.
- Take the roast out, use 2 forks to shred. Skim the fat off from the cooking juices. Put the meat back into the slow cooker, thoroughly heat. On each tortilla, put 1/2 cup meat mixture using a slotted spoon. Sprinkle cheese over. Add your favorite toppings.

Nutrition Information

- Calories: 415 calories
- Sodium: 830mg sodium
- Fiber: 1g fiber)
- Total Carbohydrate: 35g carbohydrate (5g sugars
- Cholesterol: 70mg cholesterol
- Protein: 27g protein.
- Total Fat: 18g fat (6g saturated fat)

281. Slow Cooker Corned Beef Supper

Serving: 6 servings. | Prep: 25mins | Ready in:

Ingredients

- 1 large onion, sliced
- 6 medium carrots, cut into chunks
- 4 medium potatoes, cut into chunks
- 1 corned beef brisket with spice packet (2-1/2 pounds)
- 2/3 cup unsweetened apple juice
- 4 whole cloves
- 2 tablespoons brown sugar
- 1 teaspoon grated orange zest
- 1 teaspoon prepared mustard
- 1 small head cabbage, cut into 6 wedges

Direction

- Put onion in a 6 quarts slow cooker. Put carrots, potatoes and brisket on top. Mix the

contents of spice packet, mustard, orange zest, brown sugar, cloves and apple juice; put on top of brisket. Cook for 3-1/2 to 4 hours on high while covered.
- Put in cabbage; cook for half an hour more while covered, until veggies and meat are tender. Strain and throw away cloves; serve corned beef and veggies with pan juices.

Nutrition Information

- Calories: 541 calories
- Cholesterol: 130mg cholesterol
- Protein: 29g protein.
- Total Fat: 26g fat (9g saturated fat)
- Sodium: 1585mg sodium
- Fiber: 7g fiber)
- Total Carbohydrate: 49g carbohydrate (17g sugars

282. Slow Cooker Pot Roast

Serving: 6 | Prep: 15mins | Ready in:

Ingredients

- 1 onion, sliced
- 1/4 cup all-purpose flour
- 1 (2 1/2 pound) boneless beef chuck roast
- 1 pinch salt and ground black pepper to taste
- 1 (1.2 ounce) package dry beef gravy mix
- 1 (1 ounce) package ranch dressing mix
- 1 (.7 ounce) package dry Italian-style salad dressing mix
- 1/2 cup water, or as needed
- 5 whole peeled carrots (optional)

Direction

- Use a cooking spray to coat the inside of a slow cooker then layer the onion slices at the bottom of the cooker.
- On a work surface, spread the flour out. Sprinkle salt and black pepper onto the chuck

roast and roll all sides of the roast into the flour to coat evenly. Pound the flour into the meat with the edge of a small, sturdy plate. Put the floured roast into the cooker above the layer of onions. In a bowl, stir Italian dressing mix, ranch dressing mix and beef gravy mix together with water until smooth. Pour this mixture over the chuck roast and surround the meat with carrots.
- Cover the slow cooker. On a low setting, let it cook for about 8 hours until the gravy thickens, and the roast turns tender.

Nutrition Information

- Calories: 385 calories;
- Sodium: 1288
- Total Carbohydrate: 20.8
- Cholesterol: 87
- Protein: 23.9
- Total Fat: 22

283. Slow Cooker Sauerbraten

Serving: 8 servings. | Prep: 20mins | Ready in:

Ingredients

- 1 bottle (14 ounces) ketchup
- 1 large onion, chopped
- 3/4 cup packed brown sugar
- 3/4 cup cider vinegar
- 1 tablespoon mixed pickling spices
- 3 bay leaves
- 1 boneless beef chuck roast or rump roast (3 to 4 pounds)
- 4 cups water
- 1-1/2 cups crushed gingersnap cookies (about 30 cookies)
- 2 tablespoons cornstarch
- 1/4 cup cold water

Direction

- Mix the first 6 ingredients. Put roast into a 5-quart slow cooker. Pour in water. Top with ketchup mixture. Put in the cookie crumbs. Cover and cook on low, for 6 to 8 hours, or until meat becomes tender.
- Take roast out of the slow cooker then keep it warm. Drain the cooking juices and skim fat. Put 4 cups of the juices into saucepan. Boil. Mix water and cornstarch until they become smooth; then stir into the cooking juices. Bring back to a boil; cook while stirring for 1 to 2 mins, or until thickened. Serve together with the roast.

Nutrition Information

- Calories: 475 calories
- Cholesterol: 101mg cholesterol
- Protein: 35g protein.
- Total Fat: 11g fat (3g saturated fat)
- Sodium: 858mg sodium
- Fiber: 1g fiber)
- Total Carbohydrate: 58g carbohydrate (40g sugars

284. Slow Cooker Steak 'n' Gravy

Serving: 4 servings. | Prep: 15mins | Ready in:

Ingredients

- 1 pound beef top round steak
- 1 tablespoon vegetable oil
- 1-1/2 cups water
- 1 can (8 ounces) no-salt-added tomato sauce
- 1 teaspoon ground cumin
- 1 teaspoon garlic powder
- 1/2 teaspoon salt-free seasoning blend
- 1/4 teaspoon pepper
- 2 tablespoons all-purpose flour
- 1/4 cup cold water
- 2 cups mashed potatoes

Direction

- Cut beef to 1-in. cubes; in oil, brown in a skillet. Put into 3-qt. slow cooker then cover in water; add seasonings and tomato sauce. Cover; cook till meat is tender for 4 hours on high/8 hours on low.
- Mix cold water and flour in a small bowl; mix into liquid in the slow cooker. Cover; cook till gravy is thick for 30 minutes on high; serve with potatoes.

Nutrition Information

- Calories: 361 calories
- Protein: 28g protein. Diabetic Exchanges: 3-1/2 lean meat
- Total Fat: 16g fat (0 saturated fat)
- Sodium: 336mg sodium
- Fiber: 1g fiber)
- Total Carbohydrate: 26g carbohydrate (0 sugars
- Cholesterol: 72mg cholesterol

285. Slow Cooked Barbecued Beef Brisket

Serving: 8 servings. | Prep: 10mins | Ready in:

Ingredients

- 1 teaspoon salt
- 1 teaspoon chili powder
- 1/2 teaspoon garlic powder
- 1/4 teaspoon onion powder
- 1/4 teaspoon celery seed
- 1/4 teaspoon pepper
- 1 fresh beef brisket (2-1/2 pounds), trimmed
- SAUCE:
- 1/2 cup ketchup
- 1/2 cup chili sauce
- 1/4 cup packed brown sugar
- 2 tablespoons cider vinegar
- 2 tablespoons Worcestershire sauce
- 1 to 1-1/2 teaspoons Liquid Smoke, optional
- 1/2 teaspoon ground mustard

Direction

- Mix initial 6 ingredients in small bowl; rub on brisket. Put in 3-qt. slow cooker.
- Mix sauce ingredients in small bowl. Put 1/2 on brisket; put aside leftover sauce.
- Cover; cook till meat is tender for 4-5 hours on high. Serve with reserved sauce.

Nutrition Information

- Calories: 242 calories
- Sodium: 810mg sodium
- Fiber: 0 fiber)
- Total Carbohydrate: 16g carbohydrate (14g sugars
- Cholesterol: 60mg cholesterol
- Protein: 29g protein.
- Total Fat: 6g fat (2g saturated fat)

286. Slow Cooked Green Chili Beef Burritos

Serving: 12 servings. | Prep: 30mins | Ready in:

Ingredients

- 1 boneless beef chuck roast (3 pounds)
- 1 can (14-1/2 ounces) beef broth
- 2 cups green enchilada sauce
- 1 can (4 ounces) chopped green chilies
- 1/2 cup Mexican-style hot tomato sauce
- 1/2 teaspoon salt
- 1/2 teaspoon garlic powder
- 1/2 teaspoon pepper
- 12 flour tortillas (12 inches)
- Optional toppings: shredded lettuce, chopped tomatoes, shredded cheddar cheese and sour cream

Direction

- Halve roast; put in a 3 or 4-quart slow cooker. Put broth in; cover. Cook for 8-9 hours on low till meat is tender.
- Remove beef; use 2 forks to shred meat till cool to handle. Skim fat from the cooking liquid; keep 1/2 cup of liquid. Put reserved liquid and shredded beef in the slow cooker. Mix pepper, garlic powder, salt, tomato sauce, green chiles and enchilada sauce in.
- Cover; cook for 1 hour on low till heated through. Put beef mixture down middle of tortillas; add whatever toppings you want. Roll up.

Nutrition Information

- Calories: 419 calories
- Protein: 29g protein.
- Total Fat: 17g fat (6g saturated fat)
- Sodium: 1175mg sodium
- Fiber: 5g fiber)
- Total Carbohydrate: 36g carbohydrate (2g sugars
- Cholesterol: 74mg cholesterol

287. Slow Cooked Meatball Stew

Serving: 6 servings. | Prep: 20mins | Ready in:

Ingredients

- 3 medium potatoes, peeled and cut into 1/2-inch cubes
- 1 pound fresh baby carrots, quartered
- 1 large onion, chopped
- 3 celery ribs, sliced
- 1 package (12 ounces) frozen fully cooked home-style meatballs
- 1 can (10-3/4 ounces) condensed tomato soup, undiluted
- 1 can (10-1/2 ounces) beef gravy
- 1 cup water
- 1 envelope onion soup mix
- 2 teaspoons beef bouillon granules

Direction

- Into the 5-quart slow cooker, add meat balls, celery, onion, carrots and potatoes. Mix rest of the ingredients; add on top of the meatball mixture.
- Keep it covered and cook on low setting till veggies become tender-crisp or for 9 to 10 hours.

Nutrition Information

- Calories: 291 calories
- Total Fat: 8g fat (3g saturated fat)
- Sodium: 1400mg sodium
- Fiber: 4g fiber)
- Total Carbohydrate: 41g carbohydrate (12g sugars
- Cholesterol: 51mg cholesterol
- Protein: 14g protein.

288. Slow Cooked Spaghetti Sauce

Serving: 6-8 servings. | Prep: 15mins | Ready in:

Ingredients

- 1 pound ground beef or Johnsonville® Ground Mild Italian sausage
- 1 medium onion, chopped
- 2 cans (14-1/2 ounces each) diced tomatoes, undrained
- 1 can (8 ounces) tomato sauce
- 1 can (6 ounces) tomato paste
- 1 bay leaf
- 1 tablespoon brown sugar
- 4 garlic cloves, minced
- 1 to 2 teaspoons dried basil
- 1 to 2 teaspoons dried oregano
- 1 teaspoon salt
- 1/2 to 1 teaspoon dried thyme

- Hot cooked spaghetti

Direction

- Cook onion and beef until meat is not pink anymore in a large skillet over medium heat; drain.
- Place in a 3-quart slow cooker. Add the next 10 ingredients. Cook with a cover for 7-8 hours on low or until heated through. Get rid of bay leaf. Serve with spaghetti.

Nutrition Information

- Calories: 142 calories
- Sodium: 546mg sodium
- Fiber: 3g fiber)
- Total Carbohydrate: 13g carbohydrate (8g sugars
- Cholesterol: 28mg cholesterol
- Protein: 12g protein.
- Total Fat: 5g fat (2g saturated fat)

289. Slow Cooked Stuffed Flank Steak

Serving: 8 servings. | Prep: 20mins | Ready in:

Ingredients

- 1 beef flank steak (2 pounds)
- 1 medium onion, chopped
- 1 garlic clove, minced
- 1 tablespoon butter
- 1-1/2 cups soft bread crumbs (about 3 slices)
- 1/2 cup chopped fresh mushrooms
- 1/4 cup minced fresh parsley
- 1/4 cup egg substitute
- 3/4 teaspoon poultry seasoning
- 1/2 teaspoon salt
- 1/8 teaspoon pepper
- 1/2 cup beef broth
- 2 teaspoons cornstarch
- 4 teaspoons water

Direction

- Flatten steak to 1/2-in. thickness; put aside.
- Sauté garlic and onion in butter in a nonstick skillet until tender. Add pepper, salt, poultry seasoning, egg substitute, parsley, mushrooms, and the bread crumbs; combine well.
- Pour the mixture over steak to within 1 in. of edge. Starting with a long side, roll it up like jelly; use kitchen string to tie. Transfer to a 5-qt. slow cooker; add broth. Cook, covered, for 8-10 hours on low.
- Transfer the meat to a serving platter, and keep it warm. Skim fat from the cooking juices; keep in a small saucepan.
- Combine water and cornstarch until the mixture becomes smooth; and stir into juices. Bring to a boil; cook while stirring until thickened, about 1-2 minutes. Get rid of the string before cutting steak into slices; serve with gravy.

Nutrition Information

- Calories: 230 calories
- Fiber: 1g fiber)
- Total Carbohydrate: 6g carbohydrate (0 sugars
- Cholesterol: 62mg cholesterol
- Protein: 26g protein. Diabetic Exchanges: 3 lean meat
- Total Fat: 11g fat (5g saturated fat)
- Sodium: 348mg sodium

290. Slow Simmered Burgundy Beef Stew

Serving: 4 servings. | Prep: 30mins | Ready in:

Ingredients

- 1-1/2 pounds beef stew meat (1-1/4-inch pieces)
- 3 tablespoons all-purpose flour

- 3/4 teaspoon salt
- 2 to 4 teaspoons canola oil, divided
- 2 teaspoons beef bouillon granules
- 2 teaspoons dried parsley flakes
- 1-1/2 teaspoons Italian seasoning
- 2 cups water
- 1 cup Burgundy wine or beef stock
- 3 medium potatoes (about 1-1/3 pounds), peeled and quartered
- 1 cup fresh mushrooms, halved
- 1 medium onion, cut into eight wedges
- 2 medium carrots, cut into 1-inch pieces
- 2 celery ribs, cut into 1/2-inch pieces
- Additional water, optional

Direction

- Turn oven to 350° to preheat. Combine beef with salt and flour until lightly coated; shake to remove excess. Heat 2 teaspoons oil in an oven-safe Dutch oven over medium heat. Cook beef in batches until browned. Add more oil if necessary. Take browned beef out of the pan.
- Add wine, 2 cups water, herbs, and bouillon to the same pan; bring the mixture to a boil, mixing well to loosen browned bits from the pan. Add beef, and bring the mixture to another boil. Move to oven; cover and bake for 1 hour.
- Mix in vegetables and make it thinner by adding more water if necessary. Bake, covered, for 45 minutes to 1 hour until vegetables and beef are tender.

Nutrition Information

- Calories: 419 calories
- Sodium: 949mg sodium
- Fiber: 4g fiber)
- Total Carbohydrate: 33g carbohydrate (5g sugars
- Cholesterol: 106mg cholesterol
- Protein: 37g protein.
- Total Fat: 15g fat (5g saturated fat)

291. Smoky Chuck Roast

Serving: 4-6 servings. | Prep: 10mins | Ready in:

Ingredients

- 1/4 cup water
- 1 tablespoon Liquid Smoke, optional
- 1 tablespoon brown sugar
- 1 teaspoon celery salt
- 1 teaspoon onion salt
- 1/2 teaspoon ground nutmeg
- 1/2 teaspoon mustard seed
- 1/4 teaspoon pepper
- 1 boneless beef chuck roast (2 to 3 pounds)
- 1/4 cup barbecue sauce

Direction

- In a big resealable plastic bag, mix the initial eight ingredients; put in roast. Seal the bag; keep in refrigerator for 8 hours, flip one time.
- Drain off and get rid of marinade. Put the roast into a greased 2.5-quart baking pan. Bake with cover at 325 degrees for 1.5-2 hours. Baste with BBQ sauce. Bake, with no cover, till the beef softens or for 10 to 12 more minutes.

Nutrition Information

- Calories:
- Fiber:
- Total Carbohydrate:
- Cholesterol:
- Protein:
- Total Fat:
- Sodium:

292. Smothered Round Steak

Serving: 4 servings. | Prep: 15mins | Ready in:

Ingredients

- 1/3 cup all-purpose flour
- 1/2 teaspoon salt
- 1/4 teaspoon pepper
- 1-1/2 pounds beef top round steak, cut into strips
- 1 large onion, sliced
- 1 large green pepper, sliced
- 1 can (14-1/2 ounces) diced tomatoes, undrained
- 1 jar (4 ounces) sliced mushrooms, drained
- 3 tablespoons reduced-sodium soy sauce
- 2 tablespoons molasses
- Hot cooked egg noodles, optional

Direction

- Mix beef together with pepper, salt, and flour in a 3-quart slow cooker. Mix in all the rest of the ingredients, apart from the noodles.
- Cover and cook on low for 6-8 hours, or until the meat is soft. Serve together with noodles if you like.

Nutrition Information

- Calories: 335 calories
- Protein: 42g protein.
- Total Fat: 6g fat (2g saturated fat)
- Sodium: 1064mg sodium
- Fiber: 4g fiber)
- Total Carbohydrate: 28g carbohydrate (14g sugars
- Cholesterol: 95mg cholesterol

293. South Of The Border Stuffed Peppers

Serving: 4 | Prep: 15mins | Ready in:

Ingredients

- 4 large red bell peppers, tops and seeds removed
- 1 poblano pepper
- 1 1/2 cups water
- 1 cup uncooked white rice
- 1 tablespoon vegetable oil
- 1/2 cup chopped onion
- 1 pound ground beef
- 1 clove garlic, minced
- 1 teaspoon ground cumin
- 1 teaspoon dried oregano leaves
- 1 (10 ounce) can red enchilada sauce
- salt and ground black pepper to taste
- 1 cup shredded Asadero cheese

Direction

- Preheat the oven to 200°C or 400°F. Grease the baking dish lightly.
- Put the poblano and bell peppers in the greased baking dish. Cook for 20 minutes in the preheated oven until the poblano's skin is wrinkled. Take the poblano pepper out of the dish then peel. Chop the poblano into quarter-inch portions then set it aside.
- On medium heat, boil water and rice in a pan. Turn to low heat then cover; let it simmer for 20 minutes until the rice absorbs the water. Take off heat then set it aside.
- On medium heat, cook onion in a pan for 5 minutes until soft and translucent; mix in ground beef. Cook until the beef is evenly brown and crumbly; drain. Mix in oregano, cumin, and garlic. Cook and stir for a minute until the garlic is aromatic. Sprinkle pepper and salt to taste. Mix in poblano pepper, enchilada sauce, and rice until well combined. If desired, adjust the seasoning according to taste.
- Prepare the cheese sauce. On medium heat, stir the queso asadero in a pan until smooth and melted.
- Turn the oven to 175°C or 350°F.
- Fill the bell peppers with beef mixture until heaping full. Put the excess beef mixture in the middle of the dish in between the stuffed peppers. Pour the cheese sauce all over each pepper. Use aluminum foil to cover the baking dish.

- Bake the peppers for 35 minutes in the preheated oven until the filling is completely heated and the cheese sauce is bubbling.

Nutrition Information

- Calories: 622 calories;
- Protein: 33.2
- Total Fat: 28.5
- Sodium: 478
- Total Carbohydrate: 56.3
- Cholesterol: 104

294. Southern Pot Roast

Serving: 5 servings. | Prep: 10mins | Ready in:

Ingredients

- 1 boneless beef chuck roast (2-1/2 pounds)
- 1 tablespoon Cajun seasoning
- 1 package (9 ounces) frozen corn, thawed
- 1/2 cup chopped onion
- 1/2 cup chopped green pepper
- 1 can (14-1/2 ounces) diced tomatoes, undrained
- 1/2 teaspoon pepper
- 1/2 teaspoon hot pepper sauce

Direction

- Slice half of the roast and put in a slow cooker that's 5 quart. Drizzle with some Cajun seasoning. Put onion, green pepper, and corn on top. Mix in hot pepper sauce, pepper, and tomatoes and put it on top of vegetables.
- Cover the mixture up and cook for 5 to 6 hours on low until the meat becomes tender. Place the corn mixture by using a slotted spoon, serve.

Nutrition Information

- Calories: 455 calories

- Protein: 47g protein.
- Total Fat: 22g fat (8g saturated fat)
- Sodium: 601mg sodium
- Fiber: 3g fiber)
- Total Carbohydrate: 17g carbohydrate (5g sugars
- Cholesterol: 147mg cholesterol

295. Southwest Beef Brisket

Serving: 8 servings. | Prep: 25mins | Ready in:

Ingredients

- 1 fresh beef brisket (3 pounds)
- 1 small onion, finely chopped
- 1 serrano pepper, seeded and minced
- 4 teaspoons brown sugar
- 1 tablespoon chili powder
- 1 tablespoon cider vinegar
- 2 garlic cloves, minced
- 1/2 teaspoon salt
- 1/2 teaspoon ground cumin
- 4 teaspoons canola oil
- 2-1/2 cups water
- 2 cans (10 ounces each) diced tomatoes and green chilies
- 1 medium onion, sliced

Direction

- Slice brisket in half. Mix the cumin, salt, garlic, vinegar, chili powder, brown sugar, serrano pepper and chopped onion in a big plastic bag that can be sealed. Put in the brisket; close bag and flip to coat. Chill overnight.
- Cook the brisket in oil until browned on all sides in a pressure cooker. Pour the water, sliced onion and tomatoes. Close the cover securely following manufacturers' directions.
- Over high heat, set the cooker to full pressure. Turn heat down to medium-high and cook for 55 minutes. (Pressure regulator should remain a steady, slow rocking motion or release of steam; alter the heat if necessary.) Take away

from the heat; let the pressure drop automatically. Transfer beef to a serving platter; serve together with tomato mixture.

Nutrition Information

- Calories: 271 calories
- Sodium: 500mg sodium
- Fiber: 2g fiber)
- Total Carbohydrate: 8g carbohydrate (4g sugars
- Cholesterol: 72mg cholesterol
- Protein: 36g protein. Diabetic Exchanges: 5 lean meat
- Total Fat: 10g fat (3g saturated fat)

296. Southwest Zucchini Boats

Serving: 4 servings. | Prep: 15mins | Ready in:

Ingredients

- 4 medium zucchini
- 1 pound ground beef
- 3/4 cup salsa
- 1/4 cup dry bread crumbs
- 1/4 cup minced fresh cilantro
- 1 teaspoon chili powder
- 1/2 teaspoon ground cumin
- 1/4 teaspoon salt
- 1/8 teaspoon pepper
- 1 cup shredded Monterey Jack cheese, divided
- Sour cream, optional

Direction

- Cut zucchini in half lengthwise; using a sharp knife, slice a thin layer off the bottom of each so that zucchini can sit flat. Leave 1/4-in. shells by scooping out pulp.
- Put shells in a 3-qt. microwave-safe dish that is ungreased. Microwave with a cover for 3 minutes on high, until crisp-tender; then drain and put aside.
- In the meantime, cook beef in a large skillet over medium heat until no longer pink; then drain. Take away from heat; stir in the 1/2 cup cheese, pepper, salt, chili powder, cumin, cilantro, breadcrumbs and salsa. Spoon into zucchini shells.
- Microwave without a cover for 4 minutes on high. Sprinkle top with the rest of cheese. Microwave for 3 to 4 minutes more or until zucchini are softened and cheese melts. If preferred, serve along with sour cream.

Nutrition Information

- Calories: 387 calories
- Sodium: 618mg sodium
- Fiber: 3g fiber)
- Total Carbohydrate: 15g carbohydrate (6g sugars
- Cholesterol: 95mg cholesterol
- Protein: 30g protein.
- Total Fat: 23g fat (11g saturated fat)

297. Southwestern Beef Burritos

Serving: 8 servings. | Prep: 15mins | Ready in:

Ingredients

- 2 to 2-1/2 pounds beef top round steak, cut into 1-inch cubes
- 2 tablespoons canola oil
- 2 large onions, chopped
- 2 garlic cloves, minced
- 1 can (15 ounces) enchilada sauce
- 1 can (14-1/2 ounces) diced tomatoes, undrained
- 1 to 2 cans (4 ounces each) chopped green chilies
- 1 teaspoon salt
- 1/4 teaspoon pepper

- 2 tablespoons all-purpose flour
- 1/4 cup cold water
- 8 flour tortillas (10 inches)
- Diced tomatoes, sliced ripe olives, shredded cheddar cheese, sour cream, chopped green onions, shredded lettuce and/or guacamole, optional

Direction

- Over medium heat, brown meat in oil in a large skillet. Let it drain. Stir in and cook garlic and onions for 2 minutes. Put in pepper, salt, chilies, tomatoes, and enchilada sauce and let it boil. Lower the heat. Simmer with cover until meat becomes tender, about 2 hours.
- Mix together water and flour. Put in the beef mixture and stir continuously. Let it boil. Cook, while stirring, until it thickens, about 1 minute.
- Heat the tortillas and put about half cup of the filling over them, off center on each one. Fold base and sides on top of the filling and roll the tortillas up. Put a bit more of the filling over the burritos. Serve right away. If you want, you can garnish it with guacamole or lettuce, onions, sour cream, cheese, olives, and tomatoes.

Nutrition Information

- Calories: 446 calories
- Protein: 34g protein.
- Total Fat: 12g fat (3g saturated fat)
- Sodium: 973mg sodium
- Fiber: 9g fiber)
- Total Carbohydrate: 43g carbohydrate (6g sugars
- Cholesterol: 64mg cholesterol

298. Southwestern Burgers

Serving: 2 servings. | Prep: 25mins | Ready in:

Ingredients

- 1/4 cup mayonnaise
- 2 tablespoons spicy brown mustard
- 1 tablespoon ground cumin
- 1/4 teaspoon lemon juice
- 1/8 teaspoon salt
- 1/8 teaspoon pepper
- 1 medium green pepper
- 1/2 pound lean ground beef
- 2 slices cheddar cheese
- 2 hamburger buns, split
- 2 slices tomato
- 2 slices onion
- 2 lettuce leaves

Direction

- Mix together pepper, salt, lemon juice, cumin, mustard and mayonnaise in a small bowl; put into refrigerator with a cover until ready to serve.
- Put green pepper on grill grate over medium heat with a cover for about 6 minutes until the skin blisters. Rotate pepper with tongs a quarter turn. Continue the process of grilling and rotating until every side is blackened. Transfer pepper to a bowl right away; let it stand with a cover for 15 to 20 minutes.
- At the same time, form beef into 2 patties. Put them on grill grate over medium-hot heat without a cover until a thermometer reaches 160 degrees, about 7 to 9 minutes per side.
- Peel off and discard charred skin of a green pepper; discard seeds and stem. Cut pepper into 2 equal pieces. Add cheese and green pepper on top of each patty; continue grilling for the cheese to melt, another 1 minute.
- Put the buns on grill grate, cut side down, until toasted, about 1 to 2 minutes. Use mayonnaise mixture to spread on the bun bottoms; put lettuce, onion, tomato and burgers on top the buns to serve. Replace bun tops.

Nutrition Information

- Calories: 406 calories
- Sodium: 1183mg sodium
- Fiber: 5g fiber)
- Total Carbohydrate: 36g carbohydrate (10g sugars
- Cholesterol: 72mg cholesterol
- Protein: 32g protein.
- Total Fat: 13g fat (4g saturated fat)

Nutrition Information

- Calories: 240 calories
- Total Fat: 8g fat (4g saturated fat)
- Sodium: 676mg sodium
- Fiber: 2g fiber)
- Total Carbohydrate: 30g carbohydrate (7g sugars
- Cholesterol: 26mg cholesterol
- Protein: 11g protein.

299. Spaghetti Goulash

Serving: 12-16 servings. | Prep: 25mins | Ready in:

Ingredients

- 1 package (16 ounces) thin spaghetti, broken in half
- 3/4 pound ground beef
- 3/4 pound Jones No Sugar Pork Sausage Roll sausage
- 1 medium green pepper, chopped
- 1 medium onion, chopped
- 2 cans (14-1/2 ounces each) diced tomatoes
- 1 bottle (12 ounces) chili sauce
- 1 can (8 ounces) mushroom stems and pieces, drained
- 1 tablespoon Worcestershire sauce
- 1 teaspoon salt
- 1/4 teaspoon pepper
- 1 cup shredded cheddar cheese, divided

Direction

- Follow directions on package to cook spaghetti. Drain off water. Cook sausage, onion, beef, and green pepper in a big frying pan on medium heat until meat is not pink. Drain excess grease. Mix in tomatoes, cover, and gently boil for 45 minutes. Take away from heat. Mix in pepper, chili sauce, salt, spaghetti, mushrooms, and Worcestershire sauce. Move to a 4-qt. greased dish or put in two 2-qt. greased dishes. Sprinkle cheese on. Cover; bake in a 350-degree oven until cooked through, 35-40 minutes.

300. Spaghetti Hot Dish

Serving: 4 servings. | Prep: 20mins | Ready in:

Ingredients

- 1 pound lean ground beef (90% lean)
- 2 medium onions, diced
- 3 celery ribs with leaves, diced
- 1/4 cup butter, cubed
- 5 tablespoons all-purpose flour
- Salt and pepper to taste
- 3-1/2 cups milk
- 2 tablespoons chopped pimientos
- 1 to 2 teaspoons soy sauce
- 1-1/4 cups broken spaghetti, cooked and drained
- 1 cup finely crushed butter-flavored crackers (about 25 crackers)

Direction

- Cook celery, onions and beef over medium heat in butter in a large skillet until no longer pink; drain. Stir in pepper, salt and flour until blended. Add pimientos, soy sauce and milk gradually. Bring to boiling; cook while stirring until thickened or for 2 minutes. Stir in spaghetti.
- Place into a greased 11x7-in. baking dish. Scatter with cracker crumbs. Bake without a

cover at 350° until heated through or for 30-35 minutes.

Nutrition Information

- Calories: 653 calories
- Protein: 35g protein.
- Total Fat: 33g fat (16g saturated fat)
- Sodium: 587mg sodium
- Fiber: 4g fiber)
- Total Carbohydrate: 54g carbohydrate (17g sugars
- Cholesterol: 115mg cholesterol

301. Spaghetti Squash Meatball Casserole

Serving: 6 servings. | Prep: 35mins | Ready in:

Ingredients

- 1 medium spaghetti squash (about 4 pounds)
- 1/2 teaspoon salt, divided
- 1/2 teaspoon fennel seed
- 1/4 teaspoon ground coriander
- 1/4 teaspoon dried basil
- 1/4 teaspoon dried oregano
- 1 pound lean ground beef (90% lean)
- 2 teaspoons olive oil
- 1 medium onion, chopped
- 1 garlic clove, minced
- 2 cups chopped collard greens
- 1 cup chopped fresh spinach
- 1 cup reduced-fat ricotta cheese
- 2 plum tomatoes, chopped
- 1 cup pasta sauce
- 1 cup shredded part-skim mozzarella cheese

Direction

- Halve squash lengthwise; throw seeds. On a microwave-safe plate, put the halves, cut side facing down. Allow to microwave on high without cover for 15 to 20 minutes, till soft. Let cool slightly.
- Preheat an oven to 350°. Combine quarter teaspoon salt with the rest of the seasonings; put to beef, combining slightly yet well. Form into 1-1/2-inch rounds. Brown meatballs in a big skillet over medium heat; take off from pan.
- Heat oil in same pan over medium heat; sauté the onion for 3 to 4 minutes till soft. Put the garlic; let cook and mix for a minute. Mix in the rest of the salt, ricotta cheese, spinach and collard greens; take off from heat.
- Part strands of squash spaghetti with a fork; mix into greens mixture. Put to an oiled baking dish, 13x9-inch in size. Put cheese, sauce, meatballs and tomatoes on top. Allow to bake without cover for 30 to 35 minutes, till meatballs are cooked completely.

Nutrition Information

- Calories: 362 calories
- Protein: 26g protein. Diabetic Exchanges: 3 lean meat
- Total Fat: 16g fat (6g saturated fat)
- Sodium: 618mg sodium
- Fiber: 7g fiber)
- Total Carbohydrate: 32g carbohydrate (7g sugars
- Cholesterol: 69mg cholesterol

302. Spaghetti With Italian Meatballs

Serving: 10 servings. | Prep: 20mins | Ready in:

Ingredients

- 3/4 cup chopped onion
- 1 tablespoon olive oil
- 1 garlic clove, minced
- 1 can (28 ounces) Italian crushed tomatoes, undrained

- 1 can (6 ounces) tomato paste
- 1 cup water
- 1-1/2 teaspoons dried oregano
- 1/2 teaspoon salt
- 1/2 teaspoon pepper
- MEATBALLS:
- 4 slices white bread, torn
- 1/2 cup water
- 2 eggs, lightly beaten
- 1/2 cup grated Parmesan cheese
- 1 garlic clove, minced
- 1 teaspoon dried basil
- 1 teaspoon dried parsley flakes
- 1/2 teaspoon salt
- 1 pound lean ground beef (90% lean)
- 2 teaspoons olive oil
- 1 package (16 ounces) spaghetti

Direction

- In a large saucepan, cook onion in oil until softened. Add garlic; cook for 1 more minute. Stir in the tomato paste, tomatoes, oregano, water, pepper and salt. Allow to boil. Lower heat; simmer while covered for nearly 30 minutes.
- In the meantime, in a small bowl, soak bread in water for 5 minutes. Squeeze out excess liquid. In a large bowl, combine the cheese, eggs, basil, garlic, parsley, bread and salt. Crumble beef over mixture and mix well. Form into balls, about 1-inch each.
- In a large nonstick skillet, use cooking spray to coat then brown meatballs in batches in oil over medium heat.
- Add meatballs to sauce; boil again. Decrease heat; uncover and simmer for approximately 30 minutes until meatballs are no longer pink.
- Cook spaghetti following the instructions on the package; drain. Serve with meatballs and sauce.

Nutrition Information

- Calories: 368 calories
- Sodium: 661mg sodium
- Fiber: 3g fiber)
- Total Carbohydrate: 50g carbohydrate (9g sugars
- Cholesterol: 73mg cholesterol
- Protein: 20g protein. Diabetic Exchanges: 2-1/2 starch
- Total Fat: 9g fat (3g saturated fat)

303. Spiced Pot Roast

Serving: 6-8 servings. | Prep: 15mins | Ready in:

Ingredients

- 1/3 cup all-purpose flour
- 1 teaspoon salt
- 1/4 teaspoon pepper
- 1 boneless beef rump or chuck roast (3 pounds)
- 2 tablespoons vegetable oil
- 1-1/2 cups beef broth
- 1/2 cup chutney
- 1/2 cup raisins
- 1/2 cup chopped onion
- 1-1/2 teaspoons curry powder
- 1/2 teaspoon garlic powder
- 1/2 teaspoon ground ginger

Direction

- Mix pepper, salt and flour; rub over the whole roast. Brown all sides of roast in oil in a Dutch oven. Combine the rest of ingredients and pour over the roast.
- Bake with a cover for 3 hours at 325°, until meat becomes tender. If desired, thicken gravy.

Nutrition Information

- Calories: 400 calories
- Total Fat: 20g fat (7g saturated fat)
- Sodium: 524mg sodium
- Fiber: 1g fiber)

- Total Carbohydrate: 19g carbohydrate (13g sugars
- Cholesterol: 111mg cholesterol
- Protein: 35g protein.

304. Spicy Beef Brisket

Serving: 4 | Prep: 10mins | Ready in:

Ingredients

- 2 pounds beef brisket
- 1 (10.5 ounce) can beef broth
- 1/4 cup white wine
- 2 tablespoons olive oil
- 2 teaspoons seasoning salt, or to taste
- 1 teaspoon ground allspice
- 2 tablespoons whole black peppercorns
- 5 cloves garlic, minced
- 1/4 cup dried onion flakes
- 1 tablespoon red pepper flakes
- 1 bay leaf
- 2 tablespoons cornstarch
- 1/4 cup cold water

Direction

- Cut off most of the visible fat from brisket, and put in slow cooker. Add olive oil, white wine and beef broth. Add bay leaf, red pepper flakes, onion flakes, garlic, peppercorns, allspice and seasoning salt to taste. Place a cover, and cook for 3 to 4 hours on Low or till roast is tender enough to easily prick with fork.
- Transfer roast onto a serving platter. Mix cold water and cornstarch together; stir into juices in slow cooker. Increase to High, and cook for only several minutes till thickens. Get rid of bay leaf, and serve it over roast as the gravy.

Nutrition Information

- Calories: 510 calories;

- Total Fat: 38.8
- Sodium: 767
- Total Carbohydrate: 12
- Cholesterol: 93
- Protein: 25.4

305. Spicy Beef Burritos

Serving: 6 | Prep: 30mins | Ready in:

Ingredients

- 6 ounces sliced jalapeno peppers
- 1 tomato, diced
- 1 (4 ounce) can chopped green chile peppers
- 1 green bell pepper, diced
- 1 red bell pepper, diced
- 1 onion, diced
- 1 1/2 tablespoons hot sauce
- 1/4 teaspoon ground cayenne pepper
- 1 pound ground beef
- 1 (1 ounce) package burrito seasoning
- 1 (14 ounce) can refried beans
- 6 (10 inch) flour tortillas
- 1 (10 ounce) bag shredded lettuce
- 1 (8 ounce) container sour cream
- 1 (8 ounce) package shredded sharp Cheddar cheese

Direction

- Mix cayenne pepper, hot sauce, onion, red and green bell pepper, green chile peppers, tomato and jalapeno peppers in a big bowl.
- Cook beef in a big skillet on medium high heat for 5 minutes, mixing to break clumps up. Drain extra grease. Add burrito seasoning and jalapeno pepper mixture; cook, occasionally mixing, for 10 minutes till flavors merge, covered.
- Put refried beans in a saucepan on medium low heat; mix and cook for 5 minutes till heated through.
- In microwave, warm each tortilla for 15-20 seconds till soft. Spread refried beans layer

over; divide beef mixture to tortillas. Top with cheddar cheese, sour cream and lettuce. Fold opposite edges of every tortilla in; roll up to a burrito.

Nutrition Information

- Calories: 723 calories;
- Cholesterol: 108
- Protein: 34
- Total Fat: 38.9
- Sodium: 2042
- Total Carbohydrate: 59.9

306. Spicy Orange Beef

Serving: 4 | Prep: 15mins | Ready in:

Ingredients

- 2 tablespoons vegetable oil
- 1 pound round steak, cut into thin strips on the diagonal
- 1/4 cup orange peel, cut into slivers
- 1 clove garlic, minced
- 1/2 teaspoon ground ginger
- 2 tablespoons cornstarch
- 1 cup beef broth
- 1/4 cup soy sauce
- 1/4 cup sherry
- 1/4 cup orange marmalade
- 1/2 teaspoon crushed red pepper flakes

Direction

- Heat oil on medium high heat in a wok/skillet. 1/3 at 1 time, add beef strips; stir-fry till brown for 3 minutes, transferring done pieces onto paper towel-lined plate.
- Put all beef in wok. Mix in ginger, garlic and orange peel; stir-fry for 1 minute.
- Mix red pepper, marmalade, sherry, soy sauce, broth and cornstarch in a medium bowl; put mixture on beef, constantly mixing. Boil on medium heat; cook for 1 minute then serve hot.

Nutrition Information

- Calories: 397 calories;
- Sodium: 1263
- Total Carbohydrate: 22.7
- Cholesterol: 73
- Protein: 24.9
- Total Fat: 22.3

307. Spicy Shepherd's Pie

Serving: 6 servings. | Prep: 15mins | Ready in:

Ingredients

- 1 package (6.6 ounces) instant mashed potatoes
- 1 pound ground beef
- 1 medium onion, chopped
- 1 can (14-1/2 ounces) diced tomatoes, undrained
- 1 can (11 ounces) Mexicorn, drained
- 1 can (2-1/4 ounces) sliced ripe olives, drained
- 1 envelope taco seasoning
- 1-1/2 teaspoons chili powder
- 1/2 teaspoon salt
- 1/8 teaspoon garlic powder
- 1 cup shredded cheddar cheese, divided

Direction

- Prepare the mashed potatoes following the package directions. In the meantime, over medium heat, cook beef and onion in a large skillet, until the meat is no more pink; drain. Add garlic powder, salt, chili powder, taco seasoning, olives, corn and tomatoes. Bring to a boil; cook, stir for around 1-2 minutes.
- Next, transfer to a greased 2-1/2-qt. baking dish. Lay 3/4 cup cheese on top. Spread atop with the mashed potatoes; dust with the

leftover cheese. Uncover and bake at 350° until the cheese is melted, for 12-15 minutes.

Nutrition Information

- Calories:
- Sodium:
- Fiber:
- Total Carbohydrate:
- Cholesterol:
- Protein:
- Total Fat:

308.   Spinach Beef Bake

Serving: 6-8 servings. | Prep: 10mins | Ready in:

Ingredients

- 1 pound ground beef
- 1 jar (4-1/2 ounces) sliced mushrooms, drained
- 1 medium onion, chopped
- 2 garlic cloves, minced
- 1-1/2 teaspoon dried oregano
- 1-1/4 teaspoon salt
- 1/4 teaspoon pepper
- 2 packages (10 ounces each) frozen chopped spinach, thawed and squeezed dry
- 1 can (10-3/4 ounces) condensed cream of celery soup, undiluted
- 1 cup sour cream
- 1 cup uncooked long grain rice
- 1 cup shredded part-skim mozzarella cheese

Direction

- Brown beef in a frying pan; drain. Add pepper, salt, oregano, garlic, onion and mushrooms. Add rice, sour cream, soup and spinach; combine well.
- Move the mixture to a 2-1/2-quart baking dish coated with cooking spray. Dredge mozzarella cheese over top. Set oven at 350°, bake while

covered until the rice gets tender, about 45 to 50 minutes.

Nutrition Information

- Calories: 342 calories
- Protein: 19g protein.
- Total Fat: 17g fat (9g saturated fat)
- Sodium: 835mg sodium
- Fiber: 3g fiber)
- Total Carbohydrate: 27g carbohydrate (3g sugars
- Cholesterol: 69mg cholesterol

309.   Spinach Beef Stew

Serving: 4 servings. | Prep: 15mins | Ready in:

Ingredients

- 1 medium onion, chopped
- 1 tablespoon olive oil
- 2 garlic cloves, minced
- 1/3 cup cider vinegar
- 2 tablespoons dry red wine or beef broth
- 1 can (29 ounces) tomato sauce
- 1 cup water
- 1/3 cup chopped roasted sweet red peppers
- 3 bay leaves
- 3 tablespoons brown sugar
- 3 teaspoons beef bouillon granules
- 1 teaspoon dried oregano
- 1/2 teaspoon dried basil
- 1/4 teaspoon dried thyme
- 1/4 teaspoon pepper
- 1/3 cup uncooked long grain rice
- 1/2 pound cubed cooked roast beef
- 2 cups chopped fresh spinach
- Sour cream and grated Parmesan cheese, optional

Direction

- Sauté onion in oil in a Dutch oven until soft. Add garlic, sauté for another 1 minute. Mix in wine and vinegar. Boil it; cook until the liquid has mostly evaporated.
- Add seasonings, bouillon, brown sugar, bay leaves, peppers, water, and tomato sauce. Boil it. Mix in rice. Lower the heat, simmer with a cover until the rice is soft, about 15-20 minutes.
- Remove the bay leaves. Add spinach and beef; cook while stirring until thoroughly heated and the spinach has wilted. Enjoy with Parmesan cheese and sour cream if wanted.

Nutrition Information

- Calories:
- Fiber:
- Total Carbohydrate:
- Cholesterol:
- Protein:
- Total Fat:
- Sodium:

310. Spinach Steak Pinwheels

Serving: 6 servings. | Prep: 15mins | Ready in:

Ingredients

- 1-1/2 pounds beef top sirloin steak
- 8 bacon strips, cooked
- 1 package (10 ounces) frozen chopped spinach, thawed and squeezed dry
- 1/4 cup grated Parmesan cheese
- 1/2 teaspoon salt
- 1/8 teaspoon cayenne pepper

Direction

- Make shallow and diagonal cuts into the steak with 1-inch intervals into its top. Follow the same cuts going the opposite direction. Tightly seal the steak with plastic wrap and pound it into 1/2-inch thickness using the meat mallet. Unwrap the plastic and remove the steak.
- At the center of the steak, position the bacon widthwise. Combine all the remaining ingredients in a bowl and pour it all over the bacon. Roll the steak like a jelly-roll style, starting from the shortest side of the steak. Secure the steak with toothpicks and cut it into six slices.
- Grease the grill rack with cooking oil. Place the pinwheels into the coated rack and cover it. Grill each side for 5-6 minutes until the beef meets its desired doneness. Thermometer readings will depend on your desired doneness; for medium-rare cooked, it should read 145°F and for medium cooked it should be 160°F. Remove and throw the toothpicks before serving.

Nutrition Information

- Calories: 227 calories
- Sodium: 536mg sodium
- Fiber: 1g fiber)
- Total Carbohydrate: 3g carbohydrate (0 sugars
- Cholesterol: 60mg cholesterol
- Protein: 31g protein. Diabetic Exchanges: 4 lean meat
- Total Fat: 10g fat (4g saturated fat)

311. Spinach Beef Spaghetti Pie

Serving: 8 servings. | Prep: 20mins | Ready in:

Ingredients

- 6 ounces uncooked angel hair pasta
- 2 large eggs, lightly beaten
- 1/3 cup grated Parmesan cheese
- 1 pound ground beef
- 1/2 cup chopped onion
- 1/4 cup chopped green pepper
- 1 jar (14 ounces) meatless pasta sauce

- 1 teaspoon Creole seasoning
- 3/4 teaspoon garlic powder
- 1/2 teaspoon dried basil
- 1/2 teaspoon dried oregano
- 1 package (8 ounces) cream cheese, softened
- 1 package (10 ounces) frozen chopped spinach, thawed and squeezed dry
- 1/2 cup shredded part-skim mozzarella cheese

Direction

- Following the package instructions, cook the pasta; then drain. Put in Parmesan cheese and eggs. Press up the sides and onto the bottom of a 9-inch deep-dish pie plate coated with cooking spray. Bake for 10 minutes at 350 degrees.
- At the same time, cook green pepper, onion, beef over medium heat until the meat is not pink anymore; then drain. Stir in the seasonings and pasta sauce. Boil. Turn down the heat; put on a cover and simmer for 10 minutes.
- Roll out the cream cheese to form into a 7-inch circle between 2 pieces of waxed paper. Fill into the crust. Put the meat sauce and spinach on top. Dust with mozzarella cheese. Bake at 350 degrees until set, 20-30 minutes.

Nutrition Information

- Calories: 377 calories
- Cholesterol: 130mg cholesterol
- Protein: 22g protein.
- Total Fat: 21g fat (11g saturated fat)
- Sodium: 544mg sodium
- Fiber: 3g fiber)
- Total Carbohydrate: 24g carbohydrate (5g sugars

312. Spiral Pepperoni Pizza Bake

Serving: 12 servings. | Prep: 30mins | Ready in:

Ingredients

- 1 package (16 ounces) spiral pasta
- 2 pounds ground beef
- 1 large onion, chopped
- 1 teaspoon salt
- 1/2 teaspoon garlic salt
- 1/2 teaspoon Italian seasoning
- 1/2 teaspoon pepper
- 2 cans (15 ounces each) pizza sauce
- 2 eggs, lightly beaten
- 2 cups 2% milk
- 1/2 cup shredded Parmesan cheese
- 4 cups shredded part-skim mozzarella cheese
- 1 package (3-1/2 ounces) sliced pepperoni

Direction

- Set oven to 350 degrees and start preheating. Follow package instructions to cook pasta.
- At the same time, cook onion and beef for 8 to 10 minutes on medium heat in a Dutch oven or until beef is not pink anymore and broken into crumbles. Drain. Sprinkle seasonings over top. Mix in pizza sauce then take away from heat.
- Stir Parmesan cheese, milk, and egg in a big bowl. Drain pasta then place into the egg mixture; toss to mix. Move to an oiled 3-quart baking dish. Arrange pepperoni, mozzarella cheese, and beef mixture over top.
- Bake for 20 minutes with cover. Remove cover and bake for 20-25 more minutes or until heated through and golden brown.

Nutrition Information

- Calories:
- Protein:
- Total Fat:
- Sodium:
- Fiber:
- Total Carbohydrate:
- Cholesterol:

313. Star Of The North Pasties

Serving: 4 servings. | Prep: 30mins | Ready in:

Ingredients

- 2 cups all-purpose flour
- 1/2 teaspoon salt
- 1/2 teaspoon baking powder
- 1/2 cup shortening or lard
- 1/2 cup milk
- 1/2 cup cubed uncooked potatoes
- 1/2 cup cubed uncooked rutabagas
- 1/2 cup cubed uncooked carrots
- 1/4 cup chopped onion
- 1/2 pound ground beef or diced beef top sirloin steak, browned

Direction

- Combine the first 3 ingredients, cut the shortening into the mixture to get the big pea-size crumbs. Add milk little by little, mix just enough to stick them together. Form the dough gently into 4 balls, let rest for 5 minutes.
- In the meantime, mix the meat with vegetables. Take it to a light-floured surface, roll each ball into a circle. Put 1/4 of the vegetable-meat mixture on one side of each circle, brush water on the crust edges, fold in half to cover the filling. Crimp the edges to seal. Lay on an uncoated baking tray and use a fork to poke the tops. Set oven at 350°, bake for 60 minutes.

Nutrition Information

- Calories: 588 calories
- Total Fat: 31g fat (9g saturated fat)
- Sodium: 409mg sodium
- Fiber: 3g fiber)
- Total Carbohydrate: 57g carbohydrate (5g sugars
- Cholesterol: 32mg cholesterol
- Protein: 18g protein.

314. Steak Pinwheels

Serving: 6 servings. | Prep: 20mins | Ready in:

Ingredients

- 1-1/2 pounds beef flank steak
- 1/4 cup olive oil
- 2 tablespoons red wine vinegar
- 2 teaspoons Worcestershire sauce
- 2 teaspoons Italian seasoning
- 1-1/2 teaspoons garlic powder
- 1-1/2 teaspoons salt, divided
- 1-1/2 teaspoons pepper, divided
- 1/2 cup shredded cheddar cheese
- 2 garlic cloves, minced
- 1/4 cup finely chopped onion
- 1/4 cup minced fresh parsley

Direction

- Press the beef until it's 1/4-inch thick. Combine Worcestershire sauce, garlic powder, Italian seasoning, vinegar, oil, and 1 tablespoon each of salt and of pepper in a big resealable plastic bag. Insert the steak and seal the bag up then turn to coat the meat. Keep it refrigerated for 8 hours or through the night then drain the meat and discard the marinade. Mix the rest of the salt and pepper with parsley, onion, garlic and cheese then scatter it over the steak within 1-inch of the edges. Starting with the long side, roll it up in jellyroll style and tie at 1-inch intervals with kitchen string. In every piece where it's tied up, insert a skewer then cut them up into 1 1/4-inch rolls. Drip cooking oil on paper towel to moisten it and use long-handled tongs to coat the grill rack with it lightly. Over medium-hot heat, grill the steak until the meat is at desired doneness, about 6 to 8 minutes on each side. For medium-rare meat, a thermometer should register at 145°F and for medium, it should be 160°F. For well-done meat, it should read 170°F.

Nutrition Information

- Calories:
- Total Fat:
- Sodium:
- Fiber:
- Total Carbohydrate:
- Cholesterol:
- Protein:

315. Steak Potpie

Serving: 4-6 servings. | Prep: 01hours35mins | Ready in:

Ingredients

- 3/4 cup sliced onions
- 4 tablespoons canola oil, divided
- 1/4 cup all-purpose flour
- 1 teaspoon salt
- 1/2 teaspoon pepper
- 1/2 teaspoon paprika
- Pinch ground allspice
- Pinch ground ginger
- 1 pound beef top round steak, cut into 1/2-inch pieces
- 2-1/2 cups boiling water
- 3 medium potatoes, peeled and diced
- Pastry for single-crust pie

Direction

- Sauté the onions in a large skillet in 2 tablespoons of oil until golden. Allow to drain and put aside.
- Combine dry ingredients in a large resealable plastic bag; put in the meat and shake to coat. In the same skillet, brown the meat in remaining oil. Pour water; simmer, covered, for 60 minutes, until the meat is soft.
- Add potatoes; uncover and continue to simmer until the potatoes are softened, or for 15-20 minutes. Pour the mixture into a greased 1-1/2-qt. baking dish. Lay onion slices on top. Roll the pastry to fit the baking dish. Next, put over the hot filling and seal to edges of the plate. In the crust, make slits.
- Bake at 450° until golden brown, or for 25-30 minutes. Use foil to cover the edges of the crust if necessary to prevent from over-browning.

Nutrition Information

- Calories: 422 calories
- Total Fat: 21g fat (6g saturated fat)
- Sodium: 551mg sodium
- Fiber: 1g fiber)
- Total Carbohydrate: 37g carbohydrate (3g sugars
- Cholesterol: 49mg cholesterol
- Protein: 20g protein.

316. Steak Tortillas

Serving: 6 servings. | Prep: 15mins | Ready in:

Ingredients

- 2 cups thinly sliced cooked beef ribeye or sirloin steak (about 3/4 pound)
- 1 small onion, chopped
- 1/4 cup salsa
- 1/2 teaspoon ground cumin
- 1/2 teaspoon chili powder
- 1/4 teaspoon garlic powder
- 1-1/2 teaspoons all-purpose flour
- 1/2 cup cold water
- 6 flour tortillas (8 inches), warmed
- Shredded cheese, chopped lettuce and tomatoes and additional salsa, optional

Direction

- Sauté onion and steak for a minute in a large non-stick skillet. Mix in the garlic powder, chili powder, cumin and salsa.
- Mix water and flour in a small bowl until smooth; put to the skillet gradually. Take to a

boil; cook and mix until it thickens for 1 to 2 minutes. Put beef mixture on tortillas; put extra salsa, tomatoes, lettuce and cheese on top as desired. Fold in sides.

Nutrition Information

- Calories: 253 calories
- Protein: 22g protein. Diabetic Exchanges: 3 lean meat
- Total Fat: 6g fat (1g saturated fat)
- Sodium: 313mg sodium
- Fiber: 0 fiber)
- Total Carbohydrate: 28g carbohydrate (1g sugars
- Cholesterol: 43mg cholesterol

317. Steak And Black Bean Burritos

Serving: 2 servings. | Prep: 15mins | Ready in:

Ingredients

- 4 ounces beef flank steak
- 1/8 teaspoon salt
- 1/8 teaspoon pepper
- 1/2 teaspoon canola oil
- 2 flour tortillas (8 inches), warmed
- 1/2 cup cold cooked rice
- 1/2 medium ripe avocado, peeled and diced
- 1/2 cup canned black beans, rinsed and drained
- 2 tablespoons sour cream
- 1 tablespoon salsa
- 1 tablespoon finely chopped onion
- 1-1/2 teaspoons minced fresh cilantro

Direction

- Drizzle pepper and salt on the steak. Over medium high heat, cook the steak in oil in a small skillet coated with cooking spray until you achieve your desired doneness of the steak, about 3-4 minutes on each side. A thermometer should read 145° for medium rare, 160° for medium and 170° for well-done.
- Cut the steak thinly across the grain. Put in the middle of the tortillas. Put cilantro, onion, sour cream, beans, avocado, salsa and rice on top. Roll up the tortillas then serve immediately.

Nutrition Information

- Calories: 449 calories
- Sodium: 589mg sodium
- Fiber: 6g fiber)
- Total Carbohydrate: 51g carbohydrate (2g sugars
- Cholesterol: 37mg cholesterol
- Protein: 21g protein.
- Total Fat: 18g fat (5g saturated fat)

318. Steaks With Cherry Chipotle Glaze

Serving: 4 servings. | Prep: 15mins | Ready in:

Ingredients

- 1/4 cup sherry vinegar
- 1/4 cup balsamic vinegar
- 1/4 cup Worcestershire sauce
- 1/4 cup olive oil
- 2 garlic cloves, minced
- 2 teaspoons Dijon mustard
- 1/4 teaspoon salt
- 1/4 teaspoon pepper
- 2 beef flat iron or top sirloin steaks (1 pound each)
- GLAZE:
- 2 tablespoons cherry preserves
- 1 tablespoon brown sugar
- 1 tablespoon olive oil
- 1 chipotle pepper in adobo sauce, minced

Direction

- Mix the initial 8 ingredients in a shallow bowl. Stir in meat and toss it thoroughly to coat. Store the mixture for 4 hours inside the refrigerator.
- Pour and whisk the glaze ingredients in a separate bowl. Drain the meat and discard its marinade. Grill each side of the meat, covered, over medium heat for 4 minutes, or you can broil the meat 4-inches away from the heat source until the desired temperature of the meat is reached (for medium-rare, 135°F; for medium, 140°F; for medium-well, 145°F). Be sure to baste the meat using glaze at the final 2 minutes of cooking. Before serving, cut the steaks in half and arrange it in a serving platter.

Nutrition Information

- Calories: 510 calories
- Cholesterol: 146mg cholesterol
- Protein: 43g protein.
- Total Fat: 31g fat (10g saturated fat)
- Sodium: 260mg sodium
- Fiber: 0g fiber)
- Total Carbohydrate: 12g carbohydrate (11g sugars

319. Stew For A Crowd

Serving: 120 (1-cup) servings. | Prep: 60mins | Ready in:

Ingredients

- 25 pounds beef stew meat
- 5 pounds onions, diced (about 16 cups)
- 2 bunches celery, cut into 1-inch pieces (about 14 cups)
- About 5 quarts water
- 1/2 cup browning sauce, optional
- 1/4 cup salt
- 3 tablespoons garlic powder
- 3 tablespoons dried thyme
- 3 tablespoons seasoned salt
- 2 tablespoons pepper
- 12 bay leaves
- 15 pounds red potatoes, cut into 1-inch cubes (about 16 cups)
- 10 pounds carrots, cut into 1-inch pieces (about 24 cups)
- 10 cups frozen peas
- 10 cups frozen corn
- 4 cups all-purpose flour
- 3 to 4 cups milk

Direction

- Separate celery, onions, and stew meat into different big stockpot or Dutch oven. Fill each pan half full with water. Add seasoning and browning sauce (if using).
- Bring to a boil. Lower heat; simmer, covered until meat is tender, or about 1 hour and 30 minutes. Add carrots and potatoes; bring to a boil. Lower heat; simmer, covered until vegetables are softened, or about 30 minutes.
- Add corn and peas; bring to another boil. Lower heat; simmer without a cover until thoroughly heated, or for 15 minutes.
- Whisk flour with enough milk until a creamy, smooth paste forms; slowly stir into the stew. Bring to a boil. Cook, stirring until thickened, or for 2 minutes. Remove bay leaves.

Nutrition Information

- Calories: 244 calories
- Fiber: 4g fiber)
- Total Carbohydrate: 23g carbohydrate (6g sugars
- Cholesterol: 60mg cholesterol
- Protein: 22g protein.
- Total Fat: 7g fat (3g saturated fat)
- Sodium: 434mg sodium

320. Stout Shiitake Pot Roast

Serving: 6 servings. | Prep: 30mins | Ready in:

Ingredients

- 3 tablespoons olive oil, divided
- 1 boneless beef chuck roast (2 to 3 pounds)
- 2 medium onions, sliced
- 1 garlic clove, minced
- 1 bottle (12 ounces) stout or nonalcoholic beer
- 1/2 ounce dried shiitake mushrooms (about 1/2 cup)
- 1 tablespoon brown sugar
- 1 teaspoon Worcestershire sauce
- 1/2 teaspoon dried savory
- 1 pound red potatoes (about 8 small), cut into 1-inch pieces
- 2 medium carrots, sliced
- 1/2 cup water
- 1/2 teaspoon salt
- 1/4 teaspoon pepper

Direction

- Heat 1 tablespoon oil in a Dutch oven over medium heat. Cook roast in heated oil until all sides are brown; take out of the pan.
- Heat the remaining oil in the same pan. Add garlic and onions; cook and stir in heated oil until softened. Pour in beer, whisking to loosen any browned bits from pan. Mix in savory, Worcestershire sauce, brown sugar, and mushrooms. Put roast back into the pan. Bring to a boil. Lower heat; cover and simmer for 1 hour and 30 minutes. Add the remaining ingredients; mix well. Bring to a boil. Lower heat; cover and simmer until vegetables and meat are tender, for 15 to 25 minutes longer. Ladle off fat and thicken pan juices for gravy, if desired.

Nutrition Information

- Calories: 441 calories
- Sodium: 293mg sodium
- Fiber: 3g fiber)
- Total Carbohydrate: 24g carbohydrate (9g sugars
- Cholesterol: 98mg cholesterol
- Protein: 33g protein.
- Total Fat: 21g fat (7g saturated fat)

321. Stuffed Flank Steak With Mushroom Sherry Cream

Serving: 6 servings (1-1/2 cups sauce). | Prep: 45mins | Ready in:

Ingredients

- 1 beef flank steak (1-1/2 pounds)
- 1/3 cup garlic-herb spreadable cheese
- 2 tablespoons prepared pesto
- 3/4 pound whole fresh mushrooms, thinly sliced, divided
- 2 cups fresh baby spinach
- 1 jar (7 ounces) roasted sweet red peppers, drained and julienned
- 1 teaspoon coarsely ground pepper
- 1/2 teaspoon salt
- 2 tablespoons olive oil, divided
- 1 shallot, sliced
- 2 cups reduced-sodium beef broth
- 1 cup sherry
- 1 cup heavy whipping cream

Direction

- From a long side, horizontally split steak within 1/2-in. from opposing side. Flip steak so long side faces you; so it lies flat, open steak. Cover in plastic wrap; flatten to 1/4-inch thick. Remove plastic.
- Within 1/2 in. from edges, spread cheese on steak; layer with salt, pepper, red peppers, spinach, 1 3/4 cups mushrooms and pesto. Roll up, rolling the steak away from you, jellyroll style. Tie in 1 1/2-in. intervals with kitchen string; rub 1 tbsp. oil.
- Brown all sides of steaks in a big ovenproof skillet; bake in skillet for 40-50 minutes at 375° till meat gets desired doneness; 170° well done, 160° medium and 145° medium rare on thermometer. Remove from pan then cover; keep warm.

- Sauté leftover mushrooms and shallot in leftover oil till tender in same skillet. Put sherry and broth in pan; boil. Cook for 15 minutes till liquid reduces by half. Add cream; boil. Cook for 10 minutes till liquid reduces by half; serve with sliced beef.

Nutrition Information

- Calories: 489 calories
- Protein: 27g protein.
- Total Fat: 36g fat (18g saturated fat)
- Sodium: 681mg sodium
- Fiber: 1g fiber)
- Total Carbohydrate: 8g carbohydrate (3g sugars
- Cholesterol: 127mg cholesterol

322. Summer Beef Skewers

Serving: 8 servings. | Prep: 15mins | Ready in:

Ingredients

- 1 cup pineapple juice
- 1 cup red wine or beef broth
- 1/2 cup soy sauce
- 1/2 cup Worcestershire sauce
- 1 medium onion, chopped
- 1 teaspoon dried thyme
- 1 teaspoon dried rosemary, crushed
- 1/2 teaspoon pepper
- 3/4 pound cherry tomatoes
- 1/2 pound whole fresh mushrooms
- 3 small zucchini, cut into 1/2-inch slices
- 2 small yellow summer squash, cut into 1/2-inch slices
- 2 pounds beef sirloin tip steak, cut into 1-1/4-inch cubes
- Hot cooked rice, optional

Direction

- In a bowl, mix the first eight ingredients well, then take a cup of the marinade to put into a large re-sealable plastic bag with the vegetables. Take another re-sealable bag, add the beef and pour the remaining half of the marinade over the beef. Seal both bags, turn to coat, and marinate in the refrigerator for 4-6 hours or overnight, turning the bags over occasionally. Drain the beef, discarding its marinade. Drain the vegetables and save its marinade. Alternately cue the beef, mushrooms, tomatoes, summer squash, and zucchini. Cook on an open grill over medium heat for 3 minutes per side. Baste and turn frequently for 8-10 minutes, or until meat is done to liking. Meat is medium-rare when the thermometer reads 145 deg, medium at 160 deg, and well-done at 170 deg. Serve over warm rice, if desired.

Nutrition Information

- Calories: 266 calories
- Sodium: 459mg sodium
- Fiber: 1g fiber)
- Total Carbohydrate: 9g carbohydrate (0 sugars
- Cholesterol: 74mg cholesterol
- Protein: 24g protein. Diabetic Exchanges: 3 lean meat
- Total Fat: 13g fat (5g saturated fat)

323. Summer Steak Kabobs

Serving: 6 servings. | Prep: 20mins | Ready in:

Ingredients

- 1/2 cup canola oil
- 1/4 cup soy sauce
- 3 tablespoons honey
- 2 tablespoons white vinegar
- 1/2 teaspoon ground ginger
- 1/2 teaspoon garlic powder

- 1-1/2 pounds beef top sirloin steak, cut into 1-inch cubes
- 1/2 pound whole fresh mushrooms
- 2 medium onions, cut into wedges
- 1 medium sweet red pepper, cut into 1-inch pieces
- 1 medium green pepper, cut into 1-inch pieces
- 1 medium yellow summer squash, cut into 1/2-inch slices
- Hot cooked rice

Direction

- Mix the first six ingredients in a large bowl. Toss the beef in the bowl to coat with the marinade. Cover and store in the refrigerator for 8 hours or overnight. Discard the marinade and alternately skewer beef and vegetables on 12 metal or water-soaked wooden skewers. Cook in a covered grill at medium heat, turning occasionally for 10-12 minutes or until beef is done to liking. Serve over rice.

Nutrition Information

- Calories: 257 calories
- Total Carbohydrate: 11g carbohydrate (7g sugars
- Cholesterol: 46mg cholesterol
- Protein: 27g protein. Diabetic Exchanges: 3 lean meat
- Total Fat: 12g fat (2g saturated fat)
- Sodium: 277mg sodium
- Fiber: 2g fiber)

324. Super Spaghetti Sauce

Serving: 2-1/2 quarts. | Prep: 10mins | Ready in:

Ingredients

- 1 pound ground beef
- 1 pound Johnsonville® Fully Cooked Polish Kielbasa Sausage Rope, cut into 1/4-inch slices
- 2 jars (24 ounces each) spaghetti sauce with mushrooms
- 1 jar (16 ounces) chunky salsa
- Hot cooked pasta

Direction

- Put the beef in a Dutch oven placed over medium heat. Allow the beef to cook until no visible pink color on the meat; drain and place aside. Using the same pan, cook the sausage for roughly 5-6 minutes over medium heat or until the sausages turned brown.
- Mix in the spaghetti sauce, reserved beef and the salsa; heat well. Serve alongside the pasta.

Nutrition Information

- Calories: 325 calories
- Fiber: 2g fiber)
- Total Carbohydrate: 18g carbohydrate (11g sugars
- Cholesterol: 60mg cholesterol
- Protein: 17g protein.
- Total Fat: 21g fat (7g saturated fat)
- Sodium: 1378mg sodium

325. Supreme Roast Beef

Serving: 8 servings. | Prep: 10mins | Ready in:

Ingredients

- 1 large onion, sliced into rings
- 2 tablespoons Worcestershire sauce
- 4 to 5 teaspoons coarsely ground pepper
- 1 beef rump roast or bottom round roast (4 to 5 pounds)
- 6 to 8 bay leaves

Direction

- Arrange onion in a greased shallow roasting pan. Rub roast with pepper and Worcestershire sauce. Arrange roast over

onion; add bay leaves on top. Bake, covered for 1 3/4 to 2 1/4 hours at 325° until desired doneness of meat is reached.
- Discard bay leaves. Allow meat to rest for 10 to 15 minutes before carving. Thicken juices in pan if desired.

Nutrition Information

- Calories: 301 calories
- Cholesterol: 136mg cholesterol
- Protein: 45g protein.
- Total Fat: 11g fat (4g saturated fat)
- Sodium: 114mg sodium
- Fiber: 1g fiber)
- Total Carbohydrate: 3g carbohydrate (1g sugars

326. Sweet And Savory Pulled Beef Dinner

Serving: 6 servings. | Prep: 25mins | Ready in:

Ingredients

- 1 teaspoon salt
- 1 teaspoon ground mustard
- 1 teaspoon barbecue seasoning
- 1 teaspoon paprika
- 1 teaspoon chili powder
- 1/2 teaspoon pepper
- 1 boneless beef chuck roast (3 pounds)
- 3 tablespoons olive oil
- 1 large onion, halved and sliced
- 1 large sweet red pepper, sliced
- SAUCE:
- 1 can (8 ounces) tomato sauce
- 1/3 cup packed brown sugar
- 3 tablespoons honey
- 2 tablespoons Dijon mustard
- 2 tablespoons Worcestershire sauce
- 2 tablespoons soy sauce
- 5 garlic cloves, minced
- 4 teaspoons balsamic vinegar
- 3/4 teaspoon salt
- Cooked egg noodles

Direction

- Mix the first six ingredients. Slice the roast in half; then rub with seasonings. Cook all sides of beef to brown with oil in a large skillet. Move into a 4- or 5-qt. slow cooker. Put red pepper and onion on top.
- Combine the vinegar, salt, garlic, soy sauce, Worcestershire sauce, mustard, honey, brown sugar and tomato sauce in a small bowl; pour over vegetables. Cook with a cover for 6-8 hours on low, or until the meat is tender.
- Take out the roast; allow to cool slightly. Strain off the cooking juices, keeping 1-1/4 cups of juices and vegetables; remove fat from the saved juices. Use two forks to shred beef and put back to slow cooker. Stir in the saved cooking juices and vegetables; heat through. Serve along with noodles.

Nutrition Information

- Calories: 571 calories
- Protein: 47g protein.
- Total Fat: 29g fat (9g saturated fat)
- Sodium: 1604mg sodium
- Fiber: 2g fiber)
- Total Carbohydrate: 31g carbohydrate (24g sugars
- Cholesterol: 147mg cholesterol

327. Swift Spaghetti

Serving: 4-6 servings. | Prep: 10mins | Ready in:

Ingredients

- 5-1/2 cups water
- 1 package (7 ounces) spaghetti
- 1 envelope onion soup mix

- 1 pound ground beef
- 1 can (8 ounces) tomato sauce
- 1 can (6 ounces) tomato paste
- 1 tablespoon dried parsley flakes
- 1 teaspoon dried oregano
- 1/2 teaspoon dried basil
- 1/4 to 1/2 teaspoon garlic powder

Direction

- Bring water in a big saucepan to a boil. Put in dry soup mix and spaghetti. Cook until spaghetti is softened without draining, about 12 to 15 minutes. In the meantime, cook beef in a big skillet on moderate heat until it is not pink anymore, then drain. Stir in garlic powder, basil, oregano, parsley, tomato paste and tomato sauce, then put all into the spaghetti mixture and heat through.

Nutrition Information

- Calories:
- Protein:
- Total Fat:
- Sodium:
- Fiber:
- Total Carbohydrate:
- Cholesterol:

328. Swiss Steak Burgers For 2

Serving: 2 servings. | Prep: 5mins | Ready in:

Ingredients

- 2 tablespoons A.1. steak sauce, divided
- 3 teaspoons Dijon mustard, divided
- 1/2 pound ground beef
- 2 slices Swiss cheese
- 2 hamburger buns, split and toasted

Direction

- Mix 1-1/2 teaspoons of mustard and a tablespoon of steak sauce together in a small bowl. Crumble beef and add into mixture; combine well. Form into 2 patties.
- Cover and grill burgers over medium heat or broil 4 inches from the heat for 5-7 minutes per side till juices are clear and a thermometer reads 160 degrees. Use cheese to place on top. Allow to grill till cheese melts, about 1 more minute.
- Use remaining mustard and steak sauce to spread buns; place a burger on top of each.

Nutrition Information

- Calories: 471 calories
- Cholesterol: 111mg cholesterol
- Protein: 34g protein.
- Total Fat: 24g fat (11g saturated fat)
- Sodium: 782mg sodium
- Fiber: 1g fiber)
- Total Carbohydrate: 26g carbohydrate (5g sugars

329. Swiss Steak Dinner

Serving: 6 servings. | Prep: 20mins | Ready in:

Ingredients

- 1/2 cup all-purpose flour
- 2 teaspoons salt, divided
- 1/2 teaspoon pepper
- 2 pounds beef top round steak, cut into 1/2-inch pieces
- 2 to 3 tablespoons canola oil
- 6 medium onions, thinly sliced
- 7 to 9 small red potatoes (about 1-1/4 pounds), halved
- 1 bay leaf
- 1 can (10-3/4 ounces) condensed tomato soup, undiluted
- 2 cups frozen cut green beans, thawed

Direction

- In the big resealable plastic bag, mix pepper, 1.5 teaspoons of salt and flour. Put in the beef, several pieces at a time, and shake to cover.
- In the big skillet on medium heat, brown the beef in oil on all of the sides. Move into a greased 3-quart baking dish. Add the potatoes and onions on top. Scatter the rest of the salt over; toss lightly to coat. Put in bay leaf. Scoop the tomato soup on top.
- Bake with cover at 350 degrees for 1.5 hours. Add the beans around edge of the dish. Bake till the veggies and meat soften or for 15 to 20 minutes more. Get rid of the bay leaf.

Nutrition Information

- Calories: 440 calories
- Protein: 40g protein.
- Total Fat: 9g fat (2g saturated fat)
- Sodium: 1187mg sodium
- Fiber: 7g fiber)
- Total Carbohydrate: 47g carbohydrate (15g sugars
- Cholesterol: 85mg cholesterol

330. Taco Bake

Serving: 6 servings. | Prep: 30mins | Ready in:

Ingredients

- 1 pound ground beef
- 1 small onion, chopped
- 3/4 cup water
- 1 package (1-1/4 ounces) taco seasoning
- 1 can (15 ounces) tomato sauce
- 1 package (8 ounce) shell macaroni, cooked and drained
- 1 can (4 ounces) chopped green chilies
- 2 cups shredded cheddar cheese, divided

Direction

- In a skillet, brown onion and ground beef over medium heat; let drain. Mix in the tomato sauce, taco seasoning and water; mix. Let boil; decrease heat and simmer for around 20 minutes. Stir in 1 and a half cups of cheese, chilies and macaroni. Pour into a greased baking dish of 1 and a half quart. Use the rest cheese for sprinkling. Bake at 350° for approximately 30 minutes or till heated through.

Nutrition Information

- Calories: 380 calories
- Sodium: 1205mg sodium
- Fiber: 2g fiber)
- Total Carbohydrate: 22g carbohydrate (2g sugars
- Cholesterol: 90mg cholesterol
- Protein: 26g protein.
- Total Fat: 20g fat (12g saturated fat)

331. Taco Crescents

Serving: 8 servings. | Prep: 15mins | Ready in:

Ingredients

- 3/4 pound ground beef
- 1/4 cup chopped onion
- 1 package (1-1/4-ounces) taco seasoning
- 1 can (4-1/4-ounces) chopped ripe olives, drained
- 2 large eggs, lightly beaten
- 1/2 cup shredded cheddar cheese
- 2 tubes (8-ounces) tubes refrigerated crescent rolls

Direction

- Cook onion and beef in a large skillet until the meat is not pink anymore; then drain. Stir in olives and taco seasoning; then put aside to allow to cool. Put in cheese and eggs.

- Unroll the crescent roll dough and form separately into triangles. On a grease-free baking sheet, arrange triangles. Put on each triangle with 2 tbsp. of meat mixture, then roll and form into crescents. Bake at 375 degrees until lightly browned, 10-15 minutes.

Nutrition Information

- Calories: 255 calories
- Fiber: 1g fiber)
- Total Carbohydrate: 17g carbohydrate (3g sugars
- Cholesterol: 81mg cholesterol
- Protein: 13g protein.
- Total Fat: 15g fat (5g saturated fat)
- Sodium: 842mg sodium

332. Taco Meat Loaves

Serving: 2 meat loaves (6 servings each). | Prep: 25mins | Ready in:

Ingredients

- 3 large eggs, lightly beaten
- 2 cups picante sauce, divided
- 1 can (16 ounces) kidney beans, rinsed and drained
- 1 can (11 ounces) Mexicorn, drained
- 1 medium onion, chopped
- 2 cans (2-1/4 ounces each) sliced ripe olives, drained
- 3/4 cup dry bread crumbs
- 1 envelope taco seasoning
- 1 teaspoon ground cumin
- 1 teaspoon chili powder
- 2 pounds ground beef
- 2 cups shredded cheddar cheese
- Additional picante sauce, optional

Direction

- Mix chili powder, cumin, taco seasoning, bread crumbs, olives, onion, corn, beans, 1/2 cup picante sauce, and eggs together in a large mixing bowl. Crumble beef over mixture; stir to combine.
- Press beef meat mixture into 2 ungreased 9x5-inch loaf pans. Bake without covering for 50 to 55 minutes at 350° until no longer pink inside and a thermometers reaches 160°.
- Spread top of each meatloaf with remaining picante sauce; scatter top with cheese. Bake until cheese is melted, for 10 to 15 minutes more. Allow to stand for 10 minutes before cutting. Serve meatloaves with more picante sauce, if desired.

Nutrition Information

- Calories: 354 calories
- Total Fat: 18g fat (8g saturated fat)
- Sodium: 1001mg sodium
- Fiber: 3g fiber)
- Total Carbohydrate: 23g carbohydrate (4g sugars
- Cholesterol: 112mg cholesterol
- Protein: 23g protein.

333. Taco Muffins

Serving: about 16 muffins. | Prep: 35mins | Ready in:

Ingredients

- 1 pound ground beef
- 3/4 cup water
- 1 envelope taco seasoing
- 1/4 cup butter, softened
- 1/4 cup sugar
- 1 large egg
- 1-3/4 cups all-purpose flour
- 4 teaspoons baking powder
- 1/4 teaspoon baking soda
- 1/4 teaspoon salt
- 1 cup buttermilk

- 1 cup salsa
- 1 cup shredded cheddar cheese

Direction

- In the big skillet, cook the beef on medium heat till not pink anymore; drain off. Pour in the taco seasoning and water; let simmer, while uncovered, for 15 minutes. Let cool down.
- In the big bowl, cream the sugar and butter till becoming fluffy and light. Whisk in the egg. Mix the dry ingredients; put into creamed mixture alternately with the buttermilk, whisking thoroughly after each addition. Fold in the meat mixture.
- Fill the greased muffin cups 2/3 full. Bake at 425 degrees till turning golden brown or for 12 to 15 minutes. Gently transfer the muffins into the greased 13x9-inch baking dish. Add the cheese and salsa on top of each. Bake till cheese melts or for 5 more minutes.

Nutrition Information

- Calories:
- Sodium:
- Fiber:
- Total Carbohydrate:
- Cholesterol:
- Protein:
- Total Fat:

334. Tacoritos For Two

Serving: 2 servings. | Prep: 40mins | Ready in:

Ingredients

- 1 tablespoon butter
- 1 tablespoon all-purpose flour
- 1 cup water
- 1 tablespoon chili powder
- 1/4 teaspoon garlic salt
- 1/4 pound ground beef
- 1/4 pound Jones No Sugar Pork Sausage Roll sausage
- 1 tablespoon chopped onion
- 1/4 cup refried beans
- 2 flour tortillas (8 inches), warmed
- 3/4 cup shredded Monterey Jack cheese
- Optional toppings: shredded lettuce, chopped tomatoes, sliced ripe olives and sour cream

Direction

- Melt butter in a saucepan. Stir in flour until smooth and add water gradually. Boil; cook and stir until thickened, about 1 minute. Stir in garlic salt and chili powder. Bring to a boil. Lower the heat; simmer while uncovered for 5 minutes.
- Over medium heat, cook onion, sausage, and beef in a skillet until the meat is no more pink; allow to drain. Stir in refried beans until heated through.
- In a greased 8-in. baking dish, spread 1/4 cup sauce. Continue to spread each tortilla with 1 tablespoon sauce; arrange the center of each with 2/3 cup of the meat mixture. Lay 1/4 cup cheese on top each. Roll up and arrange in the prepared dish with the seam side down. Pour the leftover sauce over the top; dust with the remaining cheese.
- Bake while uncovered for 10-15 minutes at 350°, or until bubbly and the cheese is melted. If desired, enjoy with optional toppings.

Nutrition Information

- Calories: 630 calories
- Total Fat: 40g fat (19g saturated fat)
- Sodium: 1141mg sodium
- Fiber: 3g fiber)
- Total Carbohydrate: 37g carbohydrate (2g sugars
- Cholesterol: 111mg cholesterol
- Protein: 32g protein.

335. Tamale Pie For Two

Serving: 2 servings. | Prep: 15mins | Ready in:

Ingredients

- 1/3 pound lean ground beef (90% lean)
- 3 tablespoons chopped onion
- 3/4 cup stewed tomatoes, chopped
- 1/8 teaspoon garlic powder
- 1/8 teaspoon chili powder
- Dash salt and pepper
- 2 flour tortillas (6 inches)
- 2/3 cup shredded Monterey Jack cheese
- 2 tablespoons sliced ripe olives, drained

Direction

- Cook onion and beef in a small skillet on moderate heat until meat is not pink anymore then drain. Stir in pepper, salt, chili powder, garlic powder and tomatoes; take away from the heat.
- Put a tortilla into a 3-cup, cooking spray coated, round baking dish. Put cheese and half of the meat mixture on top, repeat the layers. Sprinkle olives over; bake at 350 degrees without a cover until heated through, about 15 to 20 minutes.

Nutrition Information

- Calories: 365 calories
- Sodium: 947mg sodium
- Fiber: 1g fiber)
- Total Carbohydrate: 23g carbohydrate (6g sugars
- Cholesterol: 67mg cholesterol
- Protein: 29g protein.
- Total Fat: 18g fat (8g saturated fat)

336. Tangy Meatballs

Serving: 12 servings. | Prep: 50mins | Ready in:

Ingredients

- 2 large eggs
- 2 cups quick-cooking or rolled oats
- 1 can (12 ounces) evaporated milk
- 1 cup chopped onion
- 2 teaspoons salt
- 1/2 teaspoon pepper
- 1/2 teaspoon garlic powder
- 3 pounds lean ground beef (90% lean)
- SAUCE:
- 2 cups ketchup
- 1-1/2 cups packed brown sugar
- 1/2 cup chopped onion
- 1 to 2 teaspoons liquid smoke
- 1/2 teaspoon garlic powder

Direction

- Whisk eggs in a big bowl. Add garlic powder, pepper, salt, onion, milk, and oats. Add ground beef, stirring thoroughly. Form into balls, about 1 1/2 each ball. On racks coated with cooking spray in shallow baking pans, put the meatballs. Bake without a cover for 30 minutes at 375°; strain.
- In one of the pans, put all the meatballs. Boil all the sauce ingredients in a saucepan. Add onto the meatballs. Put back into the oven and bake without a cover until the meatballs have been done, about 20 minutes.

Nutrition Information

- Calories: 423 calories
- Cholesterol: 100mg cholesterol
- Protein: 27g protein.
- Total Fat: 12g fat (5g saturated fat)
- Sodium: 991mg sodium
- Fiber: 2g fiber)
- Total Carbohydrate: 51g carbohydrate (35g sugars

337. Tangy Sirloin Strips

Serving: 4 servings. | Prep: 5mins | Ready in:

Ingredients

- 1/4 cup canola oil
- 2 tablespoons Worcestershire sauce
- 1 garlic clove, minced
- 1/2 teaspoon onion powder
- 1/2 teaspoon salt
- 1/4 teaspoon pepper
- 1 pound beef top sirloin steak (1 inch thick)
- 4 bacon strips
- Lemon-pepper seasoning
- GLAZE:
- 1/2 cup barbecue sauce
- 1/2 cup steak sauce
- 1/2 cup honey
- 1 tablespoon molasses

Direction

- Mix all the first 6 ingredients together in a big Ziplock plastic bag. Slice the steak into 4 wide strips and put it into the marinade. Seal the Ziplock bag and turn to coat the steak strips with marinade; keep it in the fridge for 2-3 hours or throughout the night, flip it once.
- Drain the marinated steak strips and throw away the marinade mixture. Use a strip of bacon to wrap each strip of steak and secure the ends with a toothpick. Season it with lemon-pepper. Use tongs to lightly rub an oiled paper towel on the grill rack.
- Put the bacon-wrapped steak on a grill over medium-low heat then cover and grill or put the steak in a broiler and let it broil 4 inches away from heat for 10-15 minutes while turning the steak from time to time until the preferred meat doneness is achieved (a thermometer inserted on the meat should indicate 170°F for well-done, 160°F for medium and 145°F for medium-rare). Mix all glaze ingredients together and use a brush to coat the steaks with the glaze. Continue grilling until the glaze is heated through. Throw away the toothpicks.

Nutrition Information

- Calories:
- Protein:
- Total Fat:
- Sodium:
- Fiber:
- Total Carbohydrate:
- Cholesterol:

338. Tangy Stuffed Peppers

Serving: 4 servings. | Prep: 20mins | Ready in:

Ingredients

- 4 large green peppers
- 1 pound ground beef
- 1 small onion, chopped
- 1-1/2 cups cooked long grain rice
- 1/4 cup grated Parmesan cheese
- 6 teaspoons Worcestershire sauce, divided
- 1/2 teaspoon salt
- 1 can (15 ounces) tomato sauce
- 1/3 cup water
- Additional Parmesan cheese, optional

Direction

- Remove the tops and seeds of the peppers. Chop pepper tops finely and set aside. Add whole pepper to boiling water in a big saucepan, cook for 3 to 5 minutes. Drain them, use cold water to rinse and set aside.
- Add chopped peppers, onion and beef to a big frying pan, cook over medium heat until the vegetables get tender and the meat is not pink any longer; drain. Take away from the heat. Mix in the salt, 4 teaspoons of Worcestershire sauce, Parmesan cheese and rice. Fill the mixture into peppers.

- Use cooking spray to coat a 2-quart baking dish and lay the peppers over the dish. Mix the rest of Worcestershire sauce with water and tomato sauce and drizzle on top of peppers.
- Set oven at 350°, bake while covered until the peppers get tender, about 25 to 30 minutes. If preferred, dredge more Parmesan cheese over top.

Nutrition Information

- Calories: 359 calories
- Fiber: 4g fiber)
- Total Carbohydrate: 36g carbohydrate (7g sugars
- Cholesterol: 60mg cholesterol
- Protein: 27g protein.
- Total Fat: 12g fat (6g saturated fat)
- Sodium: 1039mg sodium

339. Tasty Tacos

Serving: Makes 5 servings, 2 tacos each. | Prep: 15mins | Ready in:

Ingredients

- 3/4 cup VELVEETA® Salsa Dip
- 1/2 lb. ground beef, cooked, drained
- 10 TACO BELL® Crunchy Taco Shell s
- 1 cup shredded lettuce
- 3/4 cup chopped tomato

Direction

- Combine cooked meat and VELVEETA salsa dip.
- Scoop into taco shells evenly, then put tomato and lettuce on top evenly.

Nutrition Information

- Calories: 260

- Sodium: 500 mg
- Total Carbohydrate: 19 g
- Cholesterol: 45 mg
- Protein: 14 g
- Sugar: 3 g
- Total Fat: 15 g
- Saturated Fat: 6 g
- Fiber: 2 g

340. Tater Topped Casserole

Serving: 4-6 servings. | Prep: 15mins | Ready in:

Ingredients

- 1 pound lean ground beef (90% lean)
- 1/2 cup chopped onion
- 1/3 cup sliced celery
- 1/2 teaspoon salt
- 1/4 teaspoon pepper
- 1 can (10-3/4 ounces) condensed cream of celery soup, undiluted
- 1 package (16 ounces) frozen Tater Tots
- 1 cup shredded cheddar cheese

Direction

- Cook the celery, onion and beef in a large skillet until the vegetables become tender and the meat is not pink anymore; let drain. Stir in pepper and salt.
- Place the mixture into a 3-quart baking dish coated with cooking spray. Place with soup. Put the frozen potatoes on top. Bake at 400 degrees until bubbling, 40 minutes. Dust with cheese. Bake until the cheese melts, 5 minutes.

Nutrition Information

- Calories: 353 calories
- Protein: 21g protein.
- Total Fat: 20g fat (8g saturated fat)
- Sodium: 1040mg sodium
- Fiber: 3g fiber)

- Total Carbohydrate: 25g carbohydrate (2g sugars
- Cholesterol: 59mg cholesterol

341. Tender Barbecued Brisket

Serving: 12 servings. | Prep: 10mins | Ready in:

Ingredients

- 1 bottle (10 ounces) soy sauce
- 1 tablespoon Liquid Smoke, optional
- 2 teaspoons pepper
- 2 teaspoons Worcestershire sauce
- 1 teaspoon garlic salt
- 1 teaspoon onion salt
- 1 teaspoon celery salt
- 1 fresh beef brisket (about 5 pounds)
- BARBECUE SAUCE:
- 1 bottle (14 ounces) ketchup
- 1 to 2 tablespoons sugar
- 1 tablespoon cider vinegar
- 1-1/2 teaspoons prepared mustard
- 1 teaspoon Worcestershire sauce
- 1 teaspoon soy sauce

Direction

- Mix the first seven ingredients in a big resealable plastic bag; then put in the brisket. Close the bag and flip to coat. Place in refrigerator either overnight or for 8 hours; drain off the marinade and discard. Take a large piece of heavy-duty foil and wrap brisket with it. Make sure to seal tightly. Put the brisket in a greased 15x10x1-in. pan. Bake in a 325-degree oven until meat is tender, 4 hours. Remove the beef and let it sit for 20 minutes. Cut across the grain into thin slices. Put it in a 13x9-in. pan without grease. Mix the sauce ingredients and pour over beef. Cover; bake until heated, 1 hour. You can freeze the meat for up to 3 months.

Nutrition Information

- Calories: 297 calories
- Protein: 42g protein.
- Total Fat: 8g fat (3g saturated fat)
- Sodium: 2417mg sodium
- Fiber: 0 fiber)
- Total Carbohydrate: 11g carbohydrate (11g sugars
- Cholesterol: 80mg cholesterol

342. Teriyaki Beef Stir Fry For 3

Serving: 3 servings. | Prep: 10mins | Ready in:

Ingredients

- 1/2 cup water
- 1/3 cup reduced-sodium soy sauce
- 1/4 cup honey
- 4 garlic cloves, minced
- 1 tablespoon minced fresh gingerroot
- 1 beef flank steak (3/4 pound), cut into thin strips
- 2 teaspoons canola oil
- 2 cups broccoli florets
- 1 medium onion, chopped
- 1/2 cup coarsely chopped green pepper
- 1/2 cup coarsely chopped sweet red pepper
- 1 cup sliced fresh mushrooms
- 1 teaspoon cornstarch
- Hot cooked brown rice, optional

Direction

- Mix the first 5 ingredients in a small bowl. Transfer 1/2 cup of the mixture into the resealable plastic bag. Add the beef inside the bag. Seal the bag and flip it to coat. Place the bag inside the fridge for at least 1 hour. Cover the remaining marinade and place it inside the fridge.
- Drain the beef, discarding the marinade. Working in batches, stir-fry the beef in a wok

or large nonstick skillet with oil for 2-3 minutes until the beef is no longer pink. Remove from the skillet and keep it warm.
- Add the peppers, onion, and broccoli into the pan. Stir-fry the vegetables for 4 minutes. Add the mushrooms. Stir-fry for 1-2 minutes until the vegetables turn tender. Place the beef back into the pan. Mix the reserved marinade and cornstarch until smooth and add it into the beef mixture. Let the mixture boil. Cook and stir until it is already thick. If desired, you can serve this dish over rice.

Nutrition Information

- Calories: 320 calories
- Fiber: 4g fiber)
- Total Carbohydrate: 29g carbohydrate (0 sugars
- Cholesterol: 59mg cholesterol
- Protein: 28g protein. Diabetic Exchanges: 3 lean meat
- Total Fat: 11g fat (4g saturated fat)
- Sodium: 695mg sodium

343. Teriyaki Flank Steak

Serving: 4 | Prep: 15mins | Ready in:

Ingredients

- 1/2 cup wine
- 1/2 cup soy sauce
- 1/4 cup olive oil
- 1/4 cup brown sugar
- 1/4 cup grated fresh ginger root
- 2 cloves garlic, crushed
- 1 teaspoon ground black pepper
- 1 1/2 pounds beef flank steak

Direction

- Combine soy sauce, brown sugar, garlic, pepper, olive oil, ginger, and wine together in a big resealable plastic bag. Add the steak into the bag and seal it. Store the bag inside the refrigerator and allow it to marinate for 8 hours up to overnight.
- Set the outdoor grill to medium-high heat to preheat.
- Discard the marinade from the bag and arrange the steak into the grill. Cook each side for 6-8 minutes until the desired doneness was reached. If you want it rarely done, its temperature must be 145°F (63°C). Slice the steak across its grain 5 minutes after cooking. Serve.

Nutrition Information

- Calories: 355 calories;
- Sodium: 1849
- Total Carbohydrate: 14
- Cholesterol: 38
- Protein: 22.8
- Total Fat: 20.5

344. Texas Beef Stew

Serving: 4 servings (1 quart). | Prep: 15mins | Ready in:

Ingredients

- 1-1/4 pounds beef stew meat, cut into 1-inch pieces
- 1 to 2 tablespoons vegetable oil, optional
- 1/4 cup chopped onion
- 1-1/2 teaspoons garlic powder
- 1/4 teaspoon pepper
- 1 cup water
- 1 can (14-1/2 ounces) diced tomatoes, undrained
- 1 tablespoon ground cumin
- 1 teaspoon salt

Direction

- Cook beef in a large saucepan or Dutch oven until no longer pink inside, adding oil if needed; drain. Add water, pepper, garlic powder, and onion; bring to a boil. Lower heat; simmer, covered until meat is nearly tender, about 45 minutes.
- Add salt, cumin, and tomatoes; bring back to a boil. Lower heat; simmer, covered until meat is tender, about 15 to 20 minutes more.

Nutrition Information

- Calories: 239 calories
- Sodium: 782mg sodium
- Fiber: 2g fiber)
- Total Carbohydrate: 7g carbohydrate (4g sugars
- Cholesterol: 88mg cholesterol
- Protein: 28g protein.
- Total Fat: 10g fat (4g saturated fat)

345. Texas Style Brisket

Serving: 20 servings. | Prep: 35mins | Ready in:

Ingredients

- 1 whole fresh beef brisket (12 to 14 pounds)
- 1/2 cup pepper
- 1/4 cup kosher salt
- Large disposable foil pan
- About 6 cups wood chips, preferably oak

Direction

- Cut off fat from brisket to half-inch thick. Massage salt and pepper on brisket; put in a big non-reusable foil pan, fat side facing up. Chill with cover, for a few hours or up to overnight. In the meantime, in water, immerse the wood chips.
- To have grill ready for indirect slow cooking, fix vents of grill making upper vent mid open and under vent is open just 1/4 of the way. On opposing sides of the grill, create 2 arrangements of 45 unlit coals, keeping the middle of grill open. Light 20 more coals till covered in ash; scatter evenly on unlit coals. On top of lit coals, scatter 2 cups of the immersed wood chips.
- Put back the grill rack. Close the grill and for about 15 minutes, let grill temperature reach 275°.
- In the middle of grill rack, put the foil pan of brisket; put cover on grill and cook for 3 hours, keep the grill closed. Occasionally monitor grill temperature to keep a temperature of 275° during cooking. Adjust the temperature by opening vents to increase the temperature and closing the vents partially to reduce the temperature.
- To every side of grill, put 10 more unlit coals and a cup of the wood chips. Let brisket cook with cover for 3 to 4 hours more or till easily pricked with fork, a thermometer pricked in brisket must register approximately 190°; put in more wood chips and coals as necessary to keep a grill temperature of 275°.
- Take brisket off grill. Cover securely in foil; rest for 30 minutes to an hour. Slice brisket against the grain into pieces.

Nutrition Information

- Calories: 351 calories
- Cholesterol: 116mg cholesterol
- Protein: 56g protein.
- Total Fat: 12g fat (4g saturated fat)
- Sodium: 1243mg sodium
- Fiber: 1g fiber)
- Total Carbohydrate: 2g carbohydrate (0 sugars

346. Thick Beef Stew

Serving: 3 servings. | Prep: 5mins | Ready in:

Ingredients

- 1 portion Triple-Batch Beef, thawed
- 3 medium red potatoes, quartered and cut into 1/4-inch slices
- 1-1/4 cups water
- 1 to 1-1/2 teaspoons dried oregano
- 1 teaspoon salt
- 1 cup frozen peas
- 1 tablespoon cornstarch
- 2 tablespoons lemon juice

Direction

- Mix salt, oregano, water, potatoes, and beef together in a big saucepan. Boil it. Lower the heat, simmer with a cover until the potatoes are soft, about 10-15 minutes. Put in peas and heat through.
- Mix lemon juice and cornstarch until the mixture is smooth; slowly pour in the beef mixture. Boil it, cook while stirring until bubbly and thickened, about 2 minutes.

Nutrition Information

- Calories:
- Total Fat:
- Sodium:
- Fiber:
- Total Carbohydrate:
- Cholesterol:
- Protein:

347. Three Cheese Meatball Mostaccioli

Serving: 10 servings. | Prep: 15mins | Ready in:

Ingredients

- 1 package (16 ounces) mostaccioli
- 2 large eggs, lightly beaten
- 1 carton (15 ounces) part-skim ricotta cheese
- 1 pound ground beef
- 1 medium onion, chopped
- 1 tablespoon brown sugar
- 1 tablespoon Italian seasoning
- 1 teaspoon garlic powder
- 1/4 teaspoon pepper
- 2 jars (24 ounces each) pasta sauce with meat
- 1/2 cup grated Romano cheese
- 1 package (12 ounces) frozen fully cooked Italian meatballs, thawed
- 3/4 cup shaved Parmesan cheese
- Minced fresh parsley or fresh baby arugula, optional

Direction

- Set oven at 350° to preheat. Follow the package instructions to cook the mostaccioli until tender but firm enough to bite then drain. In the meantime, mix the ricotta cheese with eggs in a small bowl.
- Add onion and beef to a 6-quart stockpot, cook for 6 to 8 minutes until the beef is not pink any longer, crumbling the beef and drain. Mix in seasonings and brown sugar. Add the mostaccioli and pasta sauce and mix to combine.
- Take half of the pasta mixture to a 13x9-inch baking dish coated with cooking spray. Lay the ricotta mixture and the rest of pasta mixture over top. Scatter with Romano cheese. Add Parmesan cheese and meatballs on top.
- Bake in the preheated oven while uncovered until heated through, about 35 to 40 minutes. Add parsley on top if preferred.

Nutrition Information

- Calories: 541 calories
- Fiber: 5g fiber)
- Total Carbohydrate: 55g carbohydrate (13g sugars
- Cholesterol: 105mg cholesterol
- Protein: 34g protein.
- Total Fat: 23g fat (11g saturated fat)
- Sodium: 1335mg sodium

348. Three Pepper Beef Wraps

Serving: 6 servings. | Prep: 25mins | Ready in:

Ingredients

- 1 each large green, sweet red and yellow peppers, julienned
- 1 medium onion, halved and sliced
- 2 tablespoons olive oil, divided
- 3/4 pound lean ground beef (90% lean)
- 1 can (16 ounces) kidney beans, rinsed and drained
- 3/4 cup salsa
- 1/4 teaspoon steak seasoning
- 1/4 teaspoon pepper
- 6 flour tortillas (8 inches), warmed
- 1/2 cup shredded reduced-fat cheddar cheese

Direction

- Sauté onion and peppers together in a big nonstick skillet with 1 tbsp. of oil until tender-crisp. Take out and keep mixture warm.
- Cook beef in the same skillet on moderate heat until it is not pink anymore, then drain. In a food processor, put kidney beans, leftover oil and salsa, then place the cover and process mixture until chopped. Put into beef. Sprinkle pepper and steak seasoning over top of beef mixture, then cook and stir until heated through.
- Scoop down the center of each tortilla with 1/3 cup of beef mixture, then put 1/2 cup of pepper mixture on top of each. Sprinkle cheese over top, then fold sides as well as ends over filling. Roll up tortilla.

Nutrition Information

- Calories: 390 calories
- Sodium: 637mg sodium
- Fiber: 6g fiber)
- Total Carbohydrate: 43g carbohydrate (5g sugars
- Cholesterol: 34mg cholesterol
- Protein: 23g protein. Diabetic Exchanges: 2-1/2 starch
- Total Fat: 14g fat (4g saturated fat)

349. Tomato Beef And Rice Casserole

Serving: 6 servings. | Prep: 10mins | Ready in:

Ingredients

- 1 pound lean ground beef (90% lean)
- 3 cups canned diced tomatoes, undrained
- 1 medium green pepper, chopped
- 1 cup uncooked long grain rice
- 1 large onion, chopped
- 1 teaspoon chili powder
- 1/2 teaspoon salt
- 1/4 teaspoon pepper

Direction

- Combine all ingredients in a large bowl. Arrange in a greased 2-qt. baking dish. Bake at 400°, covered, for 1-1/2 hours, stirring once or twice. During the last 15 minutes, uncover to get brown.

Nutrition Information

- Calories: 267 calories
- Protein: 18g protein.
- Total Fat: 6g fat (2g saturated fat)
- Sodium: 413mg sodium
- Fiber: 3g fiber)
- Total Carbohydrate: 34g carbohydrate (6g sugars
- Cholesterol: 37mg cholesterol

350. Tortilla Pie

Serving: Makes 4 main-course servings | Prep: 20mins | Ready in:

Ingredients

- 1 (15-oz) can black beans, drained and rinsed
- 1 (10-oz) package frozen corn kernels, thawed
- 1 cup mild tomato salsa
- 1 (8-oz) can tomato sauce
- 6 oz pepper Jack cheese, coarsely grated (2 cups)
- 1/2 cup chopped fresh cilantro
- 2 scallions, thinly sliced
- 1/2 teaspoon ground cumin
- 4 (10-inch) flour tortillas (burrito-size)
- 1 tablespoon olive oil
- Accompaniment: sour cream

Direction

- To make the preparation: Position the oven rack in lower third of oven and preheat oven to 450 degrees F.
- In a big bowl, mix cumin, scallions, cilantro, cheese, tomato sauce, salsa, corn and beans.
- Heat one 12-in. heavy skillet on high heat till smoking. Brush both sides of each tortilla using oil and fry, flipping one time, for roughly 1 minute or till puffed and golden in spots.
- Add one tortilla into a well-oiled 15x10-in. shallow baking pan, and then spread with 1 1/3 cups of filling. Repeat the layers two times, and then add the leftover tortillas on top, pushing lightly to help layers adhere.
- Bake for roughly 12 minutes or till filling is thoroughly heated. Move using a big metal spatula to a platter, then chop the pie into wedges using a serrated knife.

Nutrition Information

- Calories: 679
- Cholesterol: 59 mg(20%)
- Protein: 30 g(60%)
- Total Fat: 29 g(44%)
- Saturated Fat: 14 g(70%)
- Sodium: 1260 mg(53%)
- Fiber: 11 g(46%)
- Total Carbohydrate: 76 g(25%)

351. Tortilla Salsa Meat Loaf

Serving: 8 servings. | Prep: 15mins | Ready in:

Ingredients

- 2 slices day-old white bread
- 2 eggs, lightly beaten
- 1 cup salsa
- 1/2 cup crushed tortilla chips
- 1/2 cup each chopped green pepper, onion and celery
- 1 jalapeno pepper, seeded and chopped
- 6 garlic cloves, minced
- 1 teaspoon pepper
- 1/2 teaspoon Italian seasoning
- 1/4 teaspoon seasoned salt
- 1 pound ground beef
- 1 pound ground pork

Direction

- Put the bread into the ungreased 9x5-inch loaf pan; put aside. In the big bowl, mix the seasoned salt, Italian seasoning, pepper, garlic, jalapeno, celery, onion, green pepper, tortilla chips, salsa, and eggs. Break up the pork and beef on top of the mixture; stir thoroughly. Pat into the prepped pan.
- Bake, while uncovered, at 375 degrees till the thermometer reaches 160 degrees or for 1.25-1.5 hours. Invert the meat loaf onto the serving platter; get rid of the bread. Allow to rest for 5 minutes prior to slicing.

Nutrition Information

- Calories: 315 calories

- Protein: 24g protein.
- Total Fat: 18g fat (7g saturated fat)
- Sodium: 319mg sodium
- Fiber: 2g fiber)
- Total Carbohydrate: 10g carbohydrate (2g sugars
- Cholesterol: 129mg cholesterol

352. Traditional Boiled Dinner

Serving: 6 servings. | Prep: 10mins | Ready in:

Ingredients

- 1 corned beef brisket with spice packet (3 pounds)
- 1 teaspoon whole black peppercorns
- 2 bay leaves
- 2 medium potatoes, peeled and quartered
- 3 medium carrots, quartered
- 1 medium onion, cut into 6 wedges
- 1 small head green cabbage, cut into 6 wedges
- Prepared horseradish or mustard, optional

Direction

- Add contents of the spice packet and brisket into the Dutch oven. Put in bay leaves, peppercorns and sufficient water to submerge; boil. Lower the heat; let simmer with cover till the meat is nearly soft or for 2 hours.
- Put in the onion, carrots and potatoes; boil. Lower the heat; let simmer with cover for 10 minutes. Put in the cabbage, let simmer with cover till soften or for 15 to 20 minutes. Get rid of the peppercorns and bay leaves. Thinly chop the meat; serve along with the horseradish/mustard and vegetables if you want.

Nutrition Information

- Calories: 558 calories
- Total Fat: 34g fat (11g saturated fat)

- Sodium: 2797mg sodium
- Fiber: 5g fiber)
- Total Carbohydrate: 25g carbohydrate (8g sugars
- Cholesterol: 122mg cholesterol
- Protein: 37g protein.

353. Ultimate Pot Roast

Serving: 8 servings. | Prep: 55mins | Ready in:

Ingredients

- 1 boneless beef chuck-eye or other chuck roast (3 to 4 pounds)
- 2 teaspoons pepper
- 2 teaspoons salt, divided
- 2 tablespoons canola oil
- 2 medium onions, cut into 1-inch pieces
- 2 celery ribs, chopped
- 3 garlic cloves, minced
- 1 tablespoon tomato paste
- 1 tablespoon minced fresh thyme or 1 teaspoon dried thyme
- 2 bay leaves
- 1 cup dry red wine or reduced-sodium beef broth
- 2 cups reduced-sodium beef broth
- 1 pound small red potatoes, quartered
- 4 medium parsnips, peeled and cut into 2-inch pieces
- 6 medium carrots, cut into 2-inch pieces
- 1 tablespoon red wine vinegar
- 2 tablespoons minced fresh parsley
- Salt and pepper to taste

Direction

- Pre-heat the oven to 325 degrees. Pat the roast dry using paper towel; tie at 2-inch intervals using kitchen string. Scatter roast with 1.5 teaspoons of salt and pepper. In Dutch oven, heat oil on medium high heat. Brown all sides of roast. Take out of pan.

- Put half teaspoon of salt, celery and onions into that pan; cook and whisk on medium heat till the onions turn brown or for 8 to 10 minutes. Put in bay leaves, thyme, tomato paste, and garlic; cook and whisk for 60 seconds more.
- Pour in wine, whisk to loosen the browned bits from pan; whisk in broth. Bring the roast back to pan. Surround roast with carrots, parsnips and potatoes; boil. Bake, with cover, for 2 to 2.5 hours or till meat becomes fork-tender.
- Take veggies and roast out of pan; keep them warm. Get rid of bay leaves; skim the fat out of cooking juices. On stovetop, boil the juices; cook for 10 to 12 minutes or till liquid decreased to roughly 1.5 cups (decreased by half). Whisk in parsley and vinegar; season to taste with pepper and salt.
- Take the string out of the roast. Serve along with sauce and veggies

Nutrition Information

- Calories: 459 calories
- Sodium: 824mg sodium
- Fiber: 6g fiber)
- Total Carbohydrate: 32g carbohydrate (8g sugars
- Cholesterol: 112mg cholesterol
- Protein: 37g protein.
- Total Fat: 20g fat (7g saturated fat)

354. Unstuffed Peppers

Serving: 6 servings. | Prep: 20mins | Ready in:

Ingredients

- 1 cup uncooked instant rice
- 1 pound ground beef
- 2 medium green peppers, cut into 1-inch pieces
- 1/2 cup chopped onion
- 1 jar (26 ounces) marinara sauce
- 1-1/2 teaspoons salt-free seasoning blend
- 1/2 cup shredded Italian cheese blend
- 1/2 cup seasoned bread crumbs
- 1 tablespoon olive oil

Direction

- Set the oven to 350°, and start preheating. Cook rice following package instructions.
- In the meantime, in a large skillet over the medium-high heat, cook onion, green peppers and beef until meat is no longer pink; drain. Mix in seasoning blend, marinara sauce and rice. Mix in cheese.
- Place to a greased baking dish of 2 quart. Toss oil and bread crumbs; sprinkle over the top. Bake until topping is golden brown and heated through, about 8-10 minutes.

Nutrition Information

- Calories: 343 calories
- Protein: 20g protein.
- Total Fat: 12g fat (5g saturated fat)
- Sodium: 469mg sodium
- Fiber: 3g fiber)
- Total Carbohydrate: 38g carbohydrate (12g sugars
- Cholesterol: 43mg cholesterol

355. Upside Down Beef Pie

Serving: 6 servings. | Prep: 10mins | Ready in:

Ingredients

- 1 pound ground beef
- 1/2 cup chopped celery
- 1/2 cup chopped onion
- 1/4 cup chopped green pepper
- 1 can (10-3/4 ounces) condensed tomato soup, undiluted
- 1 teaspoon prepared mustard

- 1-1/2 cups biscuit/baking mix
- 1/3 cup water
- 3 slices process American cheese, halved diagonally
- Green pepper rings, optional

Direction

- In a big skillet over medium heat, cook the green pepper, onion, celery and beef until the meat has no hint of pink anymore then drain. Stir the mustard and soup in. Move it into a greased 9-inch pie plate. In the meantime, combine water and dry baking mix in a big bowl until soft dough is formed. Place it on a lightly floured surface and roll into a 9-inch circle. Put this over the meat mixture. Bake at 425°F until it turns golden brown, about 20 minutes. Leave it to cool for 5 minutes. Loosen the biscuit from the plate by running a knife along the edges then flip it over onto a serving platter. Organize the cheese slices on top of it in a pinwheel pattern. If desired, decorate with green pepper rings.

Nutrition Information

- Calories:
- Cholesterol:
- Protein:
- Total Fat:
- Sodium:
- Fiber:
- Total Carbohydrate:

356. Veal Cutlets Supreme

Serving: 6 servings. | Prep: 35mins | Ready in:

Ingredients

- 6 veal cutlets (1/2 inch thick)
- 2 garlic cloves, minced
- 1 teaspoon salt, divided
- 1/4 teaspoon pepper
- 4 tablespoons butter, divided
- 2 medium onions, chopped
- 3/4 pound sliced fresh mushrooms
- 3 tablespoons crushed butter-flavored crackers
- 1 cup heavy whipping cream
- 3/4 cup dry white wine or chicken broth
- 2 tablespoons minced fresh parsley
- 3/4 cup shredded cheddar cheese

Direction

- Set the oven at 350° and start preheating. Sprinkle with 1/2 teaspoon of salt and pepper and garlic. Brown the veal in a large skillet with 2 tablespoons of butter on both sides. Place on a greased 13x9-in. baking dish.
- Sauté mushrooms and onions in the same skillet with the remaining butter till tender. Mix in the remaining salt, broth or wine, cream and cracker crumbs; cook while stirring till the mixture comes to a boil. Mix in parsley; pour over the veal.
- Bake with a cover for 20 minutes. Uncover and sprinkle cheese over. Continue baking till the cheese is melted or 5 minutes.

Nutrition Information

- Calories: 551 calories
- Total Fat: 41g fat (22g saturated fat)
- Sodium: 664mg sodium
- Fiber: 2g fiber)
- Total Carbohydrate: 11g carbohydrate (5g sugars
- Cholesterol: 184mg cholesterol
- Protein: 31g protein.

357. Vegetable Steak Stir Fry

Serving: 4 servings. | Prep: 5mins | Ready in:

Ingredients

- 3/4 pound beef top sirloin steak, cubed
- 3 teaspoons canola oil, divided
- 2 cups fresh broccoli florets
- 2 cups fresh cauliflowerets
- 2 cups julienned carrots
- 6 garlic cloves, minced
- 1 tablespoon cornstarch
- 3/4 cup beef broth
- 1/3 cup sherry or additional broth
- 1 tablespoon water
- 1-1/2 teaspoons soy sauce
- 1/4 teaspoon ground ginger
- 2 medium tomatoes, cut into wedges
- Hot cooked rice, optional

Direction

- Stir-fry steak till not pink in 2 tsp. oil in a big skillet/wok. Remove; keep warm. Heat leftover oil in same pan. Add garlic, carrots, cauliflower and broccoli; stir-fry till veggies are crisp tender.
- Mix ginger, soy sauce, water, broth, extra broth/sherry and cornstarch till smooth in a small bowl. Put beef in pan. Mix cornstarch mixture; put in pan. Boil; mix and cook till thick for 2 minutes. Add tomatoes then heat through; if desired, serve with rice.

Nutrition Information

- Calories: 251 calories
- Protein: 23g protein. Diabetic Exchanges: 3 lean meat
- Total Fat: 9g fat (2g saturated fat)
- Sodium: 364mg sodium
- Fiber: 5g fiber)
- Total Carbohydrate: 18g carbohydrate (0 sugars
- Cholesterol: 50mg cholesterol

358. Veggie Steak Fajitas

Serving: 4 servings. | Prep: 15mins | Ready in:

Ingredients

- 1 beef top sirloin steak (1 pound), thinly sliced
- 2 teaspoons ground cumin
- 1/8 teaspoon salt
- 3 teaspoons canola oil, divided
- 1 large onion, julienned
- 1 small sweet red pepper, julienned
- 1 small green pepper, julienned
- 2 tablespoons minced fresh cilantro
- 4 whole wheat tortillas (8 inches), warmed
- Optional ingredients: Shredded lettuce, chopped tomato and reduced-fat sour cream

Direction

- Sprinkle salt and cumin on beef. Sauté beef in 2 tsp. oil till not pink in a big skillet. Remove; put aside.
- Sauté peppers and onion in leftover oil till tender in same skillet; mix in cilantro. Put beef in pan; heat through.
- Put on tortillas then fold in sides; serve with sour cream (optional), tomato and lettuce.

Nutrition Information

- Calories: 344 calories
- Total Carbohydrate: 28g carbohydrate (4g sugars
- Cholesterol: 46mg cholesterol
- Protein: 29g protein. Diabetic Exchanges: 3 lean meat
- Total Fat: 11g fat (2g saturated fat)
- Sodium: 299mg sodium
- Fiber: 4g fiber)

359. Whiskey Sirloin Steak

Serving: 4 servings. | Prep: 10mins | Ready in:

Ingredients

- 1/4 cup whiskey or apple cider
- 1/4 cup reduced-sodium soy sauce

- 1 tablespoon sugar
- 1 garlic clove, thinly sliced
- 1/2 teaspoon ground ginger
- 1 beef top sirloin steak (1 pound and 1 inch thick)

Direction

- Mix initial 5 ingredients in a big resealable plastic bag; add beef. Seal bag. Turn to coat then refrigerate for 8 hours – overnight.
- Drain marinade; discard. Put beef on broiler pan coated in cooking spray; broil for 7-8 minutes per side 4-6-in. from heat till meat gets desired doneness; 170° well done, 160° medium and 145° for medium rare on a thermometer.

Nutrition Information

- Calories: 168 calories
- Total Fat: 5g fat (2g saturated fat)
- Sodium: 353mg sodium
- Fiber: 0 fiber)
- Total Carbohydrate: 2g carbohydrate (2g sugars
- Cholesterol: 46mg cholesterol
- Protein: 25g protein. Diabetic Exchanges: 3 lean meat.

360. Winter Oven Beef Stew

Serving: 6 servings. | Prep: 20mins | Ready in:

Ingredients

- 6 tablespoons all-purpose flour, divided
- 1/4 teaspoon salt, optional
- 1/2 teaspoon pepper, divided
- 1-1/2 pounds boneless beef chuck roast, cut into 1-inch cubes
- 1 medium onion, chopped
- 1 tablespoon canola oil
- 3 garlic cloves, minced
- 3 cups beef broth
- 1 can (14-1/2 ounces) stewed tomatoes, cut up
- 3/4 teaspoon dried thyme
- 3 large potatoes, peeled and cut into 1-inch cubes
- 3 medium carrots, cut into 1/4-inch slices
- 1/2 cup frozen peas, thawed

Direction

- Mix in a large resealable plastic bag 1/4 teaspoon pepper, salt (if desired), and 4 tablespoons flour. Add a few pieces of beef at a time, and shake to coat.
- In the Dutch oven, brown beef in batches in oil over medium-high heat. Take the beef out and leave it aside. Add onion to the pan and cook until tender. Add garlic; cook for an addition of 1 minute. Stir in pepper and remaining flour until blended. Stir in broth gradually. Add tomatoes, beef, and thyme. Bake at 350° for 1 and 1/4 hours, covered.
- Add in the carrots and potatoes. Bake covered for 1 more hour or until meat and vegetables are softened. Stir in peas; cover and let rest for 5 minutes before serving.

Nutrition Information

- Calories: 439 calories
- Cholesterol: 76mg cholesterol
- Protein: 30g protein.
- Total Fat: 13g fat (5g saturated fat)
- Sodium: 426mg sodium
- Fiber: 6g fiber)
- Total Carbohydrate: 50g carbohydrate (11g sugars

361. Worms For Brains

Serving: 8-10 servings. | Prep: 30mins | Ready in:

Ingredients

- 8 to 10 medium sweet orange peppers
- 1 package (16 ounces) spaghetti
- 1 pound ground beef
- 1 jar (26 ounces) spaghetti sauce

Direction

- Slice off the top portion of the peppers and put it aside; discard the membranes and the seeds. On one side of each of the prepared peppers, cut out a jack-o'-lantern face and put it aside.
- Follow the package instructions in cooking the spaghetti. While waiting for the spaghetti to cook, put the beef in a Dutch oven and let it cook over medium heat setting until it is not anymore pink in color. Drain the cooked beef.
- Drain the spaghetti then mix it into the cooked beef. Add in the spaghetti sauce then give it a thorough mix and let the mixture cook until heated through. Stuff the prepared peppers with the prepared spaghetti mixture, then put the removed pepper tops back in place.

Nutrition Information

- Calories: 334 calories
- Sodium: 404mg sodium
- Fiber: 5g fiber)
- Total Carbohydrate: 49g carbohydrate (10g sugars
- Cholesterol: 24mg cholesterol
- Protein: 17g protein.
- Total Fat: 8g fat (3g saturated fat)

362. Yankee Pot Roast

Serving: 4-6 servings. | Prep: 25mins | Ready in:

Ingredients

- 2 garlic cloves, minced
- 1 beef chuck roast (3 to 3-1/2 pounds)
- 1/4 cup all-purpose flour
- 1/4 cup canola oil
- 1 cup tomato juice
- 4 medium carrots, sliced
- 2 medium onion, chopped
- 1 cup thinly sliced celery
- 2 bay leaves
- 1 teaspoon salt
- 1/2 teaspoon dried thyme
- 1/4 teaspoon pepper
- 4 medium potatoes, peeled and quartered

Direction

- Rub the garlic on roast, then coat in flour. In a big Dutch oven, brown the roast in oil. Put in pepper, thyme, salt, bay leaves, celery, onions, carrots, and tomato juice; boil. Lower the heat; let simmer with cover for 3.5 hours, flip the meat once in a while.
- Put in potatoes; let simmer till soften or for half an hour. Take the bay leaf out. Take out the roast and chop; serve along with gravy and veggies.

Nutrition Information

- Calories: 615 calories
- Protein: 48g protein.
- Total Fat: 31g fat (10g saturated fat)
- Sodium: 669mg sodium
- Fiber: 4g fiber)
- Total Carbohydrate: 35g carbohydrate (9g sugars
- Cholesterol: 147mg cholesterol

363. Zeus Burgers

Serving: 4 servings. | Prep: 15mins | Ready in:

Ingredients

- 3 tablespoons fat-free mayonnaise
- 2 teaspoons lemon juice
- 1 garlic clove, minced
- 1/4 teaspoon dried oregano

- 1/8 teaspoon salt
- BURGERS:
- 1/4 cup frozen chopped spinach, thawed and squeezed dry
- 1/4 cup crumbled reduced-fat feta cheese
- 2 tablespoons lemon juice
- 1 tablespoon pine nuts, finely chopped
- 1 garlic clove, minced
- 1 teaspoon dried oregano
- 1/4 teaspoon salt
- 1/4 teaspoon pepper
- 1 pound lean ground beef (90% lean)
- 4 hamburger buns, split

Direction

- Mix the salt, oregano, garlic, lemon juice and mayonnaise together in a small bowl. Put on a cover and chill in the fridge until ready to serve.
- Mix together the pepper, salt, oregano, garlic, pine nuts, lemon juice, cheese and spinach in a big bowl. Crumble the beef on top of the mixture and stir well, then form the mixture into 4 patties.
- Use cooking oil to moisten a paper towel, using long-handled tongs, coat the grill rack lightly. Grill the burgers over medium heat with a cover, or broil 4 inches from the heat source for 5-7 minutes per side, or until the juices run clear and a thermometer registers 160 degrees.
- Toast the buns until light brown, about a minute, then serve the burgers with the reserved sauce on buns.

Nutrition Information

- Calories: 335 calories
- Sodium: 669mg sodium
- Fiber: 2g fiber)
- Total Carbohydrate: 26g carbohydrate (4g sugars
- Cholesterol: 73mg cholesterol
- Protein: 28g protein.
- Total Fat: 13g fat (5g saturated fat)

364. Zippy Peanut Steak Kabobs

Serving: 8 servings. | Prep: 40mins | Ready in:

Ingredients

- 3/4 cup packed brown sugar
- 3/4 cup water
- 1 cup chunky peanut butter
- 1 cup reduced-sodium soy sauce
- 3/4 cup honey barbecue sauce
- 1/3 cup canola oil
- 1 to 2 tablespoons habanero pepper sauce
- 3 garlic cloves, minced
- 2 pounds beef top sirloin steak, cut into thin strips
- 2 teaspoons ground ginger
- 1 fresh pineapple, cut into 1-inch cubes
- 2 large sweet red peppers, cut into 1-inch pieces
- Hot cooked jasmine rice

Direction

- Mix brown sugar and water in a small sauce pan. Cook with stirring on low heat until sugar is dissolved. Remove from heat and add in peanut butter, whisking until blended. Whisk in oil, barbecue sauce, soy sauce, pepper sauce, and garlic. Take 3 cups of this marinade mixture and pour into a large, re-sealable plastic bag; add the beef and seal, turning to coat the beef pieces with marinade. Keep refrigerated for 4 hours. Keep the remaining marinade covered and refrigerated until ready to serve. Drain the beef and discard its marinade. Sprinkle some ginger over the pineapples. Thread beef, red peppers, and pineapples alternately on 16 metal or wooden skewers that have been soaked. Place and cook on covered grill at medium heat for 5-7 minutes per side or until cooked to preferred doneness. Serve kabobs with rice and reserved marinade.

Nutrition Information

- Calories: 392 calories
- Fiber: 3g fiber)
- Total Carbohydrate: 30g carbohydrate (23g sugars
- Cholesterol: 63mg cholesterol
- Protein: 27g protein.
- Total Fat: 19g fat (4g saturated fat)
- Sodium: 881mg sodium

365. Zucchini Beef Lasagna

Serving: 12 servings. | Prep: 50mins | Ready in:

Ingredients

- 1 pound lean ground beef (90% lean)
- 2 garlic cloves, minced
- 2 cans (8 ounces each) no-salt-added tomato sauce
- 1/2 cup water
- 1 can (6 ounces) tomato paste
- 2 bay leaves
- 1 teaspoon minced fresh parsley
- 1 teaspoon Italian seasoning
- 1 package (16 ounces) lasagna noodles, cooked, rinsed and drained
- 1 cup (8 ounces) fat-free cottage cheese
- 1 small zucchini, sliced and cooked
- 1 cup (8 ounces) reduced-fat sour cream

Direction

- Prepare a large pan and cook on a moderate heat the beef and garlic until the beef is not anymore pinkish. Let it drain before mixing in water, bay leaves, tomato sauce, tomato paste, Italian seasoning and parsley. Let it boil before reducing the heat. Simmer while it's uncovered for about 30-40 minutes.
- Remove the bay leaves. Prepare a 13x9-inch baking pan and coat it with a cooking spray. Lay in the pan half cup of the meat sauce. Fit five noodles on the pan (cut it if necessary). Place cottage cheese and cover the layer with zucchini, five noodles, and half of the meat sauce. Cover again with sour cream and five noodles. Top the layers with the remaining meat sauce and noodles.
- At the temperature of 350°F, bake it, uncovered, for about 30-35 minutes until heated enough. Set aside for 15 minutes before cutting and serving.

Nutrition Information

- Calories: 187 calories
- Sodium: 270mg sodium
- Fiber: 2g fiber)
- Total Carbohydrate: 19g carbohydrate (0 sugars
- Cholesterol: 21mg cholesterol
- Protein: 14g protein. Diabetic Exchanges: 1 starch
- Total Fat: 8g fat (0 saturated fat)

Index

A
Apple 4,92
Asparagus 3,12,22

B
Bacon 3,8,14,15,16
Beans 3,5,20,23,60,126
Beef 1,3,4,5,6,8,11,12,18,19,20,21,22,23,24,25,26,27,28,29,30,31,32,33,39,46,48,49,50,51,54,55,57,58,66,70,71,72,73,74,75,77,78,80,81,82,88,89,91,92,94,98,99,101,104,108,116,121,124,125,126,127,134,135,139,140,141,143,144,151,153,154,155,156,158,159,160,161,163,165,168,169,174,175,176,177,184,185,186,194,195,196,197,198,201,204,207
Beer 5,140
Berry 3,32
Biscuits 5,128
Bread 4,97
Brie 3,37
Brisket 3,5,6,13,18,19,32,37,126,140,163,168,174,194,196
Broccoli 3,38
Burger 3,4,5,6,15,16,35,38,40,101,102,121,129,136,139,170,187,205
Butter 4,79

C
Cabbage 3,4,21,26,80,96
Cake 4,103
Caramel 3,28
Cashew 3,48
Cheddar 5,26,107,174
Cheese 3,4,5,6,8,14,15,16,26,35,36,38,42,45,56,65,84,119,124,129,133,197
Cherry 6,181
Chicken 3,44
Chipotle 3,6,46,160,181
Cider 3,4,48,92
Coffee 3,49,50,51
Cognac 125
Coriander 3,54
Couscous 4,67
Cranberry 3,5,37,54,134
Cream 4,5,6,26,56,57,142,183
Crumble 9,28,64,69,91,100,105,112,115,119,121,130,131,134,136,144,146,151,152,173,187,189,206
Curry 3,8

D
Dijon mustard 16,68,76,79,181,186,187
Dumplings 5,6,147,156

F
Fat 8,9,10,11,12,13,14,15,16,17,18,19,20,21,22,23,24,25,26,27,28,29,30,31,32,33,34,35,36,37,38,39,40,41,42,43,44,45,46,47,48,49,50,51,52,53,54,55,56,57,58,59,60,61,62,63,64,65,66,67,68,69,70,71,72,73,74,75,76,77,78,79,80,81,82,83,84,85,86,87,88,89,90,91,92,93,94,95,96,97,98,99,100,101,102,103,104,105,106,107,108,109,110,111,112,113,114,115,116,117,118,119,120,121,122,123,124,125,126,127,128,129,130,131,132,133,134,135,136,137,138,139,140,141,142,143,144,145,146,147,148,149,150,151,152,153,154,155,156,157,158,159,160,161,162,163,164,165,166,167,168,169,170,171,172,173,174,175,176,177,178,179,180,181,182,183,184,185,186,187,188,189,190,191,192,193,194,195,196,197,19

8,199,200,201,202,203,204,205,206,207

Flank 4,5,6,61,66,67,68,128,165,183,195

Flatbread 3,13

G

Garlic 4,5,72,73,74,94,117,146

Gorgonzola 4,75,76

Gouda 13

Gravy 3,6,29,37,44,162

H

Ham 4,81,97

Heart 4,60,84,85,86,87,88

Honey 4,94

Horseradish 3,4,5,37,68,94,142

K

Ketchup 104,105,112

L

Lemon 192

M

Macaroni 5,107,115

Madeira 5,76,123,124

Mashed potato 50

Mayonnaise 15

Meat 3,4,5,6,9,14,16,41,43,45,53,61,62,64,69,91,94,99,103,105,107,109,110,111,112,113,114,115,117,118,119,130,134,146,152,157,164,172,184,189,191,197,199

Mince 57,197

Muffins 6,189

Mushroom 4,5,6,74,99,121,122,123,144,156,183

Mustard 5,123

N

Noodles 3,4,5,11,100,156

Nut 8,9,10,11,12,13,14,15,16,17,18,19,20,21,22,23,24,25,26,27,28,29,30,31,32,33,34,35,36,37,38,39,40,41,42,43,44,45,46,47,48,49,50,51,52,53,54,55,56,57,58,59,60,61,62,63,64,65,66,67,68,69,70,71,72,73,74,75,76,77,78,79,80,81,82,83,84,85,86,87,88,89,90,91,92,93,94,95,96,97,98,99,100,101,102,103,104,105,106,107,108,109,110,111,112,113,114,115,116,117,118,119,120,121,122,123,124,125,126,127,128,129,130,131,132,133,134,135,136,137,138,139,140,141,142,143,144,145,146,147,148,149,150,151,152,153,154,155,156,157,158,159,160,161,162,163,164,165,166,167,168,169,170,171,172,173,174,175,176,177,178,179,180,181,182,183,184,185,186,187,188,189,190,191,192,193,194,195,196,197,198,199,200,201,202,203,204,205,206,207

O

Oil 97

Onion 3,4,28,71

Orange 3,5,6,11,128,175

P

Parmesan 5,17,27,38,43,44,49,56,58,62,69,77,78,85,86,87,88,89,94,101,105,112,115,119,120,121,125,127,130,132,173,176,177,178,192,193,197

Pasta 3,4,22,47,55,77

Pastry 180

Peel 170

Pepper 3,4,5,6,10,69,74,88,89,92,116,129,130,131,135,167,178,192,198,201

Pie 3,4,5,6,39,42,71,81,86,114,175,177,191,199,201

Pineapple 5,134,135

Pizza 3,4,5,6,13,27,38,65,93,113,121,136,137,138,139,178

Polenta 27

Pork 171,190

Port 5,83,139

Potato 4,5,55,104,110,112,132,133,140,147

R

Raisins 8

Rice 3,4,5,6,21,30,81,146,198

S

Salsa 4,5,6,67,96,131,193,199

Salt 43,55,108,115,136,143,144,171,200

Sausage 3,23,126,171,185,190

Savory 5,6,151,152,153,186

Sesame seeds 128

Sherry 6,183

Sirloin 3,4,5,6,39,90,135,192,203

Spaghetti 4,5,6,62,143,153,164,171,172,177,185,186

Spinach 3,6,43,50,176,177

Squash 6,172

Steak 3,4,5,6,12,17,18,35,36,44,59,61,65,66,67,68,74,79,106,109,118,119,123,125,128,131,133,147,149,157,162,165,166,177,179,180,181,183,184,187,195,202,203,206

Stew 3,4,5,6,9,25,30,31,48,50,70,73,74,77,85,86,92,98,106,117,121,128,141,144,148,153,164,165,176,182,195,196,204

Sugar 26,45,135,151,171,190,193

T

T-bone steak 152

Taco 4,6,96,97,188,189,190,193

Teriyaki 6,194,195

Tomato 3,4,6,15,17,79,198

Tortellini 4,84,98

Turkey 4,101

V

Veal 6,202

Vegetables 5,127

Venison 3,31

W

Worcestershire sauce 8,14,15,16,19,21,30,31,32,35,41,45,46,52,57,59,60,64,68,71,73,76,77,79,92,109,110,111,112,125,129,141,152,160,163,171,179,181,183,184,185,186,192,193,194

Wraps 6,198

L

lasagna 23,43,49,56,57,62,85,86,87,103,105,116,117,137,149,207